Argentina in the Global Middle East

Argentina in the Global Middle East

Lily Pearl Balloffet

Stanford University Press
Stanford, California

Stanford University Press
Stanford, California

Printed in the United States of America on acid-free, archival-quality paper

Library of Congress Cataloging-in-Publication Data

Names: Balloffet, Lily Pearl, author.
Title: Argentina in the global Middle East / Lily Pearl Balloffet.
Description: Stanford : Stanford University Press, 2020. | Includes
  bibliographical references and index.
Identifiers: LCCN 2020004592 (print) | LCCN 2020004593 (ebook) | ISBN
  9781503611740 (cloth) | ISBN 9781503613010 (paperback) | ISBN
  9781503613027 (ebook)
Subjects: LCSH: Arabs—Argentina—History. | Middle
  Easterners—Argentina—History. | Immigrants—Argentina—Social
  conditions. | Emigration and immigration—Social aspects. |
  Argentina—Emigration and immigration—History. | Middle
  East—Emigration and immigration—History.
Classification: LCC F3021.A59 B35 2020 (print) | LCC F3021.A59 (ebook) |
  DDC 982—dc23
LC record available at https://lccn.loc.gov/2020004592

Cover design: Christian Fuenfhausen

Por, y principalmente a causa de, Javier

And for Julie, the ultimate detective.

Contents

Acknowledgments

Much like the historical episodes that fill the following chapters, this book is itself the product of countless intersecting networks of people, places, and ideas. I carried the support of these networks with me over the course of the past decade, and this endeavor would have been impossible without them.

My mentors at the University of California, Davis threw their support behind this project when it was little more than a seed of an idea. The fingerprints of the scholars who guided me through the early stages of this research are to be found throughout the text: Victoria Langland, Andrés Reséndez, and Tom Holloway each gave their time and insight as I pulled together the initial strands of this story. I cannot imagine a more stalwart adviser, cheerleader, and advocate than Charles Walker, who continues to see me through my development as a scholar all these years later. The generosity of spirit of these individuals, together with others, including Shayma Hassouna, Ari Kelman, Susan Miller, and Suad Joseph, collectively taught me what it means to have an intellectual home. For this, I am forever grateful.

This book never would have seen the light of day without the monetary support of various organizations and institutions. To the dozens of strangers who read the deluge of funding proposals that I submitted over the years and decided to give this project a chance: thank you. Grants from the US Department of Education's Foreign Language and Area Studies, and Fulbright-Hays divisions, were critical in the execution of my language training and research, respectively. Aside from being an intellectual home, U.C. Davis also funded my research from the start. The History Department, Hemispheric Institute of the Americas, dean of social sciences, and office of the provost provided me with research and writing fellowships that enabled me to expand the breadth and depth of my study. I am indebted to the gifts of Kathryn Reed Smith and the late Wilson Smith, whose fellowships made possible my graduate studies. Once in the field, several institutions facilitated my archival search, including the Hemeroteca of the Biblioteca Nacional, Ministerio de Relaciones Exteriores y Culto, Club Sirio Libanés, Club Libanés, Hospital Sirio Libanés, the Asociación de Beneficencia Drusa, and Iglesia San Marón in Buenos Aires, and the Misión Maronita de Mendoza, the Parroquia San Jorge de Mendoza, the Sociedad Árabe Islámico de Mendoza, Club Sirio de Mendoza, and the Club Sirio Libanés de Salta. Salime Taha invited me to her home to work with her precious family archives and admire the tenacious Levantine cedar growing on her back patio. I also had help in digging up the historic photos that I ultimately included in this book. Many thanks to Marcelo Huernos and the Archivo del Instituto de Investigación en Arte y Cultura 'Dr. Norberto Griffa' de la Universidad Nacional de Tres de Febrero, the Archivo General de la Nación, Ricardo Simes of the Asociación de Beneficencia Hospital Sirio Libanés, and Armando and Segundo Deferrari of the Museo Las Lilas of San Antonio de Areco. Amy Lee—my dear friend, co-conspirator, and go-to expert on all things cartographic—accompanied me on my final research trip and created all of the maps for this book.

While conducting my research in Argentina, many people took it upon themselves to help me move this project forward. Mirta Naser and Fabiola Ortigala opened their home to me during my long stay in Mendoza. Ricardo Simes and Zarife Allub de Sarquis welcomed me to the Hospital Sirio Libanés and introduced me to important collaborators like Edgardo Bechara El Khoury and Christian Mouroux. Gladys Jozami hosted me for many hours of tea and coffee at La Biela, where she shared her knowledge of Middle East migration history. Toward the end of this project, I had the good fortune to connect with Marcelo Huernos of the Museo de la Inmigración in Buenos Aires. Because of his efforts and the generous invitation of the Universidad Nacional Tres de Febrero, I was able to have the gratifying opportunity to spend a week working with Marcelo and his students on their approach to creating a museum exhibit that encompasses some of the characters and institutions from this book. I realize that most historians do not get the opportunity to see their work come alive in this way, and I deeply appreciate their efforts.

Doing historical research in the field can be an isolating experience no matter where it takes place. The blissful solitude of archives did sometimes feel like a refuge to me—a ghostly sanctuary for inviting voices, faces, and ephemera from bygone worlds. On other days, it was crushingly lonely, and I relied on the smallest of human encounters to uplift me on the difficult days. Before she left us far too soon, I shared many afternoons with Nathalie Collin in the Biblioteca Nacional. She taught me to revel in the bus ride home from the library and to savor the snippets of conversation around me. To date, my colleagues Mayra Soledad Valcarcel and Mariela Luján Ramos always enliven my trips to Buenos Aires. They epitomize an unflagging dual engagement with their intellectual pursuits, and the pressing social movements of which they are a part. I aspire to the intensity of their energies on both fronts. *Estoy y estaré con ustedes. Será ley.*

As a historian of human mobilities, it is perhaps unsurprising that I think often about how it is that I came to land in California. Many years back, Alejandra Osorio taught my first Latin American history course at Wellesley College and subsequently suggested to me that I might consider Davis for graduate school. I am eternally glad to have followed her advice. As a historian of geography and space, I thought it would be amusing to calculate the geographic center to my own movements over the years that took me from Massachusetts to Argentina, Louisiana, and California. The result of this equation landed me squarely in the lush mountain folds of southern Appalachia in the western region of North Carolina. To my surprise, shortly after I made this calculation, I found myself packing my truck and heading in the direction of my geocenter to begin a postdoctoral fellowship at the Khayrallah Center for Lebanese Diaspora Studies at North Carolina State University. There, I truly found my footing as a historian of Middle East migrations, in large part thanks to daily encouragement from Akram Khater.

If Raleigh was fairly close to my calculated midpoint, the following two years that I spent at Western Carolina University were smack in the middle of it. I only wish that while I was there, I had spent more time outside in the Smoky Mountains in the company of my brilliant colleagues Brett and Pan Riggs, Rob Ferguson, and Liz Harper. The camaraderie of my Latinx studies colleagues Melissa Birkhofer and Paul Worley sustained me for those two years, and it continues to do so. Their work ethic, resilience, and commitment to meaningful inclusion is powerfully heartening. I also benefited immensely from the regional community of SECOLAS folks. Our regular lunches in Charlotte kept me connected with colleagues who shared stories of teaching and researching all things Latin

America while living in the Carolinas. I am thankful to Erika Edwards, Jackie Sumner, Greg Crider, Lyman Johnson, Steven Hyland, and Jürgen Buchenau for their good cheer and our friendship born from these gatherings.

The beauty, and occasional ache, of the strong friendships built through academic networks is the reality of having one's friends scattered across the globe. I miss the proximity of my Davis peers: among them Jordan Lauhon, Patricia Palma, Cristián Castro, Elizabeth Montañez-Sanabria, Steve Cote, and Jessica Fowler. William Paloma San Martin's companionship has been unswerving, and he is also responsible for bringing other wonderful colleagues into my orbit, such as Rafael Pedemonte, whose insights on Global South imaginaries in the Cold War helped me craft my chapter revisions. José Ragas was of crucial help to me on many occasions while writing this book. No one could ask for a better listener, reader, sympathizer, or company for a plate of *empanadas de carne* than Comrade Ragas.

Also scattered across the globe is a web of women scholars who, with their capacious intellect, discerning insights, and unfaltering solidarity, each played a role in spurring forward my writing. These include Emily Davidson, Maria Guadalupe Arenillas, Sally Howell, Elizabeth Claire Saylor, Grace Peña Delgado, Christine Mathias, Julia Sarreal, Ellen McLarney, Devi Mays, Lauren Banko, Almuth Ebke, Jessica Ordaz, Camilla Hawthorne, and Katy Seto. Stacy Fahrenthold has given her ear and shared her knowledge of Middle East migration history on countless occasions. Jessica Stites Mor's solidarity in my final years of book revision has been unwavering, and her invitation to write a piece on Syrian refugees and diasporic interlocutors for the 2016 Latin American Studies Association Forum became the springboard for the genesis of the book's concluding chapter. Rambling dog walks, phone calls, and shop talk with Marian Schlotterbeck have brought me clarity and solace for the past several years as I inched my way to the end of this manuscript and back to California.

Throughout the publishing process, the folks at Stanford University Press have been ideal collaborators. The very idea of choosing to work with a press before I fully grasped the nitty-gritty of the book publishing process could, in another circumstance, have been a fraught decision. Instead, they met me at every step of the way with transparency, efficiency, perspicacity, and patience. It has been a pleasure to work with Margo Irvin as my editor. Margo's dedication to helping this manuscript become the best possible version of itself was manifest from our earliest interactions. Many thanks as well to my two anonymous reviewers for their thoughtful engagement with my ideas.

I was beyond lucky to join the Latin American and Latino Studies Department at the University of California, Santa Cruz while I was in the final years of writing. I cannot imagine a better environment for carrying to completion this project on South-South migration. My colleagues here are deeply committed scholar-activists whose impressive work inspires me to challenge myself and advocate for our students, communities, and values. Special thanks to Gabriela Arredondo and Jessica Taft for helping me in this transition. I'm still new here, yet in many ways, this has felt like a homecoming.

Outside of this intricate patchwork of benefactors, colleagues, and mentors, many more friends and loved ones were utterly central to my completion of this project. These include Jay Haas, Didi Thompson, Zayne Turner, Cyndi Marshall, Steve Tracy, Cathy Forkas, Sasha Klein, John Nuttall, Warren Charles Jones, Allison Abresch-Meyer, Kelley Deane McKinney, Tina Morrison, Nick Walkowski, Anna McHugh, Juan Pedroza, and so very many others. The complicated web of humanity that these folks form represents the family that I have chosen for myself over the years and across the miles. That said, my biological kin aren't so bad either. I am blessed with a large family that sprawls across three continents. The story of how they came to be there lies unequivocally at the root of my interest in the history of migration. To all of my aunts, uncles, cousins, in-laws, and relatives of complex and unclassifiable relation—thank you for telling me the stories of how my family tree enveloped América in its tendrils.

Without the patience, indulgence, and care of my faithful sisters, this book certainly would not exist. Talking to Naomi on the phone from across the globe was an instantaneous tether to home. Sara's strength inspires me to tap uncharted reserves of my own fortitude. Leanna's confidence that I would complete this project was so convincing that it animated me in my darkest moments. Her antics with little S. have brought me some of my brightest ones. Benjamin Pearl has been my stalwart partner for the majority of this vast sea change in my life that began with moving to California more than a decade ago. Before I embarked on this book, I had never seen the Pacific Ocean, and now we live at its doorstep. Thank you for everything, especially your reminders to step outside so that the ferocious beauty of our natural surroundings might bring me starkly to my senses.

Finally, I thank my parents, Julie Graessle and Javier Balloffet. Words fall short of expressing the immensity of their commitment to my dreams. This book is for them.

Argentina in the Global Middle East

Introduction
Transregional Migration and Mobility

In the far northeastern region of Argentina, it is easy to fancy oneself in a different world from that of the frenetic bustle of the nation's federal capital. Red dirt roads snake across the subtropical landscape, winding through verdant forests and wetlands that reverberate with the thrum of more than half the nation's biodiversity. In contrast, a thousand kilometers away in the historic port city of Buenos Aires, the colorful crush of public bus lines streams constantly through the major arteries and countless microneighborhoods. Here, the thrum is that of careening buses, the rattle of the century-old subway system, and more than 40,000 taxis. The city's iconic 9 de Julio avenue—a veritable river of vehicles some twenty lanes wide that slices north to south through the heart of the city—by itself sees more than 200,000 commuters daily. In a place like Buenos Aires, it's not hard to imagine that this tangled, moving mass of people has its roots in a long history of human mobility—across city blocks, neighborhoods, oceans. This port city has long been a convening place. Perched at the southwestern shore of the Río de la Plata estuary, it looks on as the Atlantic intrudes into the basin of the Paraná and Uruguay Rivers. This is the topography that greeted millions of people who arrived in Argentina as part of the tectonic shifts in global migration patterns that reconfigured this planet's human landscape from the late nineteenth to the early twentieth centuries. Buenos Aires— the city, the port, and the pulsing circulation of those who make their lives and conduct their affairs there—is a poster child for the transformative process of mass migration in the American hemisphere.

The small town of Oberá in Argentina's northeasternmost province of Misiones seems a world away from the nation's furious metropolis and dra-

1

matic port landscape. A quiet city tucked into low, green hills, it sits south of the Paraná River. Energetically, the town is at best a distant cousin of the fast-paced capital. It is a place that exemplifies the striking differences between this lush northeastern region and the densely peopled federal capital. For the uninitiated, it would be all too easy to assume a cultural, historical distance from modern Argentina's immigrant past in surroundings such as these. At first glance, it may not seem to be a place that embodies the defining history of international migration that is so readily apparent in Buenos Aires. However, once a year, Oberá's Immigrant Festival dispels any such illusions. At the annual event, more than 100,000 people gather in the Park of Nations arena to sample food, watch dance performances, and mill about sixteen fanciful houses scattered across two dozen acres. Each house is meant to represent one of sixteen different national heritage groups—or *colectividades*— who have settled in the Oberá area since the late nineteenth century. A stroll through the Park of Nations leads past a Bavarian beer garden, a Japanese pergola, and the smell of fresh pasta wafting from an Italian-style villa. At the top of the sloping park, the *Casa Argentina* (Argentina House) stands triumphant, decked out in celeste and white ribbons, surrounded by smoking *asado* pits filled with splayed open cuts of beef.

Following months of archival research in Buenos Aires in 2011, this was my first stop on a meandering 6,000-kilometer bus loop through a dozen provinces in the nation's sprawling interior. Writing a book about the ties between Argentina and the Middle East born from a long history of migration left me with the urge to make my own peregrination. I wanted to see firsthand the vast distances that Middle Eastern migrants to Argentina routinely traveled for work, family, schooling, and a host of other motivations starting in the last decades of the nineteenth century. In search of the vestiges of these movements, I had arrived in Oberá in time for the opening ceremony of that year's Immigrant Festival. I watched as performers representing the *colectividad árabe* appeared onstage dancing the *dabke*–a traditional line dance form with roots in the Levantine region of Jordan, Syria, Lebanon, and Palestine. The precision footwork, billowing pants, and smart vests were more than a little reminiscent of the traditional Argentine gaucho dancers who had preceded them on the stage, regaling the audience with a vigorous *malambó* set. To mark the shift from Argentine to Arab dancing, the large screen that acted as a backdrop for the dancers faded from a projection of Argentina's flag to a new image. The flag that took its place, however, was not that of Syria or

Lebanon—the origin points of some 130,000 Middle Easterners who made their way from what was then the Ottoman Empire to Argentina by World War I. Instead, there appeared a projected image of the Saudi Arabian flag—a flag that didn't come into use until 1973. Moments later, in the parade of the elected *Reinas de Colectividades* (pageant queens), the reina árabe marched under yet another flag, neither Syrian, Lebanese, nor Saudi Arabian. Instead, her sash sported the crest of the Arab League—the federation of Arab nations established in 1945 as World War II came to an end. This chronological jumble of symbols struck me as somewhat fitting for a group described as "mythical and exotic" in the event program.

It is common for casual conversations about the role of the immigrant masses in Argentine history to entirely gloss over the presence of Middle Easterners. This silence is reminiscent of their portrayal at the festival that day in 2011: a people whose past is untethered to any specific national heritage or coherent temporality but is decidedly, excitingly, foreign in an Argentine context. In reality, Middle Eastern migration is at the very heart of Argentine history and culture. At Oberá's Park of Nations, one needed only to walk over to the Casa Argentina to be reminded of this. Drifting across the patio filled with asado smoke and waving Argentine flags were the *samba* and *chacarera* songs of Eduardo Falú, a foundational figure in Argentina's modern folk music movement. Born in 1923 in the arid northwestern province of Salta some 1,200 kilometers away from Oberá, the singer was the son of Syrian immigrants Juan and Fada Falú. By the time of his death in 2013, he was indisputably a pillar of traditional Argentine *criollo* musical culture, an obvious choice for the soundtrack of the Immigrant Festival's symbolic epicenter. On the lawn of the Casa Argentina, the convergence of geographies—from Salta, to Misiones, to Syria—is striking.

This is, at its core, the type of powerful collapsing of geographic distance and space that this book offers. From the roar of a Buenos Aires subway tunnel, to the tropical buzz of a Misiones forest, the common thread of Middle Eastern migration enables us to connect these geographies. It suddenly becomes possible to imagine Oberá, Salta, and the nation's capital as part of the same continuum of moving people, things, and ideas. We can thus integrate our vision of Argentine history by exploring the history of Argentina's ties to the Middle East. By way of tracing these mobilities so commonly thought of as somehow outside of—foreign to—the Argentine national fabric, we can challenge a host of geographic segregations that so many decades of historical scholarship naturalized by rendering a vision of Argentina as a metropolis and its corresponding *interior*. The inherent division between Buenos Aires and the rest of Argentina has been taken as a given by years of historical accounts and countless portrayals of Argentine national history in classrooms throughout the Americas and beyond. To see cities as bastions of civilization and their corresponding rural spaces as stagnant and barbarous is not unique to outdated perspectives on Argentina, but it may be one of the starker examples. This book invites us to think of geographic space and human movement as continuous and connective.

A Transregional Approach to Migrant América

From a twenty-first-century vantage point, it is easy to see relations between peoples and states in the Middle East and the Americas as yet another product of an ever-globalizing world. Indeed, new populations, commodities, and ways of thinking circulate between these regions with increasing frequency, thanks to the perfect storm of communication and transportation technology. Meanwhile, media, politicians, and international organizations tirelessly inform us that this planet is on the move. The constant onslaught of these reminders can lull one into believing that the panorama of human, material, and ideological circulation among these regions is a recent phenomenon. Engaging a historical perspective on the topic of Middle Eastern–American relations (*América* on a hemispheric scale, that is), reveals how global migration systems bound these geographies together since the nineteenth century.

Argentina lies at the nucleus of América's history of global migration booms of the mid-nineteenth to early twentieth centuries. By 1910, one of every three Argentine residents was an immigrant—twice the demographic impact that the United States experienced in the boom period from the 1860s to World War I. As a principal transatlantic migration hub, Argentina's trajectory as a modern nation played out through the experience of mass migration. The immigrant masses integrated national space through their engagement with agriculture, industry, and infrastructure. Meanwhile, elites and popular classes alike formulated ideas of national identity alternately forged in, or in opposition to, ideas about immigration and migrants themselves. The theme of immigration is central to both inward-facing histories of the development of Argentine national identities, as well as outward-facing histories of Argentine foreign relations.

It was in this context that Middle Easterners from Ottoman Syria made their way to Argentina prior to World War I and quickly spread across the high desert of the Andean Altiplano borderlands, all the way to the fabled Patagonian Land of Fire in the south. Subsequently, the communities, institutions, and businesses of this colectividad dotted the landscape of Argentina's largest cities to its most remote frontiers. Though scattered far and wide across more than 1 million square miles, these individuals were anything but isolated from one another. The movement and circulation of people, things, and ideas between urban hubs and rural outposts alike defined the geography of this migration. This migrant geography—conceived of and articulated alternately as a diaspora, imagined community, or network—can perhaps most simply be referred to as the *mahjar*. In Arabic, *mahjar* refers to the combined people and territories that constitute the human spatial map of migrant worlds constructed after the massive out-migration from Ottoman Syria since the last third of the nineteenth century. The mahjar materialized during a period of massive development and transition for American migration hubs such as Argentina, Brazil, and the United States—the three countries that became home to the largest resident communities of individuals with roots in the Arabic-speaking eastern Mediterranean. In each of these American contexts, the proliferation of new infrastructure, especially railroads, provided the circuitry for highly mobile Middle Easterners across the hemisphere.

This book traces some of the key ways in which women and men in the Argentine mahjar staked their fundraising endeavors, business ventures, and artistic projects in movement across a migrant geography that stretched beyond national boundaries. These multiple forms of mobility—not only of humans themselves, but of objects, worldviews, money, and material culture—were central to the social landscape of the mahjar. The geographic extent of these mobilities ranged from habitual microregional or local movements to dramatic forays across political borders. The constancy and diversity of these mobilities testify to the fact that the social relations of this colectividad did not simply connect two or more countries in the traditional conceptualization of "transnational" migrant groups.[1] These diverse layers and types of mobility did generate transnational relations between people in Argentina and the Middle East, but they also generated local and regional networks of relations that were intimately related to those transnational ties.[2] As a starting point, thinking of Argentina's Middle Eastern migrants in a transnational frame does indeed help us move beyond a binary mode of interpreting the movement in migrants' lives as defined by either arriving or leaving—immigration versus emigration. It opens the door to seeing cultures and social structure as something other than predicated on determined spatial boundaries or static notions of rootedness.[3]

However, conceptualizing the ties born out of Middle Eastern migration to Argentina as simply trans*national* presents certain limitations. Argentines of Middle Eastern descent can certainly trace their heritage back to particular nations very much in existence today—predominantly Syria and Lebanon. At the time of the global migration boom of the late nineteenth to early twentieth centuries, though, these nations did not exist yet; they were part of the Ottoman Empire. In other words, the advent of nation-states followed, rather than preexisted, the birth of supposedly trans*national* ties between these Latin American and Middle Eastern geographies. Furthermore, even after the establishment of the national boundaries that today delineate the nations of the Arabic-speaking eastern Mediterranean, the various mobilities that existed between those places and the Americas did not neatly abide by a fixed transnational circuit between Argentina and Syria/Lebanon. Instead, a broader set of social, political, and cultural relations drew together actors and ideas from a wider Middle Eastern and North African region, as well as a wider American region. Some scholars of the mahjar refer to this phenomenon as the birth of a public sphere that deeply affected everything from political movements to artistic forms in the modern Middle East and whose formation we can attribute to historical processes of mass migration.[4] In a similar light, this book examines the mobilities between localities, provinces, and nations as subsets of a broader spectrum of transregional relations. This is not only a more accurate description, geographically, of the panorama of ties that formed between the Middle East and Argentina—and the Americas more generally. In addition, it encourages us to more thoroughly incorporate people and places at the margins of traditional histories of mass migration and to conceive of them as unified in distinct ways by transregional systems of migration and mobility.

Locating a Global Middle East

By the time twentieth-century scholars started to examine the history of the mahjar, the legacy of Cold War area studies exerted a powerful force on the way in which we have traditionally taught about and conducted research on the "Middle East" and "Latin America." Methodological and conceptual frameworks that naturalized the bounded nature of world "areas" left little room for subjects whose realities are staked in the movement between places. Although it was during the Cold War years that the institutional consolidation of area studies gained serious traction, the tendency to isolate and segregate the globe into areas is much older. The desire to dominate through intricate regimes of labeling, delineating, and partitioning lay at the very core of colonial systems of territorial domination for centuries.[5] Questioning the supposed logic of these segregations is necessarily one of the foremost tasks at hand if we are to work toward decolonizing the way we think, write, and teach global histories.[6] There is no better way to muddy the concept of neatly packaged world regions than to delve into the histories of large-scale movement, such as mass migration, between those geographies.[7] In this way, histories of the mahjar help us to chip away at the legacy of colonial and nationalist worldviews that for so many generations enshrined their visions of the world.

None of this is to say that there are not tangible cultural, linguistic, and political histories deeply related to place that helped to shape the worldviews and customs that migrants carried with them into the mahjar. In the past, some migration scholars have understood these communities as "diasporas"—social formations with distinct sociological features, wherein scatterings of people seek out continuing connections with home both literally and metaphorically through a variety of means.[8] Others have drawn from Benedict Anderson's notion of "imagined communities"—conceptualizing diasporas as a particular form of imagined community produced through "political, symbolic and moral cosmologies that both belong to and transcend the social and territorial contexts in which they actually exist."[9] For the sake of thinking beyond traditionally bounded world regions, this study avoids engaging the idea of diaspora as a fixed yardstick against which to measure the habits of Middle Eastern migrants and their descendants in Argentina. Rather than a theoretical framework, it is most useful in the context of Argentine–Middle East relations to speak of diaspora in a geospatial sense. In sum, we can think of the mahjar as a "diaspora" in that it denotes a physical terrain comprising a collection of places from which transregional actors operate. This allows us to categorize "diasporic" politics or cultural production, for example, as activities defined by their generation within the geospatial context of the mahjar. Foregrounding the geospatial nature of the term serves as a reminder that these groups—whether we conceive of them as imagined communities, diasporas, or otherwise—were first and foremost products of intricate networks of mobility on both sides of the Atlantic. This book explores the mechanics by which these diasporic mobilities not only influenced the formation of the mahjar's social landscapes, but also played an important role in Argentine ties to the Middle East beyond the realm of migrant diasporas.

The array of social landscapes comprising the mahjar in the Americas serves as the focus for a growing number of scholars of Middle Eastern migration—past and present.[10] Honing our focus on the ways in which these cultural, social, and political forms were in play throughout the mahjar at a global scale invites us to think of the Middle East as something more than a simple geographic designation. We might imagine this new scope of analysis as a "Global Middle East." Together, new works on Middle Eastern migration in the Americas have helped us to frame the long-distance ties that bind the history of the American hemisphere with that of the Arabic-speaking eastern Mediterranean.[11] From Canada, to Cuba, to Argentina, people with transregional ties to homelands such as Syria, Lebanon, and Palestine participated in the tumultuous historical processes that shaped the modern Middle East. Meanwhile, across the hemisphere, they also became Americans. These were simultaneous and mutually influential processes by which migrants and their descendants formed multiple belongings. To ascribe too much meaning to this duality—transregionalism versus integration—risks ensnaring us in the same binary of immigration versus emigration. Moving away from these binaries offers us the opportunity to harness a vocabulary of movement that does not hinge on the crossing of national borders and does not unnecessarily segregate migratory practices that need to be studied as an inclusive system. Rather than focus on Arab American experiences as embodied by these dualities, this book organizes its analysis around the movement—business travel, mobile political campaigns, roving cultural producers, and other examples— that was truly at the core of the lived social landscapes of the mahjar and at the heart of this notion of a Global Middle East.

Imagining a Global Middle East can also help us to think differently about "Latin America" as a presumed region.[12] It can open new pathways for elucidating other types of transregional circulation and exchange between Latin America and the rest of the world. Placing migration at the center of this new globalized perspective on Latin America inevitably draws our attention to a variety of entanglements—from political to economic to cultural. These entanglements are often connected to historical processes of human migration and mobility, and the transregional relations that formed thereafter. In this vein, this study of Argentina's place in this global Middle East reveals the nexus between migrant networks and the evolution of foreign policy (what one historian has deemed "immigrant foreign relations").[13] Relations of these various sorts in turn came to bear on Argentine dealings with people, ideas, and governments from the Middle East and North Africa. The dynamic unfolded over the course of the twentieth century in the wake of the global migration boom, and it continues to shape Argentina's place in the global Middle East today.

As part of the larger project of thinking beyond traditionally limited territorial constructions of the "Middle East"—and "Latin America" too, for that matter—it is useful to explore the concept of alternative, potentially unifying geographies. One such example that this book employs as a conceptual framework is the "Global South." As a term, *Global South* emerged as a post–Cold War alternative to "Third World" and was taken up by several intergovernmental organizations. The less hierarchical nature of the term (in contrast to "Third World" or "developing countries") contributed to its increasing popularity in this century's academic research. It is a term intimately related to the impacts of capitalist globalization at the periphery of wealthy spaces and human populations. Global South studies, as a field, examines power dynamics within global capitalist systems and—most relevant to this book—the history and contemporary reality of South-South relations. We can characterize these relations as a collection of exchanges, dialogues, solidarities, and collaborations that cross national, ethnic, racial, and linguistic lines.[14] This is a particularly useful way of theorizing the ways in which post–World War II actors in Latin America and the broader Middle East/North Africa regions construed their histories and destinies as connected. Although the term was not in common parlance then, the Non-Aligned Movement that developed over the course of several decades starting in the early 1960s arose in part from the social and political ideologies of individuals who recognized their shared subjugation to globalizing capitalist powers.

Bringing the idea of a Global South to the migratory histories that connect the geographies that this book explores allows us to think of the term as an analytical lens, not just a fixed site of research. In this context, theorizing the Global South as a spatial system marked by interconnecting forms of mobility helps move us toward a clearer vision of the South-South movements of people, things, and ideas that shaped Argentina as a part of the Global Middle East. This perspective relates in key ways to other systems-based approaches to migration history that encourage us to identify the continuing transcultural linkages that arise among societies and states through processes of transborder migration, capital flow, and the circulation of ideologies.[15] The diversity of interconnections that characterize Argentine and Middle Eastern history is, in sum, what each chapter of this book sets out to delineate. The promise of these conceptual frames is that they can lead us toward a baseline of interconnectedness and shared experience rather than the territorialized nation-state as our main unit of analysis.

This doesn't mean that the existence of the nation-state disappears or becomes totally deterritorialized. In the case of this study, it means that we draw closer to a new, international history of Argentina. In conjunction with an exploration of mobilities in the mahjar, we must also necessarily examine how the Argentine state, together with various sectors of civil society, forged visions of Argentina's relationship to the Middle East–North Africa region. In part, these visions coalesced through the experience of interacting with and enacting evolving attitudes toward Middle Eastern migrant and heritage populations in Argentina and abroad. This held true from the time of liberal state builders such as Domingo Faustino Sarmiento (1811–1888) and Juan Bautista Alberdi (1810–1844) through the twentieth century into the Cold War. Taking the long view of Argentina's international history and its relationship to systems of global migration also enables us to forge new understandings of twentieth-century migrants in Latin America more generally. We can approach this book's transregional history as practice toward future framings of Latin American migrant communities as systems of overlapping mobilities. These systems in turn foster transregional relationships at multiple scales. Bringing these historically overlapping systems and pathways of mobility to light also has the power to connect diverse Latin American geographies to the history of transregional capital flows, social movements, political relations, and cultural circulations. The international, cosmopolitan nature of hub cities like Buenos Aires, Mexico City, and Havana has long encouraged us to see these places as connected to international historical processes. Bringing into focus the ways in which these urban sites were part of regional networks of migrant mobilities results in the sudden, dramatic incorporation of secondary cities, towns, villages, and outposts across the hemisphere into newly internationalized histories of Latin America. Simultaneously, we also gain a more holistic vision of the sociospatial geographies of migrant groups—like the mahjar—that were previously studied as scatterings of ethnic enclaves rather than nodes in a larger network. In other words, this book pushes us to question the genesis

of assumptions about regional and global geographies as intrinsically separate—whether at a microregional, national, or global scale.

Writing Transregional History

The point of this book is not to debunk foundational narratives about Argentina's history of Arabic-speaking migrants, its international relations with the
Middle East–North Africa region, or otherwise. It is rather to examine how the
mahjar, and other forms of transregional relations, evolved as objects of knowledge within the diaspora, in academic literature, and in popular conceptions of
those topics. My approach rests on the logic that (as defined by Foucault) we
conceive of historical truth not as "the ensemble of truths to be discovered and
accepted," but instead as "the ensemble of rules according to which the true
and the false are separated and specific effects of power attached to the true."[16]
This book takes as a point of departure the fact that academics have traditionally built conceptions of migrant or diasporic populations on evidence gathered from urban contexts—and this is in part because of the predominance
of official archives in urban over rural locations throughout Latin America.
One of the primary challenges of more effectively writing ethnic/racial minority groups into histories of migration in this hemisphere is the unevenness of
readily available archival material in any given national context. This is not a
problem unique to migration history, of course. Michel Rolph Trouillot sur-
mised that "any historical narrative is a particular bundle of silences."[17]

In addition to the varied archival landscape are additional challenges
when it comes to engaging with archival sources related to the study of the
mahjar (in Argentina or elsewhere). If historical narratives are, in essence, a
"bundle of silences," there are also at times competing profusions of articulation, terminology, and personal identities that vie with one another among
archival sources. The very same factors that complicate the notion of transnationalism in Middle Eastern migrant communities of the early twentieth
century also resulted in a diverse set of names and identities assigned to those
who lived and moved in the mahjar. The shifting political landscapes of the
Middle East in the early decades of the twentieth century meant that migrants
hailing from the Arabic-speaking eastern Mediterranean were inconsistently
identified by everyone from immigration officials to mahjar community
leaders themselves. These labels ranged from *turco* (Turk), a misnomer attributed to the Ottoman documentation that many migrants presented on
their arrival, to *Otomano, Sirio, Libanés, Sirio-Libanés, Árabe, Árabe-Argentino*

(respectively, Ottoman, Syrian, Lebanese, Syrian-Lebanese, Arab, and Arab Argentine), and various combinations thereof. While researching and writing on this group and its bearing on Argentina's history, it is crucial to revisit the following questions frequently: To what degree did these umbrella labels map to the way that migrants and communities envisioned themselves? Or are we retroactively assigning meaning as scholars?

Regardless, one thing is certain when it comes to the multiple labels historically associated with the mahjar in Argentina: there never was any consensus when it came to terminology. It is for this reason that in this book, I do not presume a consensus in my own construction of the histories of these actors and groups. In the case of the individuals' lives that this book examines, many of the archival fragments in which members of this colectividad appear come out of the archives of heritage associations or the ethnic press. Thousands of names appear in places like the membership rosters of Middle Eastern heritage associations, or Arab Argentine business directories created by the voluntary submissions of individual business owners and workers. The fact that these individuals are recorded here suggests that they felt at least some degree of connection with the idea of a Middle Eastern–Argentine colectividad. From this perspective, we can start to interpret the idea of the colectividad, of the diaspora, as a meaningful entity—or at the very least, a useful networking opportunity—in the eyes of these characters who appear fleetingly in the archival record. In this way, as a scholar of the Argentine mahjar, I am fortunate that the information that shows up about remote, undertheorized limbs of the colectividad does at least provide faint clues as to how people related to certain identity categories.

This is of course not the case (or at least it is much harder to determine) in the archival record of other groups—for example, the subjects of forced labor migration of earlier centuries. At any rate, the historian's task is to assemble a composite of sources out of the various scraps of available archival information. This is perhaps the broadest possible definition of the writing of history through archival methods. But the intricacy of weaving together that composite of archival information becomes even more delicate when the groups in question are ones whose histories, ethnicities, racial categories, religious affiliations, and cultural practices have been systematically downplayed (or even denied) in the context of official national histories. Ethnic groups whose presence in Latin American migration booms belies the fact that these were not simply masses of "European" immigrants have historically served as mere footnotes rather than focal points in the history of large-scale migration to the Americas—Latin America, in particular. In constructing this composite of sources, we also must honestly and repeatedly ask ourselves throughout the research process: What are the limits of the archival landscape? What are the limits of traditional disciplinary methods in accessing diasporic histories in Latin America?

These and others were the questions that I continuously revisited while conducting the bulk of my research in Argentina over the course of 2013 to 2015. I drew on materials from a combination of state and private archives—primarily the Biblioteca Nacional and, to a lesser extent, the Ministerio de Relaciones Exteriores, both in Buenos Aires. Alongside these collections, I relied on the holdings of several private archives held by Middle Eastern heritage associations and institutions. The latter took me out of Buenos Aires and into the provinces. There, throughout my 6,000-kilometer bus loop, I didn't always find a wealth of useful archival materials, but I consistently gained firsthand experience at traversing the long distances characteristic of the travel itineraries of so many of those who lived in the mahjar. In Misiones, Mendoza, Salta, and Tierra del Fuego, I worked in archives and visited important sites related to the history of the Argentina's many entanglements with the Middle East. I intentionally selected sites beyond provinces that have served as the geographic backdrop for previous historiographies of the Argentine mahjar, such as Tucumán, Santiago del Estero, and Córdoba, since I had the opportunity to draw from secondary literature. My determination to conduct research outside the federal capital was part of my attempt to produce a narrative of Argentine migration history that would have less bias toward urban communities.

In my own meanderings in pursuit of the archival basis of this project, I was able to work with an array of source materials including Arab Argentine and other periodicals, records from community organizations and institutions, personal correspondence, and diplomatic archives. In turn, I combined these primary sources with historical maps and records of Argentine infrastructure—especially the railroad boom of the nineteenth to twentieth century—that heavily influenced the demographic patterns of this diaspora throughout the country. In addition to this fieldwork conducted in Argentina, I also spent a summer at Stanford University's Hoover Institute Archive, whose holdings include extensively archived correspondence from Argentine president Juan Domingo Perón over the course of his exile from 1955 to 1973.

Toward the end of the project, I returned to Argentina to get a better sense of the work being done today to energize new and old connections between Argentina and the Middle East–North Africa region. On this final trip, I conducted a small batch of interviews—a process that felt like an exciting privilege for a historian who had spent several prior years of her career studying the archival traces of long-passed historical actors. Throughout the ensuing process of writing and analysis, I have done my best to draw out clues as to migrants' mental geographic maps and the ways that they intersected with other forms of Argentine–Middle East relations over time.[18] Six chapters that build an analysis of Argentina as intimately tied to, and part of, a more globalized vision of the Middle East are the result of these efforts.

The book begins with two chapters situated in the early years of the Argentine mahjar. During this period, the Middle East existed in the Argentine creole elite imagination and within the parameters of the national immigration project of the nineteenth century. Central to the rationale of statesmen-intellectuals like Sarmiento and Alberdi was the desire to consolidate national territory. It is important to place the formation of Argentina's mahjar within this context while also exploring the migrant mobilities across Argentine territory that arose during this same era. This context of state formation and mobility also invites us to employ a spatial analysis of the mahjar by way of tracing the deep infrastructural and demographic changes that Argentina experienced during mass migration. It sets the stage for tackling the question of transregional network building in the mahjar during the first half of the twentieth century. Case studies of circulating cultural producers and women's philanthropic organizations cast migrant geographies in the light of intraregional and local immigrant mobilities that offer us insight into the logistical mechanics of migrant networks rather than ascribing their connectivity to more ephemeral notions of intellectual or political currents. Chapter 5 carries the narrative further into the twentieth century by focusing on escalating transregional entanglements between Argentina and the Arab world by the 1950s and 1960s. By investigating the developing relations between Argentina and Egypt during this period, the study moves away from a typical binary analysis of a singular "homeland" and "host country," widening the scope to interrogate how migration from one country can affect the relationship between a host country and a broader geopolitical region. In keeping with the project's central themes of circulating people, goods, and ideas, the book concludes by examining the historical roots of transregional trade, migration policy advocacy, and South-South artistic collaboration today.

Collectively, these chapters investigate the history of the Argentine mahjar as a way of illuminating the interplay between migration and mobility systems over time and the ways in which they came to bear on the evolution of a host of transregional relations. This is a necessary examination to make today, in an era in which media and governments increasingly vocalize (and thus naturalize) the dominance of South-to-North migration systems.[19] Now perhaps more than ever before, we must render visible this rich history of South-South ties. From the fall of the Ottoman Empire, through the negotiation of new Third World identities and alliances in the Cold War, and up to the current day, a connected history has unfolded that defies segregation into the discrete realms of Latin America or the Middle East.

1 Imagining Nation and Migration

On November 10, 2015, a group of Argentines submitted a letter to Cristina Fernández de Kirchner in the waning days of her presidential term that began in 2007 and ended on December 9, 2015. The letter, which addressed the plight of Syrian refugees, came at the apogee of what international media termed the "Mediterranean migration crisis"—a moment when more than 1 million people attempted to cross the Mediterranean Sea seeking refuge in Europe and beyond over the course of 2015. While migrants hailed from many different countries, Syrians were the focal point for news coverage, humanitarian response, and reactionary political invective. "They wander helpless in Europe and the Middle East," decried the November 2015 letter submitted to the Argentine president. Signed by fifteen representatives of local and national institutions, as well as thirty individuals, the letter urged a succinct prescription for Argentina's response to the spike in Syrian refugees: bring Syrian refugees to Argentina. More specifically: bring them to the Argentine territories "most in need of peopling." The last sentence of the letter went even further, suggesting that in addition to "delivering marked cultural, economic and demographic benefits to Argentina," Syrian refugees had the potential to "[improve Argentina's] geopolitical situation in Patagonia, and other sensitive regions of the national territory."[1] The notion of bringing immigrants to Argentina in order to fill "unoccupied" territories and bolster geopolitical advantage in frontier zones is nothing new. With this, the letter, consciously or not, drew on rhetoric and reasoning that dates to foundational myths of the nineteenth century. In this case, of course, they applied the logic to the context of twenty-first-century forced migration.

The letter contained rhetorical echoes of nineteenth-century intellectuals who perceived a pressing need for comprehensive territorial domination as a means for consolidating political and economic control over the new republic. The signatories of the letter may have invoked a rhetorical legacy of liberal ideas about migrants as civilizing agents, but the document that they produced was a subtle subversion of the arguments of foundational intellectuals such as Domingo Faustino Sarmiento and Juan Bautista Alberdi. Sarmiento and Alberdi, after all, called for the arrival of the *European* masses on Argentine shores. Many (though not all) of those who drafted the 2015 petition to Kirchner were Argentine individuals, or institutional representatives, with heritage ties to immigrants from the Middle East. Thus, a century after Argentina's demographic revolution peaked, descendants of the immigration boom invoked key ideas about the relationship of migrants, progress, and geopolitically vulnerable space. The way these themes coalesced in a 2015 letter just as seamlessly as they did in nineteenth-century discourses serves as an apt reminder of the staying power of the ambitions and anxieties that drove the state-sponsored colonization projects that shaped modern Argentina. It is on this note that we begin our exploration of Argentina in the "global" Middle East by integrating the intellectual history of these nation-building endeavors with the social history of migration. This allows us to move toward spatial analyses of the reorganization of rural Argentina through transportation technology and human mobilities.

Despite an increasing number of studies on core urban migration destinations of the mahjar in the Americas, such as New York, Boston, São Paulo, and Buenos Aires, we still know relatively little about how these central migratory hubs related to vast networks of rural diasporic populations such as those represented by the plethora of institutions that spread across the Argentine provinces and territories. Methodologically, the transnational turn in approaches to immigration history in the Americas has illuminated the importance of recognizing the transregional exchanges of people, politics, money, and cultural production that exist between diaspora communities and their homelands. This productive methodological shift has rendered interdisciplinary work in the broader field of migration studies that has consistently pushed scholars to conceive of transnational networks as our base unit of analysis rather than neatly defined geopolitical packages. However, in part as a result of this general direction of the field, few studies of the mahjar, especially of its Latin American region, have considered the actual mechanics by which these immigrant communities formed the local networks that allowed large-scale transnational flows of culture and capital. Broadening our view in this way also enables us to think about how international migration—a particular form of human movement across geographic space—gave rise to a plethora of mobilities, not all of which took place in dramatic transoceanic fashion. Much of this movement took place within national territories or regional sub-networks, a fact that the emphasis on the particular term trans*national* might risk obscuring and which we might more aptly consider as an array of trans*regional* movements within and between diasporic geographies.

Beginning our study with a dual look at the nineteenth-century rise of mobilities and infrastructure will lay the groundwork for better apprehending the ways in which this vibrant network enabled the execution of large-scale projects that linked the provinces to the federal capital and often circulated people, money, and ideas back to the Middle East and North Africa. The linkages that formed within this network of movement and infrastructural connection fostered institutions forged from philanthropic campaigns—such as the Hospital Sirio Libanés, artistic projects, or anti-imperialist and Global South solidarities. Each of these case studies highlights scenarios that unfolded across the institutions and communities whose distribution mirrored Argentina's intricate map of rail transit. By beginning a study of the Argentine mahjar with the inception of these local networks, we can better understand the local conditions that undergirded what eventually became global pathways of circulation and exchange. This exercise in decentering our focus on the hub of the federal capital also reveals the ways in which peripheral spaces were instrumental in the construction of international networks of Arabs across Latin America and beyond.

Imagining the Liberal Immigration Project

Liberal elite plans to launch a large-scale immigration project in Argentina were intimately tied to their conceptualizations of rural, "uninhabited" spaces. These were often articulated as threats to state-driven internal colonization schemes. Practically speaking, connecting Argentina's rural spaces to its urban hubs was the key to achieving a modern economic state. Indeed, the inability of the Spanish colonial project to do as much in the Río de la Plata region in part led to its undoing as a colonial possession.[2] Thus, the nineteenth-century creole elite prescription to the diagnosed challenges of consolidating and modernizing the Argentine political apparatus and economy was a twofold investment in immigration and infrastructure. In addition to more concrete imperatives related to territorial domination and economic stimulation, the push to bring large numbers of European immigrants to Argentina was also a response to prevailing creole anxieties regarding the "barbarism" of the tumultuous post-independence decades.

Elites aimed to directly address the dual concern over an undefined frontier between Indigenous- and creole-controlled territories (as well as several South American border disputes), in conjunction with Argentina's relatively low population density overall. In the process, intellectuals staked positions on the essential qualities of the peoples and cultures whom they deemed to be potential vectors of progress—or its inverse. In other words, the immigration boom existed in the imagination before it existed in reality, especially in the minds of political theorists and statesmen such as key members of Argentina's Generation of 1837 intellectual movement. This group of self-declared Sons of the May Revolution (their moniker a nod to the May 1810 series of events that led to the first self-governing Argentine junta during the South American independence wars of the early nineteenth century) included university students, writers, and political theorists. Many of them would go on to forge the foundational documents of the Argentine Republic by midcentury. Sarmiento and Alberdi were among these individuals.

Sarmiento (1811–1888) was a liberal writer and statesman who spent many of his intellectually formative years in exile before becoming Argentina's seventh president in 1868. Alberdi was a political theorist who returned from his Uruguayan and Chilean exile after the fall of Argentina's famous caudillo, Juan Manuel de Rosas, in 1852. Alberdi's *Bases y puntos de partida para la organización política de la República Argentina* drafted many of the concepts that in turn shaped the Argentine Constitution of 1853. While Sarmiento and Alberdi clashed over the early political machinations of Justo José de Urquiza, president of the Argentine Confederation after the defeat of Rosas, they held in common a vision of mass migration as the panacea to their nation's barbarism and underpopulation.

These Generation of '37 voices were the earliest architects of Argentina's national immigration project that would culminate in the arrival of some 5.9 million immigrants by 1916, more than half of whom settled permanently. Going into this project, these men possessed a set of preconceived notions of the essential character of the inhabitants of distinct world regions. These preconceptions came to bear on the rhetorical contours of their discourses on immigration—discourses that often became enshrined in legislative and constitutional acts that shaped Argentine immigrant experiences. In Alberdi's view, "Every European that comes to [Argentine] shores brings . . . more civilization than a great many books of philosophy." In accordance with this logic, he posed the following rhetorical question in his seminal *Bases*: "Do we want to plant and nourish the qualities of English liberty, French culture, and the industriousness of men from Europe and the United States?"[3] The Argentine Constitution of 1853 echoed this directive, legally codifying the European preference at the inception of the immigration boom. The merits or drawbacks associated with the courtship of certain immigrant groups was one based on a set of preexisting frameworks in the creole elite imagination— a dynamic in which the idea of the immigrant arrived in the Argentine imagination before migrants themselves began to arrive at the Port of Buenos Aires. Much as historian Jeffrey Lesser has pointed out the case of Chinese laborers who first came to Brazil in the early nineteenth century, the idea of an Eastern Other existed in South America prior to the arrival of actual Asian migrants.[4]

In the case of the Middle East in the Argentine imaginary, the "Orient" (and an accompanying construct of an Arab Other) existed in creole elite imaginaries in ways that both dovetailed with, yet were also unique from, European Orientalist essentializations of these peoples and places. Repeatedly, nineteenth-century Argentine politicians and intellectuals reflected on the Orient's Middle Eastern and North African geographies and people as sites for comparison to their own fledgling democratic society. In the case of Sarmiento, who frequently refracted his conceptualizations of the Argentine self through Orientalist lenses, an "anxiety of similarity" characterized his repetitive associations between Argentina and the Orient in many of his writings.[5] Thus, one must look no further than the very intellectual center of Argentina's large-scale immigration project to encounter a deeply equivocal relationship to the Arab world.

Unlike the rest of Argentina's Generation of '37 protagonists, Sarmiento had spent time in the Arab Mediterranean. During his Rosas era exile, he traveled to the United States, Europe, and North Africa, all the while assiduously recording his thoughts on the workings of democratic systems and institutions that he observed. In 1847 his journey took him to Algeria, where he spent time with bedouin hosts. Riding through Algeria's Mitidja plains, Sarmiento found both the physical and human geographies reminiscent of Argentina's fertile lowland pampa. During his journey, he acquired a burnoose[6] and reveled in

his belief that this allowed him to effectively masquerade as an Arab. He compared bedouins to Argentine gauchos, the skilled horsemen of the pampa,
and he even went so far as to assert a certain degree of psychological affinity
or synchronicity between the Argentine and the Arab. The nature of his observations was exemplary of the environmental determinism that imbued his
most famous writings such as *Civilización y barbarie: Vida de Juan Facundo
Quiroga* (1845) and *Recuerdos de provincia* (1850). When his 1847 travels subsequently took him to Europe and the United States, he reenacted his bedouin
masquerade. He donned his burnoose for a clandestine, late-night gondola
ride in Venice and a walk through a crowded avenue in Cincinnati.[7] Upon his
return to Chile, he charged his sister with painting a portrait of him in which
he sported a burnoose, fez, and full beard as he sat perched atop a camel.
Sarmiento mixed this Orientalist masquerade, an almost absurdist performance of insistent affinity, with a genuine belief that the Arab world held important lessons for Argentina as a young republic.

Observing the dynamics of French colonialism in Algeria, Sarmiento's
thoughts turned toward civilizing projects in the Americas. In a letter penned
from Algiers, he wrote, "Why can't the Atlantic currents . . . shift toward the
South of América?" This could, he argued, prompt European immigrants to
bring "civilization and industry to the very edges of the concealed Saharas
[*Saharas incógnitas*] that hide in America's tropical zones."[8] Prior to spending time in North Africa, Sarmiento had already floated ideas of immigration projects as solutions to the "barbarism" present in potentially civilizable
societies, and he continued to contribute columns on the subject to Chilean
newspapers while in exile. However, Algeria was his first experience of observing a modern European settler colonial project. At the end of his time there,
he concluded that waves of European immigrant-settlers had tempered the
barbarous elements of Algerian society. Notwithstanding, his was an equivocal relationship toward Arabs and bedouins—one embodied by his impulse to
emulate them while simultaneously approving of French colonial subjugation
of Arab peoples.

This ambivalence, central in Sarmiento's writings on Arab peoples and
landscapes, also characterized other moments in the history of Argentine
policymakers, journalists, and public figures whose relationship to both the
idea of Middle Eastern immigrants, as well as the actual Arab *colectividad*,
was mutable and situational. This is a departure from a historiographical tendency to characterize discrete ethnic groups as either welcomed or unwanted

in the eyes of a host country. Moving away from this binary also allows us to investigate the ways in which immigrants from Argentina's Middle Eastern communities navigated these shifting political and social contingencies over the course of several generations.

Preferential Policies: Origins and Occupations

From the outset of Argentina's courtship of the immigrant masses, policymakers expressed a European preference.[9] Into the twenty-first century, this preference remained on the books, even though most of the Americas abandoned official European preferential legislation after 1964. Argentina never legally sanctioned the targeted ethnic, racial, or national exclusion that marked the policies of many other governments in the Americas. Elsewhere, official policies of exclusion had cyclically rippled across the hemisphere since the mid-1800s. The series of Asian exclusion acts that proliferated from the 1880s to the 1920s exemplify this broader politics of exclusion. In their longitudinal study of racist immigration policy in the Americas, David Fitzgerald and David Cook-Martín attribute Argentina's relative lack of explicitly discriminatory legislation to, among other factors, the imperative to populate Argentina's expansive geography.[10]

In general, positive expressions of preference and subjectively vague statements of the state's ability to reject unwanted arrivals were the standard rather than specific restriction or exclusion when it came to immigration policy during the height of Middle Eastern immigration to Argentina from 1880 to 1915. In 1902, congress passed the Residency Law (Ley de Residencia), formalizing the subjective discrimination that was already in practice by granting authorities the right to lawfully expel immigrants for several nebulous offenses. These included the act of "perturbing public order," in Argentina, or even in years past in their place of provenance, meriting retroactive punishment. The Law of Social Defense (Ley de Defensa Social) followed in 1910, mandating heavy fines and even prison sentences for individuals responsible for transporting people deemed detrimental to the social good into the Port of Buenos Aires.

This lack of official sanctions against particular migrant groups did not, however, equate to a lack of more or less formalized discriminatory practices. Argentine consular agents and immigration officials periodically used administrative tactics to reduce and restrict entry by, or dissuade the emigration of, Jews, *gitanos*, and Middle Easterners. These tactics included circulars and veiled directives sent to international Argentine diplomatic outposts or foreign authorities in charge of granting exit visas for potential emigrants.[11] These examples all point to a bias against the arrival of immigrants from the Arabic-speaking eastern Mediterranean—but a bias that was nevertheless left out of official legislation. This may have been due in part to the fact that there was a marked inconsistency in the classification of Ottoman immigrants once they arrived at an Argentine point of entry, meaning that, much like elsewhere in the Americas, Ottoman Syrians often found themselves in a liminal juris- dictional area between ethnic and racial categories in the eyes of many host country constitutions, censuses, and immigration policies.[12]

Whether Argentine immigration authorities understood Middle Eastern migration as conforming to or at odds with this European preference was inconsistent. In 1905, the Dirección General de Inmigración (National Im- migration Authority) classified Ottomans as Asians. Seven years later, their annual report suggested otherwise. In a full-page map labeled "Nationality of Immigrant Arrivals in the Argentine Republic from 1857–1913," the cor- responding image was nowhere close to a comprehensive cartography of all migrant nationalities represented by the demographics of this boom period. Instead, the map depicted only a floating image of the European continent, completely unmoored from any of its Asian border states. Inscribed next to each country name was the number of immigrant arrivals of origin. In the case of the Ottoman Empire, the borders outlined on the map included only land west and north of the Straits of Bosporus and the Dardanelles and was la- beled "Turkey." Written across this geographic area was the number "130,939," suggesting (erroneously) that the Ottoman administrative divisions (or vilay- ets) of Adrianople and the western half of Istanbul were the point of origin for this large number of migrants. This was of course not the case. Although they may have been labeled as *turcos* upon entry to Argentina, Ottoman arrivals hailed overwhelmingly from the vilayets of Syria, Beirut, and Aleppo and the governorates of Mount Lebanon and Jerusalem.

The elision of the correct geography of provenance for Ottomans who made their way to Argentina by 1914 was more than a clerical error, though. The erasure of that territory from the official map also achieved the erasure of Asia on a continental scale from the official imaginary of Argentina's im- migrant masses. With that, the Dirección General de Inmigración recast Ottomans as Europeans, despite having classified them as Asians less than a decade earlier. Cartographically rendering the Middle East as within the bounds of Europe at this moment may have been related to a diplomatic

Figure 1. Middle Eastern migrants on a Buenos Aires patio in 1902. Source: Archivo General de la Nación, Buenos Aires, Argentina, Inv.154999.

flare-up between Argentine and British officials. In 1912, Argentine authorities attempted to block the entrance of a small group of Indian Sikh laborers through diplomatic means and labor exclusion. All the while, the authorities insisted—in their own defense—that Argentina's immigrant masses were European, not Asian. (British authorities weren't amused and pointed out that the Sikh laborers were traveling on British colonial passports.) This may help to explain why authorities hastily reclassified these Ottoman vilayets (and by proxy more than 100,000 Ottoman migrants) as part of Europe in their records surrounding the debacle with the British.[13] In 1925, the annual report once again unambiguously classified Ottoman Syrians as Asians. Regardless of the exact set of contingencies that weighed into this inconsistency, the net result was a marked mutability in the way that the Argentine state classified the first generations of Ottoman Syrian immigrants who took up residence in cities and towns across the country (see Figure 1).

In addition to unraveling the shifting place of Middle Eastern migration within the ethnonational parameters of the creole elite's immigration project, we must also examine policymakers' concurrent desire to attract certain kinds of laborers to Argentina—namely, industrial and agricultural ones. They believed that an industrializing workforce would propel Argentina into modernity. As such, a strong occupational bias toward immigrants who would work the fields and factory lines underpinned their rationale. In this regard, Alberdi asked, "Do we want orderly, disciplined, energetic work habits to prevail in South America?" Answering this rhetorical question, he concluded, "Then let us fill our country with people who have a profound grasp of such habits. Those who are well acquainted with industrial Europe will soon form industrial South America."[14] Immigrants who arrived with the desire to work in occupations other than those perceived to fuel the industrial engine of economic progress risked backlash. The rhetoric of political theorists such as Alberdi—and the language of the 1853 Constitution—signals not only the presence of prevailing racist attitudes of the era but also the perception that pro-immigration policy had the power to fill occupational lacunae in the Argentine economy. Encouraging the arrival of migrants who would till fields and work factory lines dovetailed with goals of methodically and systematically settling Argentina's interior, as well as expanding the national economy.

Early on, Ottoman Syrians gained a reputation for tending to avoid entry into these agricultural and industrial sectors. The stereotype of the itinerant pack peddler—the *mercachifle*—became prominent in critiques leveled against Ottoman Syrians by national press organs and immigration authorities alike by the turn of the century. "We have all seen them walk down our streets, dirty and ragged dragging their wretched merchandise, which they offer from door to door," lamented Juan Alsina, director of immigration, in 1900. "Some move to towns in the provinces, while others risk going to the countryside for the same purpose. Most of these merchants are only agents of companies of the same nationality, which do business with a relatively large capital. The Syrian immigrant does not represent an efficient socio-economic factor. . . . His role as a consumer is minimal and the part he plays as a producer is non-existent," he continued.[15] Editorials in national press organs such as *La Prensa, La Nación,* and *El Mercurio* voiced similar critiques of the Syrian mercachifle in the first decade of the twentieth century.[16]

Complaints about nonsettled turco mercachifles also emanated from private citizens who saw their interests directly jeopardized by the activities of itinerant peddlers. During the 1910s, various complaints submitted to the Departamento Nacional de Trabajo (DNT; National Labor Department) shared a critique of the mobile lifestyle and business model of mercachifles. In most of the cases, the complainants were landowners who claimed that peddlers were taking advantage of naive clientele. If we dig into the details of the complaints, a pattern emerges of capitalist landowners who asserted a dangerous connection between turcos and local Indigenous groups, particularly Indians employed by the agricultural economy of these local landowners. In several instances, DNT officials appear to have bought in to these accusations. In 1914, DNT inspector Miguel Vidal traveled to Jujuy province to investigate the conditions of Indian laborers on sugar plantations (*ingenios*). He dutifully reported back to the DNT the claims made by local landowners and military officials who accused turco peddlers of duping ingenio laborers. In his report, Vidal recorded the following narrative of mercachifle activities:

> The company store . . . does not sell alcohol nor firearms. Indians come by these items once they leave the sugar mill. Strategically situated, numerous turcos co-merciantes wait for the Indians along the path that they must take to return to their village. In turn, Indians trade the horses and clothing they have acquired at the company store for a gun and ammunition. I have never witnessed this, but everyone testifies as much. . . . I believe that even with the greatest regulations to govern the Indians, they will always be at the mercy of these merchants.[17]

Later in his report he would go so far as to claim that he was "positive that [tur-cos] provide arms and war munitions [*munición de guerra*]" to the Indians.[18] Local military officer Lieutenant Mariano Aráoz de Lamadrid sent similar complaints back to the DNT in his own report. In it, he indicated that sugar cane mill owners believed that turco merchants were traveling northward from Salta Province and engaging in illegal arms trading with indio workers (*comercio furtivo de armas*).[19] It is clear that the presence of mobile turco ped-dlers was a convenient scapegoat for several interested parties, including the Argentine government, military, and owners of large agricultural enterprises. Labor inspectors could claim that all was above board in terms of wages paid to Indian laborers; if there was any exploitation, it was not at the hands of ingenio owners but rather nefarious turco peddlers. Military officials were able to continuously animate the specter of Indian armed uprising by sound-ing the alarm about the arms sales. Finally, ingenio owners could shirk re-sponsibility for underpaying laborers by claiming that their workers departed Jujuy for their home villages in the Chaco region at the end of the season with all they needed, yet were met along the way by interloping merchants. In this sense, the turco mercachifle played a linchpin role in the construction of Indians as alternately dangerous or infinitely manipulable—and either way in need of regulation. Nor was the fixation on peddlers as a risk to security and development in the region a passing complaint; it was in fact enshrined in the regulations for Indian labor contracting signed by military authorities in the Chaco as well as Jujuy-based ingenio owners. Article 6 of the contract stated that ingenio owners were obligated to give thirty days' notice to proper authorities if they observed "hawkers" (*ambulantes*). The article prohibited direct commerce with Indians and accused peddlers of "taking advantage of, and exploiting the ignorance and vices of the Indians and selling to them . . . at an unfair profit, and even selling them arms and the provisions of war."[20] Indian workers at the Ledesma ingenio rejected the contract and refused to work after new rules allowed ingenio owners to withhold a certain percent of their wages in mandatory savings. The predatory tactics of turco vendors were a major justification for this wage holding, but after Indians at least one ingenio refused to work under these new stipulations, DNT inspector Alejandro M. Unsain reported to the Buenos Aires office on the subsequent revision of the contract. Although the revised contract contained certain wage and company store pricing concessions to the Indians, it also added new language to more firmly prohibit trade with pack peddlers.[21]

Another report from the DNT, this one on living and working conditions in the Chaco and Formosa Territories, reflected similar conflicts between the activities of Middle Eastern merchants and the monopolistic desires of local agro-industrialists. The latter fought hard to ensure the primacy of the company store in the daily economy of workers but had difficulty cracking down on mobile merchants. In contrast to the DNT Inspectors Unsain and Vidal in Jujuy, the functionary sent to the Gran Chaco region appeared somewhat more skeptical of local complaints. In 1915, DNT inspector José Elías Niklison sought local testimony and evidence regarding turco pack peddlers who sold to Indian workers from the Compañía Las Palmas del Chaco Austral sugar and quebracho mill in the Presidencia Roca canton of the Chaco territory. Over the course of his trip to the area surrounding Las Palmas, the inspector took assiduous notes on the power dynamics that seemed to hold sway over local politics. Situated on the Bermejo River, the mill was by far the largest economic engine in this rural area north of Resistencia, the territorial capital. Its owner was Carlos Hardy, a wealthy man whom Niklison unflinchingly characterized as "a species of feudal lord who is feared and obeyed" and who had created in Las Palmas an environment "of autocracy and oppression."[22] Mataco, Chorote, and especially Toba Indians did the bulk of the grueling work at Las Palmas, where they received half a peso every 350 to 400 meter line of sugar cane harvested. Working in squads of fifty to eighty people, men, women, and children alike descended on the cane fields during harvest season in early June and then fed the cane into the powerful mill. Two twelve-hour work shifts daily kept the mill running around the clock during harvest season. For their labor they were paid in *fichas* or *letras*—company store scrip.[23] This system was put in place to try to maintain the circulation of wages within the company's holdings and prevent capital from escaping into the outside local economy. Any wages spent at the company store were, after all, a savings for Hardy's operation. Seemingly dissatisfied with the offerings or prices at the company store, or both, however, Indian workers took their scrip to local Middle Eastern merchants and used their fichas to purchase a variety of wares at better prices, and sometimes superior quality. This practice was strictly prohibited by the Las Palmas administrators, who became aware of the practice only after Middle Eastern vendors began appearing at the mill and demanding that the scrip be exchanged for money.[24]

In the wake of these demands from Middle Eastern peddlers, Hardy cracked down on peddling at Las Palmas. He posted public advisories warning local businesses not to accept Las Palmas scrip, and informing workers of severe consequences for spending their wages on the goods other than those purveyed by the company store. Hardy went so far as to make examples of workers who continued to violate this code—in one case, even firing an employee of eighteen years. In that instance, Cantalicio Romero, a seasonal worker from Corrientes, lost his job at Las Palmas after his wife allowed "some Arab merchants" to take rest and drink water on the patio of the Romero household. In another punitive action, Hardy fired an Italian immigrant working as a planter after the employee purchased a coat from "los turcos." Hardy denied his former employee, Cinira Fioravanti, 661.40 pesos in back pay and posted a warning to future turco vendors and their potential customers that stated the following:

TURCO PEDDLERS:

The Company does not want these people to circulate [*transitar*] its crops [*chacras*], and you must prohibit their entry. If they question you, you must explain that the law says that they are no longer to circulate here, and must only travel on public roads, and as we have no public roads here, you are thereby authorized to throw [the vendors] out. Any difficulty that results from this order, you must communicate with the Administration.

Likely feeling that Hardy wielded too much local power, Niklison actually pushed back against this crackdown on Middle Eastern merchants. He reported to the DNT that "all of the peddlers that I have known regularly pay for their [peddling license] that enables them to legally exercise this type of commerce. I was unable to confirm any infraction committed on their part. The 'turcos' disdain for the 'authority' of these large businesses is evident inasmuch as is their sincere respect for the laws of this country, and the functionaries charged with enforcing them" (see Figures 2 and 3). He also intervened firmly on the side of two merchants, Emilio Naput, and Manuel Sapagnin, who were engaged in a dispute with Las Palmas administrators over the disbursement of nearly 2,000 pesos in cash owed them after they accepted scrip payment from workers in exchange for goods vended. Following Niklison's intervention, the administration begrudgingly squared the balance with the peddlers. The DNT inspector criticized the greedy administrators, characterizing their actions as shameful, and painting an exceedingly positive (if also deeply stereotypical and racially charged) image of Middle Eastern peddlers as a group, insisting that they were "disciplined and docile." He went so far as to insist that the Ministry of the Interior would do best to pen a circular that might encourage local police forces to accord safety guarantees to traveling merchants like Naput and Sapagnin. This was necessary, he insisted, in order to "avoid events that do not coincide with the liberty, civilization, and culture of our country."[25]

While it is tempting to conclude from this episode that Niklison stood out as a government official with an exceptionally open mind about the rights of Middle Eastern migrants to circulate through the interior, it is well worth noting that not two years later, Niklison's take on turco peddling was much more in line with his colleagues Unsain and Vidal. While on a mission to Salta Province to investigate an uprising of Mataco Indian laborers, Niklison repeated the theory that unscrupulous mercachifles routinely took advantage of the seasonal labor migration of Indians en route to their villages in the Chaco after the cane harvest.[26] Overall, this reminds us that authorities' position toward Middle Eastern migrant vendors was situational, and certainly based on what was expedient given the contingencies of local, political, or economic conditions. These reports also reinforce the perspective that the mobility of these Middle Eastern migrants was often distressing to several groups, including military

Figure 2. Pack peddler's medallion, 1905. Peddlers carried these medallions on their person as a form of license to operate in a designated area. Source: Archivo del Instituto de Investigación en Arte y Cultura "Dr. Norberto Griffa" de la Universidad Nacional de Tres de Febrero, Buenos Aires, Argentina. Reprinted with permission.

forces, government officials, and land and business owners. It is important that we view the ways in which individuals like Hardy and Lieutenant Lamadrid characterized peddler threats as intertwined with other anxieties about the settlement of frontier spaces, and the exercise of control over their Indigenous inhabitants.

Back in Buenos Aires, while immigration port authorities did not officially deny rights or services to Ottoman Syrians across the board, they did take measures to disincentivize their choice to become entrepreneurs rather than industrial or agricultural workers. In 1910, for example, Argentine immigration officials permitted only Syrians who proclaimed that they would not become merchants to stay in the Hotel de Inmigrantes, the Buenos Aires boardinghouse stationed at the point of disembarkation for new immigrant arrivals.[27] In response to the Argentine state's negative association with the image of the itinerant merchant, Syrian community leaders, as well as the Ottoman consul general, worked with immigration officials on various schemes to encourage Syrian immigrants toward agriculture rather than petty commerce.[28] None of these efforts, however, made a serious impact on the tendency toward commerce. Instead, the first two decades of the twentieth century saw the proliferation of Middle Eastern immigrants and their descendants establish businesses throughout the Argentine provinces and territories. To understand the mechanics

Figure 3. "Mercachifle a pie" vendor license. Pack peddler Chama Abraham of Lomas de Zamora, Buenos Aires Province, carried this license with him throughout 1928. Source: Archivo del Instituto de Investigación en Arte y Cultura "Dr. Norberto Griffa" de la Universidad Nacional de Tres de Febrero, Buenos Aires, Argentina. Reprinted with permission.

of this demographic spread, it is necessary to examine the mobility of this migrant population in tandem with the history of transportation technology in Argentina. The boom in railroad technology that was concurrent with the boom in international migration to Argentina enabled the mobility between spaces that, I argue, came to characterize the South American mahjar.

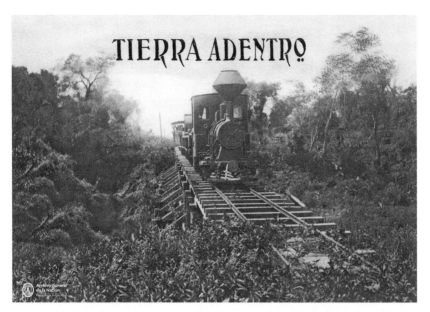

Figure 4. Narrow gauge Formosa Railroad, 1911. Source: Archivo General de la
Nación, Buenos Aires, Argentina, Caja 3073/Inv.160546.

"Filling" and Connecting Space: The Railroad Boom

The railroad boom represented a reorganization of rural space around the
technology and economy of a centralized Argentine state starting in the late
nineteenth century. By 1914, the railroad annually transported 10 million
tons of cereal, 72 million passengers, and 5 million tons of livestock.[29] By mid-
twentieth century, Argentina had the most extensive railroad system in Latin
America. The region's belle époque era of increased foreign investments, industrial growth, and urban reform manifested in a major infrastructural shift
that linked Argentina's interior to the capital more efficiently than ever before
(see Figure 4). Between 1857 and 1920, the Argentine rail system grew from
10,000 to 47,000 kilometers of track.[30] Foreign (primarily British) investment
in rail lines that cut through the pampa and extended in all directions addressed the need for large-scale transportation of agricultural goods and laborers, and livestock. The infrastructural shift in the Argentine landscape caused
by the expansion of the railroads marched forward in tandem with the demographic shift brought on by mass migration. As James Scobie points out in
his study of provincial Argentine cities, "At the outset, Buenos Aires had not

exerted the same domination over the railroad system as it had held over river transportation by virtue of its position as the major city at the mouth of the [River Plate] estuary."[31] The lack of centralized control over the construction of railways resulted in the proliferation of competing rail networks that mirrored, and emerged from, the rivalry between Buenos Aires and the provinces. While the Buenos Aires–based rail network slowly radiated outward from the Port of Buenos Aires like the spokes of a wheel, the provincial rail network pushed westward and northward to the provinces of Mendoza, San Luis, La Rioja, Catamarca, Santiago del Estero, Salta, and Jujuy. The spokes of the Buenos Aires line reached northeastward into the province of Santa Fe and up into the verdant region of Entre Ríos, Corrientes, and Misiones by the close of the nineteenth century.

In the 1880s, these two rail networks merged just as Buenos Aires officially became the federal district after decades of internecine power struggles between the Federal and Unitarian parties. Along with its federalization, Buenos Aires gained control over a railroad system on the brink of a boom. A surge in rail construction under the auspices of mainly British stakeholders accompanied the modernization of the Port of Buenos Aires and an increase in wheat farming and livestock ranching on the plains. For provincial capitals such as Mendoza and San Juan, the arrival of the railroad was a catalyst that spurred both economic growth and urban expansion.

The introduction of rail technology to the nation's most remote terrains was integral to the modernization schemes of thinkers such as Sarmiento and Alberdi. In his 1852 *Bases*, Alberdi proclaimed:

> We must bring our capitals to the coast, or rather bring the littoral to the interior of the continent. By conquering distance, the railroad and the telegraph will forge the unity of the Argentine Republic better than any congress. The congresses may declare it one and indivisible, but without the railroad to connect its most remote regions it will always remain divided and divisible, despite all the legislative decrees.[32]

From its inception, national leaders envisioned the railroad as the cornerstone of political and territorial unity. It was also inextricably bound up with their vision of how mass migration could forge a new Argentina. In this regard, Alberdi noted:

> Nor can you bring the interior of our lands within reach of Europe's immi-

grants, who today are regenerating our coasts, except with the powerful aid of the railroads. They are (or will be) to the life of our interior territories what the great arteries are to the inferior extremities of the human body: sources of life.[33]

The subtle implication of Alberdi's bio-metaphor was that without railroads to carry immigrants to distant interior territories, those lands would lie empty and fallow—devoid of human life. Yet much of the interior was not empty and fallow; rather, it was settled by Indigenous groups such as the Toba of the Chaco and the Mapuche in Patagonia. This type of rhetoric was typical in many expansionist projects of the nineteenth century, especially in North American Manifest Destiny narratives. As American studies scholar David Nye reminds us, "In most foundational narratives there is no mention of any previous inhabitants, as though the continent had been completely raw and undeveloped, waiting for the axe, the sawmill, and the arrival of the first railroad."[34]

In this light, the railroad served as the technological arm of conquest that followed military campaigns against Argentina's Indigenous communities that took place over the course of the 1870s and 1880s. In the case of the Chaco Territory, Gastón Gordillo confirms, the expansion of the railroads was "imagined as the last stage of the conquest of the Chaco. Now that Indigenous armed resistance had been defeated, progress demanded modifying the form of the geography to make it more amenable to mobility and speed."[35] The railroads continued to occupy an important place in the national imaginary well into the twentieth century, reaching a "symbolic landmark" in 1948 when President Juan Domingo Perón nationalized British-owned tracks to create the state-owned Ferrocarriles Argentinos. The following decades saw the railroads become "emblems of an assertive Argentine nationality, and also of the Peronist welfare state that partly eroded the power of the old elites."[36] As James Scobie notes, from the outset, "the prospect of railroad communication captivated everyone's imagination."[37] This was of course not limited to the imagination of elite intellectuals such as Alberdi or Sarmiento. For thousands of Arab migrants who arrived in Argentina at the peak of the nation's rail construction fever, the newly laid tracks offered access to frontier regions and provincial urban centers where they could work in an entrepreneurial capacity.

The development of the rail system dramatically reorganized rural space in Argentina. By the last decade of the nineteenth century, all of the provincial capitals were connected to the increasingly proliferating rail lines. This was in stark contrast to the fact that prior to 1870, less than 20 percent of the national population lived within 10 kilometers of a rail line. This means that less than 20 percent of the Argentine population lived within approximately a three-hour journey by horse-drawn wagon to a rail station. With the track construction boom of the 1880s, access to rail lines by the general population drastically expanded, revolutionizing the logistics of travel. Riding the rails was cheaper than traveling by wagon and ten times faster in addition to enabling passengers to avoid some of the perils of road travel such as banditry. Railroads also altered the social landscape, with stations serving as important spaces of sociability in addition to gauntlets of commerce and transportation. In their heyday, railroads embodied a "type of inclusive national collectivity" for which many rural residents today invoke nostalgia in the wake of the almost total decommissioning of Argentina's passenger rail network in the 1990s.[38]

Equally in its logistical, technological, and symbolic dimensions, the railroad boom represents the most prominent example of state-driven colonization and organization of national territorial resources. Though it was a moment of looking inward toward the farthest reaches of the interior, from contested Patagonian borderlands to the rugged Chaco, it was also a globalizing moment for a relatively young republic. The expansion of the rail network came to fruition through large-scale foreign investment and a continuous circulation of prospectors who sought to bring their expertise to the Argentine frontier. As North American and European onlookers eagerly appraised the possibilities of rail investment in Argentina, foreign observers noted the logic of peopling "empty" space that served as an imperative to liberal presidents such as Bartolomé Mitre (1862–1868). "President Mitre is working heaven and earth to people his deserted country, and drive it ahead" reported the US resident minister in Buenos Aires, Robert Kirk, in a cable to the US State Department in 1863.[39] In addition to dramatically deepening Argentine links to global systems of capital investment, this moment created the infrastructural means by which a wide array of international peoples and cultures infused rural and urban spaces starting in the final quarter of the nineteenth century. It is crucial to situate the arrival of Middle Eastern migrants to Argentina within this context of the revolution in travel and mobility that the railroad boom represents. Only then can we properly appraise the modes and roles of mobility in the Argentine mahjar.

In the vast landscape of Argentina's provinces and national territories, the migration of Arab Argentines contributed to the establishment of new towns, as well as population spikes of already-established municipalities made possible by the developing rail system. This pattern of rail, municipal, and demographic development emerged in provinces and national territories across the country. A handful of the hundreds of examples where this occurred illustrate this dynamic. In Córdoba Province, the town of Villa Deán Funes was established in 1875 when the Ferrocarril Central del Norte reached the area, and the town of Cruz del Eje was established in 1890, one year prior to the completion of the train station. In 1891, Cruz del Eje became an important railroad junction, causing a spike in both population and industry. In Buenos Aires Province, Berabevú was established in 1902 with the inauguration of the railroad, and an associate from the Empresa Ferrocarriles Argentinos purchased the first tracts of land that would go on to comprise that small agricultural municipality. Also in Buenos Aires Province, Berisso and Sierras Bayas were important mining towns in the early years of the railroad. Between 1895 and 1905, *conchilla* quarries in Berisso provided a calcareous material used as ballast in train cars, and Sierras Bayas also had a calcium quarry. Tandil, now a bustling university city, had fewer than five hundred inhabitants before the arrival of the train line, which infused the area with immigrants who expanded the ranching and mining industries. Similarly, the city of Pergamino grew around Estación Pergamino after its construction by the French enterprise Compañía General de Ferrocarriles en la Provincia de Buenos Aires in 1908.[40] These are but a few emblematic examples of the transformations that characterized the interior at the turn of the century and the decades that immediately followed. Middle Eastern immigrants made their way to all these municipalities: Deán Funes, Cruz del Eje, Berabevú, Berisso, Sierras Bayas, Tandil, and Pergamino.

Business prospects often depended on the growth of new markets and populations clustered around rail line hubs. Many Middle Eastern families strategically based their settlement on the path of the railroad, at times even setting up shop beyond the end of a rail line in the hopes that the line would extend. This was precisely the gamble that the Sapag family took when they purchased land in the southern Territory of Neuquén in 1912. They hoped that the trains (and the potential consumers that they carried) would follow.[41] Their gamble paid off, and in 1913, the British-owned Ferrocarril del Sud inaugurated a large station at Zapala—precisely where the Sapag family had

set up their grocery and dry goods store. It is likely that their economic success permitted—or at least encouraged—the chain migration of additional
family members from Mayrouba in Mount Lebanon. The next generation of
the Sapag family expanded their commercial enterprises westward in lockstep
with the rail line, which opened the Plaza Huincul station in 1921, some 75
kilometers west of Zapala. The Sapag family also installed themselves in the
Plaza Huincul area and opened more dry goods and grocery stores, as well as
a café and butcher shop.[42] With the discovery of petroleum in Plaza Huincul
in 1918, the area became an important economic frontier for the Patagonian
region. The Sapags were well situated and became important players in the
foundation of the nearby municipality of Cutral Có. Cutral Có would come to
represent the petrochemical epicenter of the Yacimientos Petrolíferos Fiscales
(YPF) oil fields founded by Enrique Mosconi in 1922 during the first term of
Unión Cívica Radical president Hipólito Yrigoyen. Since opening a dry goods
warehouse in Cutral Có, the careers of many Sapags mirrored the powerful
ascendancy of YPF.

In the case of the Sapag family, the early choice to invest in property and
businesses along the rail lines led to not only socioeconomic but also political opportunity for three sons in particular: Elías (b. 1911), Amado (b. 1921),
and Felipe (b. 1917). After establishing a warehouse and butcher business in
Cutral Có, Elías Sapag gained recognition of his role as one of the founding
pioneers of the community. In 1936, Colonel Enrique Pilotto, governor of the
National Territory of Neuquén, appointed Elías chair of the Comisión de Fomento Muicipal (a "settlement committee" in charge of attracting and facilitating the arrival of settlers and businesses to the area), with Felipe Sapag as
secretary. In this capacity the brothers spearheaded tax collection, infrastructural development, and municipal works projects during Elías's term in office,
which lasted until 1942. In 1945, all three brothers established the Sapag Her-
manos Sociedad Comercial Colectiva enterprise, a lucrative business that led
them to become the central beef distributor to the Argentine Army posts in
the region. It also provided them the resources to enter the local mining and
petrochemical industry. Aside from Elías's leadership in Cutral Có, Amado
went on to become mayor of the town of Zapala, the site of the original Sapag
businesses established in 1912. He served six nonconsecutive terms as Zapala's
mayor between 1952 and 1987. In the same year that Amado began his first
term as mayor of Zapala, Felipe Sapag became mayor of Cutral Có.

All three brothers became active supporters of Juan Perón after his election to the presidency for the first of three presidential terms in 1946. Known for the broad-based, coalitional politics of his Justicialist Party, Perón would be reelected in 1952 for a second term, only to have it cut short by the Revolución Libertadora military coup of 1955. He spent the next eighteen years in exile, as widespread grassroots movements of Peronist sympathizers carried out clandestine acts of sabotage against the military government during an era that came to be known as the *Resistencia peronista* (Peronist resistance). In this political context, the Sapag brothers founded the Movimiento Popular Neuquino (MPN, Neuquen People's Movement) political party, instating Elías as the party's first president. In the years that followed, Felipe would become a five-term governor of the Province of Neuquén by running on an MPN ticket between 1963 and 1999, and Elías a three-term national senator between 1963 and 1993 (also on the MPN ticket). The center-right MPN would go on to win the governorship for Neuquén Province in every election after 1963, as well as consistent representation in the National Congress and Senate in addition to numerous local elections. The Sapag family remains a political dynasty, with Elías's son Jorge serving as two-term provincial governor from 2007 to 2015.[43]

Of course, the spectacular trajectory of the Sapag family in Neuquén is not representative of the experience of the majority of Middle Eastern immigrants who staked their economic success on following (or anticipating) Argentina's rail expansion. Rather, it is much more reminiscent of a real-life episode of the rags-to-riches hagiography that came to dominate many historical narratives of the Arab Argentine community over the course of the twentieth century. The story is emblematic, however, as an example of the thousands of Middle Eastern migrant families who moved into Argentine frontier spaces in the late nineteenth and early twentieth centuries alongside, or in anticipation of, the arrival of rail transportation. This was a pattern that repeated itself across the Argentine provinces and national territories, resulting ultimately in the distribution of Arab Argentine communities throughout urban and rural spaces. Rather than consolidation around urban economic centers, this scattered settlement pattern defined this diaspora's demographics.

Studies of Argentina's Arabic-speaking immigrants generally note the dispersed nature in which the diaspora diffused across the Argentine landscape—and indeed the Americas more generally. However, this fact tends to serve as a footnote or preamble to the case studies of local communities where Middle Eastern immigrants lived in greater numbers: Córdoba, Buenos Aires, Tucumán, and Santiago del Estero, for example. By charting the history of

Middle Eastern migrant settlement through the history of Argentine transportation technology, we can construct an analytical model for interpreting the settlement patterns of this immigrant group. Because of the extensiveness of the railroad track laid from the late nineteenth to early twentieth century, this strategy offers a vision of Middle Eastern settlement in Argentina at a truly national scale. It also permits the incorporation of the hundreds of rural communities and outposts of the diaspora that blossomed around the spread of the rail system. This inclusion expands our focus beyond the urban epicenters (and their elite voices) that have been rendered as the central protagonists of the diaspora. In addition, it is important to map out this framework for cross-provincial and cross-territorial mobility as a baseline for subsequent chapters of this book that examine the circulation of people, goods, and ideas within the Argentine mahjar.

Decentering the Mahjar Map

It can be challenging to systematically recover archival documentation of the early generations of Arab immigrants who settled sparsely populated, remote regions of the Argentine map. In the case of rugged areas like the Gran Chaco or Southern Andean Yungas, Middle Eastern migrants made their way overland to settle in small villages and even contested frontier spaces. They opened dry goods shops and general and grocery stores, and they established itinerant vending routes that sustained the inhabitants of these rural spaces. They served rural communities—creole, immigrant, and Indigenous—and provided them with modest links to consumer culture, in addition to offering basic subsistence provisions for purchase. Memories of their presence, especially that of the turco mercachifle figure, appear sporadically in the writings of those who lived in or traveled through these terrains. Even the iconic artistic depictions of rural life by the painter Florencio Molina Campos (1851–1959) included these merchants in paintings such as *El Mercachifle* (1945; see Figure 5).

Many merchants tied their business prospects to the growth of new markets and populations clustered around rail stations and junctions. Criollo elites and politicians increasingly took note of the intense mobility of Middle Eastern migrants in the early decades of the twentieth century. In 1931, one functionary from the arid northwestern province of Salta commented on the Arab community's dispersal across the Argentine landscape: They "proceed from remote civilizations" and can be found in "the pampas, the mountains, populous cities, and the most remote corner of the desert."[44] This pattern of

Figure 5. El Mercachifle, (1945). Depiction of rural pack peddling by Florencio Molina Campos. Source: Museo Las Lilas Collection, San Antonio de Areco, Buenos Aires Province, Argentina. Reprinted with permission.

dispersal via pack peddling along rail routes was not unique to Argentina. In Brazil as well, Arab peddlers who serviced coffee plantations moved along trade routes that paralleled the construction of new railroad lines.[45]

In Brazil, Lesser contends that the construction of a uniquely Arab Brazilian cultural-ethnic identity was built on the foundational figure of the pack peddler (*mascate* in Portuguese). His contention is supported by the fact that the mascate was a figure later lauded in poetry and prose penned by Arab Brazilians who proclaimed themselves to be proud descendants of mascates.[46] This pack-peddling identity is less foregrounded in historiography of the Argentine mahjar, and numerous Arab Argentine press organs founded in the 1920s and 1930s that often contained editorials and other musings on the origins of Argentina's Middle Eastern colectividad. Instead, the Arab Argentine press tended to heavily emphasize figures and cultures from ancient Middle Eastern history when expounding on the roots of the Argentine mahjar throughout the first half of the twentieth century. By the 1930s and 1940s,

Arab Argentine journalists reached back to distant pasts of Phoenician traders, intellectual traditions of Arab and Persian scholars and mathematicians, or even European notions such as René Guenón's "Oriental Metaphysics" more often than they did the trope of the mercachifle.[47] This may have been a conscious disassociation by mahjar elites interested in distancing themselves from an origin narrative based on itinerant pack peddling. After all, this hypermobile profession had, in many instances, evoked negative reactions from journalists and politicians. We might recall, for example, director of immigration Juan Alsina's 1899 invective against Syrian peddlers whom he accused of "dragging their wretched merchandise . . . from door to door."[48] The reigning ideology on the role and purpose of immigration was, in addition to peopling "empty" terrains, the creation of a reliable labor source to spur agricultural and industrial development. The agricultural or industrial laborer was imagined as a predictable, static unit that would migrate from point A (country of origin) to point B (Argentine location in need of peopling or labor supply), enter the workforce, and subsequently be well within the control of the Argentine state and its developing capitalist economy. Whether the settlement and labor patterns of immigrants who entered these workforces were in reality so predictable (and they were not) is secondary. The point is that itinerant merchants did not fit within the bounds of the imagined ideal immigrant precisely because of their autonomous mobility. At any rate, by the early decades of the twentieth century, elite Arab Argentine journalists produced numerous editorials in widely distributed publications such as *Assalam* in which they pleaded with their "co-nationals" (*conacionales*) to give up peddling and commit themselves to agriculture.[49]

While some members of the colectividad joined skeptical immigration authorities who pegged aspirations of national progress to industrial and agricultural workers, other voices from Argentina's Middle Eastern diaspora at times sought to recast the image of the itinerant peddler as an agent of progress and modernity. In 1933, Syrian journalist Miguel Yapur of the provincial capital San Miguel de Tucumán published a treatise on the figure of the ubiquitous itinerant vendor:

> [The mercachifle] populated with his exoticism and strength the extensive plains of the patria. He scaled the higher mountains to bring [his wares] to even the most humble ranches in the sierras. He is the continuation of the work of the pioneer of progress who, with his pack hoisted on his shoulder, traversed the

most impassable regions of this new country in order to bring its inhabitants a touch of civilization. [50]

Here, Yapur deftly converts Middle Eastern migrants into the very civilizing force that played a central role in the rhetoric of intellectuals and statesmen like Sarmiento and Alberdi.

What we witness here is not, however, a simple tension between a settled middle and upper class versus an itinerant lower class. Subsequent chapters of this book demonstrate that in every socioeconomic category, Arab Argentines made livelihoods and derived identities from the process of travel and mobility. Artists, intellectuals, activists, philanthropists, shop owners, and workers depended on mobility of people, goods, and ideas through the diaspora. This mobility enabled people to execute projects, shape communities, and weigh in on national and international debates. It is through this matrix of mobility, capital networks, and cultural solidarities that we must interpret a diasporic history of the Middle East in Latin America, for it has shaped local realities and transnational relationships all the way up to the level of the state. In this sense, the mahjar hinged on overlapping mobilities. By delineating them, we can better understand how those overlapping mobilities drew together people, cultures, and sometimes states in ways that are often obscured by Cold War area studies systems for the organization of knowledge.

Institutions as Associational Nodes

Descriptions of first-generation Middle Eastern migrants such as those in Yapur's *Mercachifle* are fascinating, but they fall short of representing firsthand accounts from first-generation Middle Eastern migrants in rural spaces. The first generation of arrivals, many of whom ended up in the mountain ranges and prairies that Yapur describes, often did not leave behind abundant documentation as to how they made their way from their port of arrival to their destination in interior provinces or territories. For this reason, it is necessary to employ alternative methods for tracking the mahjar's expansion across Latin American terrain. One effective method for tracing this demographic spread is to track the establishment of institutions and voluntary associations that Middle Eastern migrants and their descendants founded across the Argentine map starting in the early twentieth century.

Throughout North and South America, denizens of the global mahjar intentionally created community spaces through the institutions and associations they founded: hometown clubs, mutual aid societies, intellectual circles, business bureaus, religious institutions, youth groups, and philanthropic organizations. Institutions and groups served diverse purposes but held in common the fact that they were voluntarily formed by Middle Eastern immigrants and their progeny and served as associational spaces. In these places, people could share food or a conversation in Arabic, relay news from the homeland, or seek assistance in a time of need. Voluntary associations such as São Paulo's Homs Club, the Club Sirio Libanés of Buenos Aires, and the Club Libanés Sirio Palestino of Santiago de Chile, for example, performed a variety of services for their Arab Latin American members. They were sites of medical care, informal banking, and conscious preservation of the Arabic language, among other activities. This sort of association appeared, predictably, in ethnically diverse urban centers with large immigrant populations, but also in rural towns and villages throughout the Americas.

In Argentina, the establishment of associations steadily increased starting in the late nineteenth century, and in less than a few decades, dozens of these spaces dotted the national map. We can think of the array of institutions and groups that this map represents as a series of associational nodes within the larger geography of South America and the broader cultural map of the diaspora. The cultural, political, and philanthropic activities discussed in the remaining chapters of this book relied on these associational nodes and the way that people, things, and ideas circulated among them. These nodes, which served very concrete local purposes, also acted as conduits in a larger network. This network of associational nodes had the ability to link together members of the larger Arab diaspora who looked to effect political, intellectual, or economic change at multiple geographic scales.

The spatial distribution of the Argentine mahjar's first generation of associational nodes indicates the centrality of railroad development in the spread of these points (see Map 1). The location of associations and institutions established by 1925 correlates clearly with national rail lines. This first crop of associational nodes spreads southwest along the Buenos Aires Great Southern Railway (BAGS).[51] These sites included cities and towns that also boasted rail stations, such as Olavarría, General Madariaga, Tandil, Mar del Plata, and Tres Arroyos (Buenos Aires Province), and Cipoletti and Zapala (National Territory of Río Negro). Associations also followed the Buenos Aires & Pacific (BA&P) Railroad westward to provincial capitals (Mendoza, San Juan, San Luis) and small towns with rail stations such as San Rafael and Maipú (Mendoza Province) and Villa Dolores (Córdoba Province). Nodes extended along the Central Argentine Railway (CAR) through the sierras and plains of Córdoba Province and up into the rises and canyons of Tucumán Province. Mutual aid societies and hometown associations often appeared first in provincial capitals and major cities—in the case of the CAR, this meant Córdoba, Tucumán, Santiago del Estero, Santa Fe, and Rosario. Like the BA&P and BAGS, small municipalities that consolidated around the arrival of the CAR also became hosts to associational nodes. Examples of these sites include Río Cuarto and Deán Funes (Córdoba) and Aguilares (Tucumán). South of the CAR, the Buenos Aires Western Railway (BAW) branched deep into the Province of Buenos Aires, connecting municipalities such as Pergamino and Junín to the federal capital. It then extended westward into the National Territory of the Central Pampa. Associational nodes of the mahjar appeared even in these remote frontier spaces, in towns such as General Pico, by the end of the 1920s. Together, the BA&P, BAGS, CAR, and BAW formed the "Great Four" British-owned broad-gauge (5'6"-wide) track systems that proliferated between the 1860s and first decade of the twentieth century. Middle- and narrow-gauge track (4'8", and 3'3" width, respectively) provincial lines also rapidly expanded from the mid-nineteenth to the early twentieth century.

Beyond the Great Four, British-owned middle-gauge tracks in the northeastern provinces connected associational nodes throughout that region. The Ferrocarril Nordeste Argentino (FCNEA) originated in Entre Ríos Province and ran northward, branching into Santa Fe and Corrientes Provinces. Its easternmost branch from the town of Monte Caseros terminated at the Argentine-Paraguayan border city of Posadas in Misiones Province. Track construction for this branch reached its terminus in 1912, and along with it came Middle Eastern businesses. By 1924, we see the foundation of associational nodes such as the Asociación de Beneficencia de Libaneses y Sirios de Misiones in Posadas. Other associational nodes along this line included the Sociedad Libanesa de Corrientes (established 1917). In close proximity was the Entre Ríos Railway, which linked nodes in that province such as the Sociedad Siria de Socorros Mutuos de Nogoyá (established 1925), Sociedad Sirio Árabe de Socorros Mutuos de Villaguay (established 1927), and later the Club Social y Cultural Sirio-Libanés of Gualeguaychú (established 1936).

French- and nationally owned narrow-gauge track served the remaining regions not reached by the Big Four or these northeastern middle-gauge track

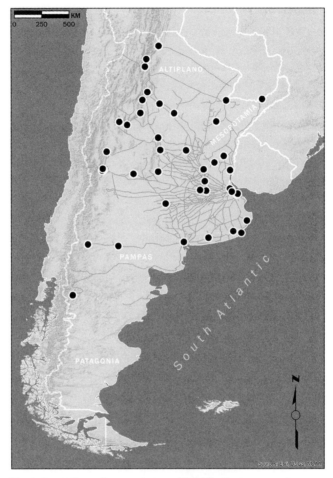

Map 1. Argentine railway system and Middle Eastern associational nodes by 1940. Data source: Cartographic rendering based on "Mapa de ferrocarriles de la Rep. Argentina" (Buenos Aires: Dirección General de Ferrocarriles, 1931). Mapoteca, Biblioteca Nacional.

lines. National government lines reached remote areas of the Chaco Plain and stretched northward through Salta and Jujuy Provinces, with the first rail transport arriving at the Argentine-Bolivian border town of La Quiaca by 1907. Associational nodes began to appear in these rugged frontier towns along remote stretches of narrow-gauge track such as the Sociedad Unión Sirio Libanesa of San Ramón de la Nueva Orán (Salta Province, established

1927). The French-owned Province of Santa Fe Railway's main line followed the Paraná River northward, terminating in Resistencia in the Chaco Territory by 1907. Similar to the nationally owned railways in the northwest, the Santa Fe line passed through a number of municipalities with associational nodes, such as the Sociedad Sirio Libanesa de Reconquista (established 1924). Collectively, this map of associational nodes that blanketed the Argentine landscape represents the geographic extent of the mobility of early generations of Middle Eastern immigrants to Argentina. It also represents the ways in which the nation's rail system stimulated the establishment of cultural, political, and economic outposts of this diasporic population. In addition to shedding light on the dynamics and demographics of this diaspora, this brings new perspective to the history of the railroad in Argentina. Beyond the vital role that the railroad played in the realm of agro-industry and infrastructure, it also shaped the geographic contours of this far-flung diaspora in its earliest generations.

Tracking the spread of associational nodes of mahjar communities in Argentina is fairly straightforward archivally. Throughout the case studies and historical episodes that fill this book, these places often served as social backdrops or key geographic plot points for the protagonists of everything from political campaigns to artistic sojourns. These institutions and associations appeared frequently in newspapers and in the annual reports for major philanthropic organizations that were in the business of organizing fundraising drives on a national level. In addition, Middle Eastern diplomatic posts in Buenos Aires today, such as the Lebanese embassy, maintain records of the dates and places where these institutions appeared starting in the early twentieth century. Furthermore, many of the nodes established in the early twentieth century continue to function today in a similar capacity to their original mission. They provide various kinds of support as well as opportunities for socialization among members of local mahjar communities. Some even continue to deal directly with the needs of newly arrived migrants from the Levant, as has been the case with the increase in new arrivals from Syria since 2011. Hometown associations such as Asociación Kalaat Yandal of Buenos Aires (established 1930) and clubs such as the Centro Sirio Libanés de Gualeguaychú of Entre Ríos (established 1936), among many others, worked with local and federal government officials to resettle individuals and families from Syria in 2015. The number of associational nodes involved in this resettlement effort has since expanded. However, when it comes to elucidating the movement and settlement of the actual individuals and families that coalesced to form these associational nodes in Argentina—and throughout the Americas—the task is more complex.

The earliest mahjar migrants often did not leave behind written accounts as to where they first settled, how they got there, or what they did to make ends meet on their arrival. The very nature of itinerant business has made it difficult to track the peregrinations of many early Arab Argentine entrepreneurs. Even for those who chose to open storefronts or work in a nonitinerant trade, it was not uncommon for them to move their businesses from one location to another in the early years. The stories that are preserved about this first generation are often the rags-to-riches narratives of peddlers-turned-industrialists or community leaders, such as the Sapag family in Neuquén. These stories are fascinating and often serve as anecdotal confirmation of the trends signaled by other data about the Argentine mahjar. However, in the long run, archivally reconstructing the livelihoods of individuals and families from newspapers, personal ephemera, and public records can quickly expand into a project in genealogy and family history. This is less practical toward the task of delineating geographical coverage and settlement patterns of this diaspora community on a national (or even transnational or regional) scale. It can also quickly turn into a historical narrative that privileges the stories of community members who enjoyed social prestige and economic and political advantage, and subsequently left behind more abundant archival record.

To approximate a macrolevel view of Middle Eastern migration not only to but through Argentine territory, it is useful to employ a spatial scaffold on which we can chart settlement and movement. As with the associational nodes, the national rail system plays an integral role in this spatial scaffold. It not only connected points of settlement but also acted as a circulatory system for a continuous movement of Arab Argentines between towns and cities in the provinces and territories. Approaching the study of the Argentine mahjar from this geospatial perspective also opens new avenues for exploring the presence of Middle Eastern migrants in provinces or national territories that have been nearly absent from the secondary literature on this population.

It is to this spatial scaffold, and some of the people who moved within it, that we now turn. By zeroing in on given railroad lines within the national rail network, rather than selecting a single city or province, we can observe the way in which thousands of Middle Eastern migrants lived in and circulated through rural frontier spaces strung out across train lines. As we will see, this reality was just as common as the more storied example of those who aggregated in urban milieus along with the rest of the immigrant masses. In this chapter, I have shown that the demographic spread of Middle Eastern diasporic populations through Argentina was a result of dual booms in international migration and infrastructure that jointly reconfigured national space in the nineteenth and twentieth centuries. From long before their arrival, Middle Eastern migrants, and the lands from which they came, flickered in the imaginations of Argentines. Their actual presence starting in the late nineteenth century was met with shifting and sometimes ambivalent responses from government agency authorities, municipal officials, and the national press. Rather than a consistent stance on the desirability (or even continental origins!) of Middle Eastern migrants, these ideas were in flux over the years during which this diaspora became established in the Americas. In other words, upon their arrival in Argentina, Middle Eastern immigrants confronted inconsistent and unfixed attitudes toward their growing colectividad. The Arab Argentine press that quickly proliferated over the early decades of the twentieth century was one way in which we see clearly the diaspora's cognizance of public opinion, political, economic, and social issues.

Chapter 2 takes as its subject the Arab Argentine ethnic press in conjunction with the geospatial framework of the railroad network. Newspapers and magazines have traditionally provided the archival basis for constructing historiographies of institution building, political debates, and economic participation in both Argentine and Middle Eastern remittance economies. At the same time, the mahjar press was one of the principal engines for generating some of the foundational myths that have long held sway on both informal and academic historiography of Arabs migration to the Americas. These foundational myths and hagiographies typically leave out the activities of nonmale, nonelite actors and groups, resulting in an incomplete vision of Arab Argentine community formation, business, and culture. Notwithstanding, the mahjar press represents some of the most extensive and well-preserved archival materials that exist regarding the history of this community. It is important to examine this tension and employ alternate strategies for deriving new narratives about the lives and livelihoods of Arab Argentines beyond the privileged urban core that largely controlled the diaspora's Fourth Estate.

2 From Mesopotamia to Patagonia

As the mahjar grew in size and geographic spread over the early decades of the twentieth century, so did a burgeoning Arab Argentine press. Readers of periodicals like *Assalam, El Eco de Oriente, El Diario Sirio Libanés*, and dozens of other publications consumed news about everything from global armed conflicts to local fundraisers. They thumbed past advertisements for tobacco brands, clothing companies, restaurants, and hotels owned by Arab Argentines across the country. Nestled amid propaganda, horse-racing schedules, steamship timetables, and the news were snippets of biographical information that fleetingly shed light on the day-to-day lives of the individuals who made up the colectividad. In one such snippet, a full-page spread on a Lebanese Argentine industrialist in rural Tucumán Province boasted laudatory text and several photographs. The subject of the piece was Julián Echivalle, an agricultural magnate who lived in the small town of Trancas, about 70 kilometers due north of the provincial capital, San Miguel de Tucumán. In bold text across the top of the page was the proclamation that Echivalle represented a "Son of Lebanon, Pioneer of Progress," and a "Champion of the Regional Economy." The article went on to extol his good character, "pureness of blood," and thriving export business. It noted that he regularly exported 1,600-ton shipments of beans to other provinces over the state-owned railway system.[1] Articles and advertisements of this nature add vivid images and details to the little information that we have about mahjar life in rural areas in the Americas. To the archivist or historian, they can seem like strokes of luck—sporadic bursts of information about individuals otherwise absent from the historical record in most cases. If we dig a bit deeper into the article on Echivalle, we can begin to garner clues as to why he appeared at all in the pages of a 1936 issue of the Tucumán-based newspaper *El Eco de Oriente.*

After describing Echivalle's lineage—his roots in a distinguished family from the Lebanese town of Bsharri—the article's author offhandedly mentions that Echivalle is the cousin of Domingo Kairuz of Buenos Aires. This small comment is an important clue as to how this rural agriculturalist ended up featured so prominently in a newspaper with national circulation. Cousin Kairuz was fabulously rich—so rich that in 1929 he purchased the estancia of the nineteenth-century caudillo and dictator Juan Manuel de Rosas, located in Matanzas, Buenos Aires Province. His prodigious wealth appeared to translate into significant power within the Buenos Aires mahjar, and he held several positions in community institutions and voluntary associations.[2] To be in Kairuz's inner circle, let alone a family member, was certainly a boon to personal prestige and no doubt accounts for some of the reason for this newspaper's public encomium of cousin Julián. Through the language and imagery used in newspapers like *El Eco de Oriente,* the mahjar press circulated ideas and hagiographies about "pioneers of progress" like Echivalle. But what of others whose stories did not appear in the pages of these publications? This chapter expands the spatial analysis of the mahjar to delve into the histories of remote limbs of the diaspora far from the hub of Buenos Aires.

There is no shortage of scholarship that duly credits the diasporic press as an important, even primary, engine in the creation of a transnational public sphere that was able to circulate information and ideas between far-flung geographies. In the pages of the press, the products of this transnational circulation, such as articulations of new political ideologies or innovations in cultural production, came to light. Understandably, we have tended to fix our gaze on this generative power of the press in transnational diasporas—the mahjar or otherwise. Beneath the surface of these exciting transregional exchanges, however, is an equally important story of movement within smaller regional contexts and the hand that it ultimately had in forging transnational communities. As a first step toward bringing into focus what we might think of as the geographic, cultural, and socioeconomic "margins" of Argentina's mahjar (and its national territory, for that matter), we can turn our attention to two regions that have not received concerted attention from secondary scholarship on Middle Eastern diasporas in the Americas. The first is the humid and verdant northeastern region that stretches through the provinces of Entre Ríos, Corrientes, and Misiones to the triborder region where the borders of Argentina, Brazil, and Paraguay meet. Denominated Argentina's "Mesopotamia" region during the colonial period, the territory occupies the interfluvial zone between the Uruguay and Paraná Rivers. The second is the Patagonian region south of the semiarid pampa, which includes the current-day provinces of Neuquén, Río Negro, Chubut, Santa Cruz, and Tierra del Fuego.

Taking this spatial approach links the history of Argentina's proliferating rail infrastructure to the story of the country's Arab colectividad. The varied geography of this diaspora spanned vast distances, yet a connective circuitry of infrastructure and human mobility linked those who made their livelihoods in these diverse locations. Although the vibrant print media of the Argentine mahjar often chose to portray bootstrapping narratives of wealthy pioneers like Julián Echivalle, its pages also contained information on the day-to-day lives of those of lesser means and without flashy connections to the Buenos Aires elite. The journalists and editors who collected and published information about everyday events and people in the Argentine mahjar necessarily found themselves moving along the same pathways of mobility that took an earlier generation of Middle Eastern migrants to the nation's interior. Across these geographies, individuals involved in the proliferation of the mahjar press moved along this circuitry to build journalistic networks that stretched beyond Argentina's borders. Although the lifestyles of these journalists and editors may seem at first to be uniquely, outstandingly mobile, they in fact mirror closely the habitual movement between diasporic nodes of much larger populations of the diaspora. People of all walks of life, it seems, moved frequently about the region for travel, leisure, medical reasons, or the pursuit of business opportunities. By fleshing out the overlapping geographies of movement that influenced the demographic spread of migrant families and the circulation of print media that followed in the wake of the diaspora's growth, this chapter reconceptualizes media organs as products of these mobilities. This new approach to print media archives takes us one step closer to decentering our vision of mahjar social and intellectual hubs away from urban nuclei such as Buenos Aires.

Geographic Margins of the Diaspora: A Spatial Framework

While differing drastically in terrain and climate, the regions of Mesopotamia and Patagonia had in common their relatively sparse settlement at the inception of the nineteenth-century migration boom. Both were also home to Indigenous groups that experienced cyclical displacement and violent persecution from the colonial era through the "Conquest of the Desert" of the 1870s and 1880s. Especially in the Patagonia region, settlers and the Argentine military increasingly pushed Indigenous communities southward, away from the choice cattle farming grasslands of Buenos Aires and La Pampa in the last quarter of the nineteenth century. Until the Boundary Treaty of 1881 (signed by Argentina and Chile), many maps rendered the Patagonian expanse as a *terra nullius*.

Mesopotamia also saw border disputes between Argentina and its neighbors in the nineteenth century—the most notable of which was without doubt the 1838 Paraguayan occupation of Misiones followed by the 1864–1879 War of the Triple Alliance. It was not until Paraguay's defeat and the ensuing peace agreement with Argentina that Paraguay withdrew its claim to the Misiones Territory. As Scobie noted in his interpretive survey of Argentine history, the status of Misiones was "vague" until the Paraguayan war came to a head.[3] Politicians pushed for colonization via immigration of areas like Patagonia and Mesopotamia, incentivizing settlement of both regions by offering agricultural contracts and subsidized transportation from Buenos Aires. Collectively, the expansive Mesopotamian and Patagonian frontier regions embodied the geopolitically "sensitive" realms that so worried the intellectual engines of the liberal immigration and colonization project of the nineteenth century.

In terms of the history of Argentina's Middle Eastern diaspora—and beyond that, of Argentina's long entanglement with the Middle East that unfolded on this foundation of international migration—regions like Patagonia and Mesopotamia tend not to figure in the key foundational narratives about how the mahjar developed over the years. Accounts of Arabic-speaking immigrants in Argentina tend to focus primarily on principal urban areas and, to a lesser extent, secondary cities, such as Santiago del Estero, Mendoza, or San Juan. The reality for many Middle Eastern migrants, however, was one shaped by often remote rural circumstances and isolation from the critical masses of compatriots typical of urban settings. Many lived far from the associational nodes of hometown clubs, mutual aid societies, or the printing presses of mahjar newspapers. For these reasons, their stories can be more difficult to track and consequently don't often appear in secondary literature. Nevertheless, archival sources confirm the presence of Middle Eastern migrants throughout Mesopotamia and Patagonia from the early twentieth century onward. If we begin by examining the railroad lines that ran through these two regions, a vision emerges of the Middle Eastern migrants who made their livelihoods throughout these frontier zones. This vision helps us to grasp the social landscapes and lived realities of a broader range of Argentine mahjar experiences and the ways in which they intersected with nascent systems of Argentine infrastructure.

Trains arrived fairly early to Argentina's Mesopotamia region. Principally, the British-owned FCNEA line ran through the provinces of Entre Ríos and Corrientes and into the National Territory of Misiones as of the late nineteenth century (see Map 2).[4] During his 1868–1874 presidential term, Domingo Faustino Sarmiento authorized the construction of the main line through the heart of Corrientes Province, from the town of Mercedes to the provincial capital. The route extended westward from Mercedes before tracking north along the Paraná River. In the decades that followed, new track extended the line to its southern terminus in the town of Concepción del Uruguay, Entre Ríos Province. From Concepción del Uruguay, the line followed the Uruguay River north along Argentina's borders with Uruguay and Brazil. After several starts and stops in construction, the track reached 1,212 kilometers in length and arrived at the Argentine-Paraguayan border city of Posadas in 1912. Surveys of Middle Eastern–owned businesses produced by printing houses in Buenos Aires and Córdoba in the first half of the twentieth century record the presence of Syrian and Lebanese business owners and workers up and down the FCNEA as early as 1917. By that time, the FCNEA boasted eighty stops—a mix of larger towns at key junctions, such as Monte Caseros and San Roque (Corrientes Province), and tiny way stations along the banks of the Uruguay and Paraná Rivers, such as Tapebicua and Pegahuo, respectively. By the time Perón nationalized the FCNEA in 1948, multiple generations of Arab Argentines lived along the length and breadth of all the line's branches.

From the early twentieth century onward, Arab Argentines lived in the towns and villages that appeared or expanded alongside the arrival of the FCNEA. Of the eighty municipalities and way stations served by the FCNEA, more than 40 percent (thirty-three of eighty) were home to mahjar communities or individuals. Those who arrived earliest to Mesopotamia tended to open dry goods and general stores, but over the course of the 1920s and 1930s, these activities diversified. By the 1940s there were barbers, shoe salesmen, mechanics, hotel owners, clockmakers, teachers, travel agents, and an array of other occupations held by members of the colectividad. The tendency of these individuals to be located along the FCNEA line, especially close to junctions or branch termini, is clear. We can observe this tendency, for example, in the

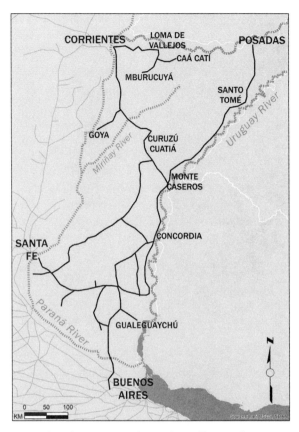

Map 2.Historic Mesopotamian region rail network. Data
source: Cartographic rendering based on "Mapa de ferrocarriles de la Rep. Argentina" (Buenos Aires: Dirección General de Ferrocarriles, 1931). Mapoteca, Biblioteca
Nacional.

lists of "Syrian-Ottoman" businesses and workers compiled by the Assalam
publishing house of Buenos Aires in 1917. Owned by the prominent Schamún
family that had emigrated to Buenos Aires from Mount Lebanon in the late
nineteenth century, the Assalam press was well known for printing the widely
distributed newspaper by the same title, *Assalam* (1902–1973).

Intended to serve as commerce guides that would encourage investment
and economic circulation within the diaspora, business directories such as
the 1917 Assalam guide provide evidence of the extensive geographic spread
of the mahjar. In the case of the Mesopotamia region, the 1917 business sur-

vey contained 314 listings for "Ottoman-Syrian" businesses or workers in the corresponding provinces of Entre Ríos, Corrientes, and the National Territory of Misiones. Just over half of the 314 listings were workers or business owners located at rail stations along the FCNEA. The percentage rises dramatically if we also factor in those living at rail stations of the other lines that serviced the Mesopotamian region, which included the British-owned Entre Ríos Railway (ERR), and shorter lines owned by the provincial or national government. Collectively, the Middle Eastern businesses and workers listed in 1917 hailed from fifty-nine locations that ranged from growing provincial cities to rural outposts. More than 80 percent of these locations (forty-nine of fifty-nine) were situated at stops along the FCNEA, ERR, or government lines. Of the 314 individuals and businesses registered across these fifty-nine locations throughout the Mesopotamia region, 295 lived at a rail station. This translates to more than nine out of every ten workers or businesses. Crossing the national boundary river into Uruguay, we can see that this pattern was by no means unique to the Argentine territory, or Mesopotamia in particular. Throughout the whole of Uruguay, 261 individuals sent their information to Assalam publishing house in 1916 with the intention of appearing in the 1917 business directory. Nearly 80 percent (207 of 261) of those listed lived at a rail station on one of Uruguay's five major rail lines: the Central, Midland, North Western, Northern, or East Coast Railways. More than a third of those listed at rail stop locations (77 of 207) were strategically located at a rail terminus. Examples include Fray Bentos, a small port town just across from Gualeguaychú on the Argentine side of the Uruguay River, and junctions such as the town of Durazno, which, in addition to being an important rail junction, was also a hub for the movement of cargo along the Yi River. All of this points to the important links between national transportation infrastructure and Middle Eastern migrants' decisions on where to pursue their livelihoods and, sometimes, build communities or institutions.

If we take the FCNEA railroad that ran through the Mesopotamian landscape as a spatial framework, we can observe instances in which people and businesses were mobile up and down rail lines over time. This represents yet another layer of mobility that we can add to the demographic picture of outlying mahjar populations in understudied provincial and territorial geographies. Taking a rail line such as the FCNEA as a base unit rather than the singular nodal point of a city or town allows us to see the mobility of people and businesses who moved up and down rail lines rather than settling permanently in one location. We see this in the case of entrepreneurs such as Miguel Yunes and José Elías, who both moved their business along the FCNEA between 1917 and 1927. Yunes reported owning a dry goods store (*almacén*) in the town of Curuzú-Cuautía in 1917. Curuzú-Cuautía was located at the junction of the Monte Caseros–Corrientes branch of the FCNEA and an extension of a narrow-gauge national government line that ran northward between the Gualeguay and Feliciano Rivers in Entre Ríos Province. Rail transport arrived in Curuzú-Cuautía in 1890, and a town began to grow up around the ensuing mobility of people and cargo through that terrain. Along with Yunes, twelve other Middle Eastern immigrants registered businesses there as of 1917, all of them grocers, general stores, and dry goods vendors (respectively, *almacenes, ramos generales, tiendas*). These businesses came to include clothing stores, tailors, and a hotel by the 1940s.

Perhaps seeking out a place to do business with little to no competition, Yunes decided to move his interests to an even more rural outpost about 50 kilometers north of his original almacén. By the time Assalam publishing house created an updated version of its business directory in 1927, Yunes was no longer in Curuzú-Cuautía, but he did register a new business located in the town of Mariano I. Loza. He did not list the municipality name as "Mariano I. Loza," however, but rather as "Justino Solari"—the name of the rail station located there, two stops north of the Curuzú-Cuatía Station on the Monte Caseros–Corrientes FCNEA line. This choice in wording is a minor detail, but nevertheless one that indicates the connection between his geographic trajectory and the presence of the rail line. Yunes was the only individual in Mariano I. Loza/Estación Justino Solari to register in the 1927 Guía Assalam directory. At that time, the haberdashery and notions shop that he reported owning would have been one of the early businesses established in Mariano I. Loza. It was only three years prior, in 1924, that Mariano I. Loza was even designated a municipality by the Corrientes provincial government after a few residents of the area formed a development committee (Comisión de Fomento) to encourage settlement.

The case of grocery store owner José Elías in the northern reaches of Corrientes Province follows a similar pattern. In 1917, Elías registered his almacén in the municipality of San Luis del Palmar, a small town approximately 30 kilometers east of the provincial capital. Narrow-gauge track connected Corrientes to San Luis del Palmar and fourteen other towns and rail stations that lay slightly south of the Paraná River and the Argentina-Paraguay border. By 1927, Elías reported his business as having moved three stops to the east along this provincial line, to the station of Lomas de Vallejos. Whereas six other Middle Eastern dry goods and grocery store owners in San Luis del Palmar registered in the 1917 directory in addition to Elías, he was the only one to report in from Lomas de Vallejos a decade later. This was likely a strategic move on his part, for Lomas de Vallejos was the junction from which the line branched south to its terminus in Mburucuyá and east to its terminus in Caá Catí. Aside from its status as a rail junction, Lomas de Vallejos represented approximately the halfway point on a long, sometimes excruciatingly slow journey from the provincial capital to the interior termini. The route from Corrientes to Mburucuyá was not terribly long—178 kilometers in distance—but the *trencito* (as locals called it) chugged along at an average pace of some 7 kilometers an hour. This sluggish crawl stretched the journey into a twenty-six-hour-long ordeal—and considerably more if bad weather or flooding complicated the journey. When famed Argentine investigative journalist Rodolfo Walsh rode the train in 1966, he delighted in christening it the "smallest, slowest, most exasperating, and most enjoyable train in the world." Renowned for its propensity to perennially run behind schedule, townspeople and passengers were known to celebrate the rare occasion of an on-time arrival by jubilantly firing off pistols.[5] In this light, the decision to set up shop at the midpoint of this arduous route may very well have opened the door to new markets of those in transit through Lomas de Vallejos. On either end of the trencito's route, Mburucuyá and Corrientes Capital were home to growing numbers of Arab Argentine businesses throughout the first four decades of the twentieth century. In Corrientes, the number of businesses registered rose from sixteen in 1917 to fifty-one by 1942. At the other end of the line in Mburucuyá, registered businesses rose from four in 1917 to ten by 1942.

Some individuals spread their business ventures along the line rather than confining them to a single location. Such was the case with a proprietor named Salvador E. Nazar, who owned a grocery store in San Luis de Palomar and also operated a haberdashery some 30 kilometers away in Corrientes. This occurred along other stretches of track in the Mesopotamian region as well. To the south of the trencito's route, along the Monte Caseros–Corrientes branch of the FCNEA, we also see cases of individuals and families spreading out their business interests along the path of the rails. The Yaya family is a prominent example. Between 1917 and 1942, the family opened a series of grocery, dry goods, haberdashery, and general stores along a 170-kilometer stretch of rail line from Mercedes to San Lorenzo. By 1927 they owned six businesses in Merecedes and Saladas, and by 1942 they had expanded another two stops northward (about 30 kilometers) along the FCNEA to open general stores in San Lorenzo as well. One individual, Tobías Yaya, owned businesses in both San Lorenzo and Saladas by 1942, which suggests that he likely moved frequently up and down the rail line to attend to his ramos generales stores at each location.

Women as well as men owned these rural businesses—a fact that rarely, if ever, received mention in the ethnic press but is readily observable in these archival materials. In the Yaya family, Ana and Zulema Yaya owned grocery and dry goods stores in Saladas in 1942. Though many more men than women registered their businesses starting in 1917, female business owners were still significantly represented. Of the forty-nine rail station locations in the Mesopotamian region, close to 20 percent were home to women who owned grocery stores, haberdasheries, dry goods and general stores, and other types of businesses. In many cases, a woman took over ownership of a business after her husband passed away. This was the case with grocery store owner Rosa Kury in Posadas, Misiones, who assumed ownership of the business after her husband, Felipe, passed away at some point between the compilation of 1927 and 1942 business listings published by Assalam press. This was also the case with the widows (first names not listed) of Miguel Richa in Curuzú-Cuautía and Nicolás Caram of Empedrado, Corrientes Province in 1927.

Sometimes, women chose to geographically shift their business investments up or down a rail line after the death of their spouse. This transpired when José Marún of Curuzú-Cuautía died, and his widow shuttered their grocery business in order to move across the province to the town of La Cruz on the banks of the Uruguay River. There she opened a notions shop in this small town on the Argentina-Brazil border, where only one other Arab Argentine individual registered his presence in 1942: a lone landowner and part-time teacher named Felipe Magua. Elsewhere, women worked and owned businesses independently of inheriting ventures from deceased husbands. In the town of San Roque, Corrientes Province, María Suerte registered her grocery store in the 1927 directory. San Roque was yet another potentially strategic rail junction, located at the split between the Goya and Corrientes branches of the FCNEA. Five stops south of San Roque, in Mercedes, Mariana Simhan worked as a dressmaker (*modista diplomada*), and Lydia Asuad Labibe worked as an instructor at a normal school. These cases and countless others from across the provinces affirm that the application of a rail-based spatial analysis can illuminate the presence—and mobilities—of populations not typically written into historical narratives of the mahjar.

These patterns of mobility, business ownership, and population in rural spaces were by no means unique to the Mesopotamian region. We can apply a similar spatial framework based on rail lines in the Patagonian region to access the histories of people and places long excluded from official histories of the mahjar. There is slightly more secondary scholarship dedicated to Middle Eastern migration to Patagonia compared with the dearth on Mesopotamia. However, focal points tend to be the famous success stories of those like the Sapag family, whose story we explored in Chapter 1. Nevertheless, studies of Arab Argentines in Patagonia are still far outnumbered by those set in Buenos Aires and a handful of provincial capitals. In the Patagonian region, an area so readily conceived of as "empty" by many since the famous pronouncements of Alberdi and Sarmiento, there was in fact a robust circulation of foreign capital, technology, and international migration that overlapped with ongoing processes of Indigenous displacement since the nineteenth century.

The proliferation of the Patagonian rail network in the early twentieth century represented the convergence of international capitalist investment and the increased availability of the material components of railroad construction in the aftermath of World War I. The result of this convergence was a series of broad- and narrow-gauge rail lines that connected key Atlantic ports to the Patagonian interior (see Map 3). Aside from the broad-gauge British-owned Ferrocarril del Sud (Buenos Aires Great Southern Railway), along which the Sapag family built their fortune, the Río Negro National Government Line was the second major broad-gauge line that transected the Patagonian territory. Early plans by the national government envisioned extensive branches that would connect these lines to various ports along the Atlantic coast, such as Puerto Madryn, Comodoro Rivadavia, and Puerto Deseado. By the 1930s, it was clear that the rail network would never be as integrated as planned; rather, it was characterized by several lines of narrow-gauge "Decauville-style" track that for the most part did not connect with one another. Decauville track was minimum gauge—the same variety as that which constituted the famously laconic trencito line in Mesopotamia. It was light and imminently transportable; to lay a new line required nothing more than setting down ready-made sections of light steel track. It was an innovation in the global history of rail transport that transformed everything from Mexican henequen plantations to French colonial expeditions into North Africa. Patagonia's infusion with many kilometers of Decauville track came in the wake of World War I, as lines previously used to carry troops and supplies to the battlefront were disassembled and sold off to bidders like the Argentine government and British railway companies. The Patagonian light rail network that emerged in the postwar period thus represents one of the ways in which this rugged landscape was part of a global circulation of materials and expertise related to transportation technology.

By the mid-1930s, narrow-gauge lines such as Central Chubut, Comodoro Rivadavia, Austral Fuegino, and Puerto Deseado Railways snaked through both coastal and inland Patagonian landscapes from Neuquén all the way south to the Santa Cruz territory. Today the best known of these is La Trochita—the Old Patagonian Express—made famous to international audiences by the romantic renderings of writers such as Paul Theroux. Construction of La Trochita began at Ingeniero Jacobbaci on the Río Negro Government Line in 1922, and by 1945 it had reached Esquel, some 400 kilometers to the south in the Chubut Territory. As laborers laid Decauville track through the south of Río Negro and along the Chubut River valley in the 1920s, freight gradually began running along completed sections of track. Aside from it being the most iconic of the Patagonian lines—today considered a heritage railway that still runs for touristic purposes—the chronology of La Trochita's construction also coincides with the demographic information recorded in Arab Argentine commerce guides printed in the first half of the twentieth century (1917, 1928, 1942).

Over these years, we can observe several mobilities and settlement patterns similar to those that characterized mahjar life along the Mesopotamian rail lines. From 1917 to 1942, as the Trochita line expanded, Arab Argentines reported in from a growing number of towns where stations were located. By the time the first train ran the full length of the Trochita line in 1945, Middle Eastern businesses and workers had been established along the length of the track from Ingeniero Jacobacci to Esquel, as well as several stops in between— Ojos de Agua, Río Chico, Ñorquincó, and El Maitén. Like the example of Tobías Yaya in Corrientes Province, who owned multiple businesses on the FCNEA, we see this transpire on the Trochita route as well. In the Río Negro territory, Simón Rahal likely moved between the grocery and dry goods stores that he owned at the Río Chico and Ñorquincó stations of la Trochita. In the Río Negro and Chubut territories, Abraham Breide owned general and dry

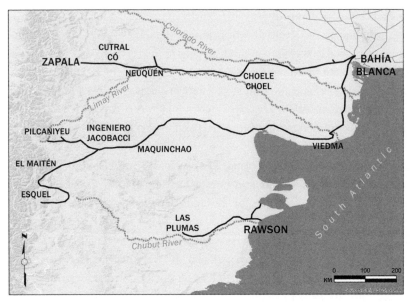

Map 3. Historic Patagonian Region rail network. Data source: Cartographic rendering based on "Mapa de ferrocarriles de la Rep. Argentina" (Buenos Aires: Dirección General de Ferrocarriles, 1931). Mapoteca, Biblioteca Nacional.

goods stores at two consecutive rail stations about 30 kilometers apart from one another, in the towns of Ñorquincó and El Maitén. Breide registered these businesses as early as 1917, meaning that he had likely set up shop in the strategic interim between the government's announcement of their plans to extend the line (1908) and the actual arrival and inauguration of the line some decades later.

Much like the Sapag family in Neuquén, the Breide family also appears to have made strategic decisions about where to invest in business based on projections for rail construction. Beyond Abraham, several other members of the family also opened grocery and general stores in Ingeniero Jacobacci and acquired land with the money they made. For example, Mansour Breide, born in Mount Lebanon in 1895, immigrated to Ingeniero Jacobacci in the Río Negro territory in 1926 and opened a general store there. Although he lived far from the federal capital, he remained intimately connected to the thriving Arab Argentine press based in Buenos Aires. By 1929, he served as a news correspondent for the Buenos Aires–based *La Gaceta Árabe*, a bilingual newspaper then in its second year of publication. In this capacity, he traveled widely throughout rural areas in Río Negro and Chubut to gather news stories that he would then relay back to the capital for publication. These sojourns took him to tiny towns like Paso Flores and Paso Chacabuco along the Limay River, which formed the boundary between the Río Negro and Neuquén Territories. It also took him westward into the foothills of the Andes—to San Carlos de Bariloche, San Martín de los Andes, and Cerro Tipilihuque.[6]

By the early 1940s, Breide had purchased land surrounding the Trochita line in the 25 de Mayo and Ñorquincó Departments, intent on expanding his business ventures. In an attempt to gain mining concessions for his property, he traveled to Buenos Aires at least four times between 1943 and 1947. He successfully dealt with the Secretaría de Industria y Comercio and gained official authorization from the Dirección de Minas y Geología to mine for industrial minerals such as kaolinite and diatomite on his land.[7] Over the years, Breide stitched together a life and livelihood deeply rooted in interprovincial (and interterritorial) mobility. Though often on a somewhat smaller geographic scale, this was the case for many others who moved between windswept Patagonian outposts or across the humid Mesopotamian region. Individually, the thread of their movement can at times be difficult to follow due to scarce archival trails, but collectively the picture that their stories paint is one of a diaspora in motion. It is this baseline of motion—rather than the implicit fixity of settlement, integration, or assimilation—that must form our point of departure for studying the mahjar.

Excavating this circulation along rail lines and through rural spaces helps us to delineate the lesser-known demographic areas of the mahjar. Furthermore, it provides a framework on which we can better analyze other forms of circulation through the diaspora such as cultural projects, print media, philanthropic campaigns, and other forms of movement that lie at the core of this book. It also draws our attention to the reality of so many Arab Argentines who lived far from the diasporic aggregations of urban spaces. Studies of the mahjar frequently focus on communities and institutions, but rarely on the numerous cases of individuals who lived alone or in proximity to only one or two other members of their diasporic group. Yet there were many, including some of the individuals explored in this chapter, who lived in geographic isolation from the areas that we have typically defined as the central hubs of diasporic community. The frequency of this reality becomes clear if we consider, for example, the number of rail station locations from which five or fewer Middle Eastern business owners or workers registered their presence. In 1917, nine Mesopotamian rail stations along the FCNEA and provincial lines fit this description, with the number growing to twelve by 1927 and fifteen by 1942.

Recently, Latin American diaspora scholars have called on the field to address the experiences of diasporic Latin Americans who were unaffiliated with the formal institutional or religious structures of their broader ethnic communities as a way of nuancing our vision of Latin American Jews, Arabs, and other groups.[8] In the case of Middle Eastern migration to Argentina, this must include attending to the experiences and actions of rurally located individuals such as Miguel Yunes, José Elías, and the widow of José Marún. Although a pervasive paucity of archival information characterizes the case of many like those mentioned here from the Mesopotamian region, we can nevertheless piece together information about their geographic trajectories and examine the ways in which their mobility related to broader patterns of movement, commerce, and circulation within the diaspora. In turn, this can lead us to interrogate the very parameters of affiliation, or, rather, what it meant to be meaningfully connected with the idea of a larger diaspora. Methodologically, this approach has a certain degree of similarity to that employed by other migration scholars, especially those of forced migration, whose historical subjects often left behind little or no documentation. It is in the search for these broader trends that we can start to consider the utility—and risks—of constructing what some scholars have deemed "collective biographies" of migrant populations at the edges of the archival record.[9] In general, we would do well to critically reconsider some of the delineations that have traditionally characterized methodological differences between scholarship of forced versus voluntary migration and migrant lives. In this case at least, the notion of stitching together sparse evidence to offer insight into lived experiences in the rural Argentine mahjar can prove useful.

The idea of the diaspora as a highly mobile entity appeared clearly in the discourses of elites in Buenos Aires who assumed the role of official chroniclers of the mahjar. "After the Jesuits, the Syrian is the new Christian missionary," stated the prefatory remarks of the 1917 *Siria Nueva* business directory published by Assalam press. The preface went on to affirm that members of the colectividad were pioneers in places like the Pampa and the Chaco.[10] Argentine immigration authorities in the early twentieth century also imagined Middle Eastern migrants as inclined toward commerce and mobility rather than an idealized vision of sedentary agriculturalists. In turn, scholarship produced on the South American mahjar has taken as a presumed baseline that this diaspora made its way to every corner of the continent. In general, though, these movements and migrations through peripheral spaces have not tended to adopt a methodological perspective that sheds light on the lived realities of diasporic individuals like Mansour Breide or the Yaya family. To remedy this, we can apply a combination of intellectual, social, and spatial history to examine diasporic mobilities in tandem with prevailing ideologies about national territory. Such an approach not only brings new dimensions to the way we think about rural space and the national immigration project in Argentina. It is also an important step toward integrating methodological approaches in the service of depicting what we might conceive of as a *demography of movement* in the Argentine mahjar, and the Arab Americas more broadly.

Mobility and Connectivity: The Mahjar Press

Of the many individuals whose stories weave together a larger picture of this demography of movement, the peregrinations of the Patagonian Arab Argentine Monsour Breide serve as a bridge to our next consideration: the role of the press (journalists, publishers, and the media that they produced) in knitting together the disparate geographic limbs of the mahjar. Traditional histories of vibrant mahjar print media tend to start (and often end) in the urban centers that housed the Arab Americas' first printing presses and largest publishing houses. In reality, the media that came out of these urban centers were intimately tied to the physical circulation of individuals throughout the full territorial extent of the diaspora. By taking this as our point of departure, we can draw connections between rural and urban diasporic spaces and ultimately gain a picture of how the press connected Arab Argentines across the vast spaces where they settled, from Mesopotamia to Patagonia. This stands in stark contrast to approaching rural spaces as ones lacking the intellectual and cultural engines of production aggregated in hub cities. Instead, I focus here on the overlaps between the pathways of mobility that account for the demographic spread of the mahjar across Argentina's national space and the routine travels of individuals involved in the production of Arab Argentine news organs. This is the first step toward analyzing the information contained within the prominent press organs against the grain. It is an approach that offers a new set of parameters for analyzing the mahjar press that move beyond a traditionally narrow focus on engagement in local versus international politics. Ultimately, this can lead us to tackle the question of Latin America–Middle East network building from the angle of intraregional immigrant mobilities. In many ways, this is more instructive than relying on ephemeral notions of intellectual or political currents often used to describe the dynamics and genesis of what some scholars have begun to refer to as the mahjar's transnational public sphere. These ephemeral notions of currents also tend to obscure the presence of larger diaspora communities beyond the privileged, urban, intellectual core.

In the case of Monsour Breide, his work for the Buenos Aires–based *La Gaceta Árabe* meant that he was part of a broad network of mobile news correspondents scattered throughout Argentina. This weekly publication, like many other Arab Argentine press organs, represented a geographic network of circulating news correspondents and information. From its outset, *La Gaceta Árabe* boasted a list of provincial news correspondents (*corresponsales del interior*). These individuals reported on births, deaths, social events, and institutional goings on in mahjar communities throughout Argentina, as well their neighbors in Uruguay, Chile, Brazil, and Bolivia. By the early 1930s, the *Gaceta* had thirty-five corresponsales reporting in from the provinces of Buenos Aires, Córdoba, Corrientes, Entre Ríos, Jujuy, La Rioja, Mendoza, Salta, San Luis, Santa Fe, San Juan, Santiago del Estero, and Tucumán. Corresponsales also worked in national territories not yet founded as provinces, such as Misiones and Río Negro. Beyond national borders, the *Gaceta* contracted with corresponsales in Montevideo, Uruguay, and La Paz, Bolivia. While the publication's printing press was in the federal capital and its director was a prominent member of the Buenos Aires–based, or *porteño*, community, to classify it as simply a porteño newspaper would be inherently misleading.

At first glance, Argentine Arab print media appear to be heavily concentrated in the nation's capital, with a handful of publications that emerged from Tucumán and Córdoba by the mid-twentieth century. When it came to the physical locations of the printing presses that churned out mahjar media, these cities were indeed the epicenters. The spread of Arabic printing press technology to South American urban outposts increased rapidly after the first Arabic wax linotype machine appeared in New York in 1910. After emigrating from Lebanon by way of Cairo to the United States, prominent newspaperman Sallum Mukarzil developed the linotype press that would allow for smaller-scale and more affordable printing of Arabic-language media throughout the Americas. Undoubtedly the spread of Mukarzil's wax linotype printing system transformed what Stacy Fahrenthold aptly deems the mahjar's printing capitals of São Paulo, Buenos Aires, and New York City. As she notes, this "shaped an entire generation of educated Syrian and Lebanese profession-als."[11] The wave of print technology rippled farther afield than these cities, to places like Tucumán shortly thereafter. Mahjar intellectuals and community leaders urgently sought to procure printing presses. Such was the case when merchant and poet Elias Turbay successfully lured Buenos Aires–based jour-nalist Simón Hamati to relocate to San Miguel de Tucumán with the promise that he would procure for him a printing press, typesets, paper, and other supplies. Hamati agreed and moved his family to Tucumán in 1913. Much to Turbay's chagrin, there was some delay in the shipping of the promised print-ing press—reportedly, he rushed to apologize to Hamati upon his arrival at the Tucumán train station and quickly assured him that the machine was in transit. Delays aside, the press eventually arrived, and Tucumán came to boast nine regular periodicals by 1922, less than a decade later.[12]

Following the advent of Arabic wax linotype came a proliferation of mah-jar print media in the American hemisphere, and Argentina was no exception. More than fifty periodicals emerged from Arab Argentine printing presses in the twentieth century, with the peak of publications appearing in the 1920s and 1930s. Many publications were short lived, but others weathered several decades, including Tucumán's *El Eco de Oriente* (1917–1959) and *Assalam* (1902–1970) of Buenos Aires. A few continue to exist even today but in digital form, such as *El Diario Sirio Libanés* (established 1929, Buenos Aires). By the 1940s, more than twenty Arab Argentine printing presses operated across the country. Although they were concentrated primarily in Buenos Aires, a hand-ful of presses had set up in secondary cities such as the provincial capitals of Tucumán and Córdoba. Still others appeared scattered through Santa Fe and Santiago del Estero, as well as rural areas of Tucumán and Córdoba provinces. The densely packed *microcentro* area of Buenos Aires without a doubt boasted the most pronounced cluster of printing houses starting in the 1910s. How-ever, preoccupation with this primacy in the consolidation of printing press technology can risk obscuring the mechanics of mobility involved in the con-tent production of the periodicals that emerged from mahjar printing houses. Isolating the trajectories of individual news correspondents, such as Monsour Breide, adds important complexity to a vision of the geographic networks to which each periodical or printing press maintained connections. By examin-ing the mobilities of journalists and newspaper editor-owners, we are able to disaggregate this geography of mahjar print capitals from the geography actu-ally represented by publications' content and readership.

The reports and news items that corresponsales like Monsour Breide remitted to editorial desks in Buenos Aires reveal that these correspondents were not simply stationed at a fixed point somewhere in the "interior." Rather, they acted as roving collectors of news, surveying the reaches of the Argentine mahjar and sharing their observations with newspaper audiences. Frequently, they set out on "tours" (*giras*) of several provinces or across large swaths of unincorporated national territory. Tours could last anywhere from several weeks to months and required multiple modes of transportation. These were opportunities to not only gather news but also to interact with social, business, or other networks. On one of his tours, Breide made a forty-five-day circuit of the Patagonian towns of San Carlos de Bariloche, Paso Flores, Paso Chacabuco, San Martín de los Andes, Tipilinke, and Ingeniero Jacobacci. In reports remitted to his editor in Buenos Aires, he reflected on his interactions with Arab Argentines living far from the hub of Buenos Aires. Describing one of the families who hosted him on his journey, Breide drew special attention to their daughter. At only a few years old, the child was able to recite "with clear diction two poems, one in honor of the fatherland, and the other of welcoming to the guests." He credited her highly educated parents for her precociousness—descendants, he claimed, of Lebanese aristocrats.[13] By drawing attention to the refinement of this young family in Patagonia, Breide signaled that they were part of the mahjar's vibrant transnational public sphere (even if he did not conceive of it quite as such). Regardless, this image, however fleeting, of Lebanese parents raising their toddler to recite poetry about the homeland to a distinguished visitor is an excellent reminder. It affirms the expansive reach of practices of cultural production—in this case, poetry and oral culture—in the Argentine mahjar. Furthermore, it reminds us that these practices were not merely the purview of urban literary salons and elite families with well-known surnames.

In addition to the circulation of corresponsales throughout the country, the editor-owners of many Argentine mahjar publications also routinely made extensive tours. When Elias Amar, the owner, editor, and director of the *La Gaceta Árabe*, went on a tour in winter 1928, he stated that his motivations were a combination of "commercial venture, and a chance at a bit of rest and relaxation."[14] The letters that he penned to his staff at the *Gaceta* while on the road indicate that beyond leisure, Amar's tour did indeed represent a chance of networking and expanding community contacts. Over the course of several months, he covered thousands of kilometers of terrain and interfaced with Arab Argentine residents of cities and towns across the northern half of the country. Upon embarking on his tour, he departed the federal capital and traveled westward on the BA&P railway. He made an early stop in the town of Junín in Buenos Aires Province, home to a growing mahjar community. Officially incorporated in 1906, Junín sat at the crossroads of the CAR and BA&P lines. In this sense, it represents a quintessential example of rail technology's power to transform small municipalities across the interior that suddenly found themselves at rail junctions or other important way stations. In the case of Junín, the opening of the BA&P rail equipment factory (Talleres Ferroviarios de Junín) compounded the impact of the rail lines' arrival to that small town in the 1880s. By the turn of the century, sixteen hundred of the town's twelve thousand residents worked at the factory, and that number doubled by the time Amar arrived in 1928.[15] Meanwhile, the growing railroad town was also home to a growing number of Arab Argentine residents.

Increasing numbers of these residents chose to submit information about their occupation and employment to widely circulated Syrian-Lebanese business directories over the first half of the twentieth century. When Amar's train pulled into the station at Junín, an expanding mahjar business community met him. The business directory that the Assalam press published the same year that Amar visited reported fifty-six small businesses owned by Arab Argentines in Junín. This was up from fifteen reported by the *Siria Nueva* directory of 1917 and signaled the steady growth that would continue in subsequent decades.[16] In other words, Junín was quickly becoming a bustling node of mahjar business and voluntary associations, even if it was still a small, rural town in comparison to the provincial and federal capitals. Perhaps for this reason, Amar was eager to visit. He quickly connected with his colleague Luis M. Yebrin upon arriving at the train station. Yebrin owned a notions shop (*tienda y mercería*) only a few blocks from the train terminal on Lavalle Street. Aside from operating his small business, Yebrin also worked as a correspondent for *La Gaceta Árabe*, and thus was in routine contact with Amar. Yebrin was highly mobile himself, moving frequently back and forth between Junín and the federal capital. Much like other correspondents, such as Monsour Breide, Yebrin maintained his local business interests amid a busy schedule of regional travel. The year that Amar visited him in Junín, Yebrin shuttled between Buenos Aires and his hometown at least six times (January, February, May, June, August, and October 1928).[17] Even when traveling for pleasure or on business unrelated to the newspaper, Yebrin would often du-

tifully stop by Amar's editorial desk to greet him, reinforce their social connection, and express his support for the publication. When his editor came to
visit his hometown on one of the first stops of his tour, Yebrin took it upon
himself to show Amar around town. Together, they toured local associational
nodes such as the Sociedad Siria Ortodoxa de Junín. In a letter that Amar later
wrote back to the *Gaceta*'s editorial team in Buenos Aires, he described his
visit with members of the voluntary association. The Sociedad, he noted, already boasted eighty members and was awaiting legal recognition (*personería
jurídica*) by the provincial government. This clearly impressed Amar, who
went on to advocate that other towns take the Arab community of Junín's
ambition to organize as an aspirational goal.[18] With this ringing endorsement,
Amar took his leave of Junín and boarded a northbound CAR line coach.

Some 90 kilometers and six rail stops later, the newspaperman reached the
town of Pergamino near the northern border of Buenos Aires Province. Like
Junín, Pergamino was also a town transformed by the arrival of rail transport.
Pergamino Station, inaugurated in 1860, lay on one of the early routes of the
Argentine government–owned Ferrocarril Oeste de Buenos Aires and served as
an important junction for both passengers and freight. At the time of Amar's
visit, the line had long since been bought by British investors and served as the
point of convergence for five regional branches of the CAR. As in Junín, the
mahjar community in Pergamino grew steadily over the first half of the twentieth century. The number of individuals who chose to register their businesses
with national directories jumped from 17 in 1917, to 50 a decade later, and then
to 128 by 1942. Although he spent much of his visit touring this burgeoning
mahjar community, Amar was not solely interested in connecting with Middle
Eastern kinsmen or associates. He also wanted to meet local authorities and
pitch the mission of his newspaper. When granted an audience with the town
mayor, Amar informed him that he was determined to make the *Gaceta* into
"a news organ that is useful and influential in the defense of the interests that
our community proposes to uphold."[19] In seeking out opportunities to interface
with local officials, Amar revealed that he saw himself as an advocate and journalist beyond a mere reporter. He took keen interest in advertising his desire
to engage with local issues and work with community leaders. Touring small
towns like Junín and Pergamino was, for Amar, much more than the "commercial venture . . . rest, [or] relaxation" that he originally stated at the outset of his
1928 travel circuit. These visits were opportunities for advocacy and the active
maintenance of social networks across long distances.

Although they rarely stated it directly, it is likely that a similar mixture of moral and material motivations prompted the mobilities of correspondents like Breide and Yebrin. Amar's tours afforded him the opportunity to reaffirm shared partnership in the larger journalistic mission of the *Gaceta* with these important collaborators—his *corresponsales*. Just as he had sought out Yebrin in Junín, Amar also sought out his correspondent in Pergamino, a comerciante by the name of Azíz Dib. Amar connected with Dib upon his arrival, and they toured the town together. Much like his colleagues, Dib was a hypermobile character himself. The year that Amar visited him in his hometown, Dib made at least eleven long-distance trips around the region. He traveled often between Pergamino and the Federal Capital, often taking the time to stop by the *Gaceta*'s offices to greet the staff, and check in with Amar. In 1928 alone —in January, April, August, September, October, and December—he made the trip from Pergamino to Buenos Aires, a straight shot eastward on the CAR line. Sometimes he traveled much farther, such as a trip to Tintina in Santiago del Estero Province in July that year. This trip was his farthest afield and would have involved a long trek of about 900 kilometers northward along the CAR line, followed by another 400 kilometers of travel on the state-owned Ferrocarril Argentino del Norte. For the most part, though, he traveled to other towns in his immediate region, including Junín and San Nicolás de los Arroyos, a port town on the Paraná River and terminus for one of the CAR branches emanating from Pergamino. His most extensive tour that year was a circuit of several small towns surrounding Pergamino, which he made under the auspices of the *Gaceta*, a journey that the newspaper in turn referred to as a "press tour" (*gira periodistica*).

Over the course of May and June 1928, Dib rode the rails back and forth across the northern limits of Buenos Aires Province and visited at least eight locations. Rather than take the CAR line (which he frequented on all of his other trips that year), he began by heading southwest along a stretch of narrow-gauge track operated by the French-owned Compañía General de Buenos Aires (CGBA). He made stops at three stations on the CGBA line just south of Pergamino—Pinzón, Carabelas, and Ferré, sparsely populated rural outposts that coalesced around the construction of railroad stations. The CGBA inaugurated Pinzón station in 1908, followed by Carabelas and Ferré in 1910. Two decades later, at the time of Amar's visit, they were small towns with fewer than two thousand inhabitants. In short, these were by no means bustling hubs of mahjar populations. A single entry for Pinzón appears in the 1928

Guía Assalam—that of a general store [*ramos generales*] owned by Salomón José. Likewise, only one individual from Carabelas sent information to the *Guía*—a shop owner (*tienda*) named Salvador Chida. For Ferré, nothing appears. Nevertheless, Dib included these small towns on his tour and made a point of stopping at them. In addition to these stations, he went on to several more rural stations along the CGBA line, as well as an intersecting branch of the BA&P. These included Ascención, General Arenales, Vedia, and Arribeños. Like Carabelas or Pinzón, these BA&P stations were also tiny outposts home to a handful of Middle Eastern migrants who operated general stores, vended dry goods, and sold basic clothing staples.[20] In sum, touring under the auspices of a mahjar newspaper was not merely a strategy for maximizing subscription rolls or courting lucrative connections with mahjar institutions in the interior. If this were the case, why commit oneself to regularly visiting sparsely populated way stations? Instead, this evidence suggests that in many cases, Arab Argentines formulated ideas about their community, identity, and values from the experience of travel. The resulting patterns of mobility brought them into contact with limbs of the mahjar spread out across broad geographic space.

In building a network of contacts, ostensibly for the sake of the newspaper, these individuals repeatedly interacted with the lifestyles and daily realities of a diverse range of Arab Argentines. At times, they paused to reflect on the ways in which they felt that their home communities could change or improve based on their observations. We saw this during Amar's trip to Pergamino, when he admired the number of mahjar institutions seeking personería jurídica and advocated for readers elsewhere in the Argentine mahjar to take note. Earlier that year, after visiting various sites in the provinces of Salta and Tucumán on a tour of the northwest, he made similar observations followed by exhortations aimed at the Buenos Aires mahjar community. In the northwest, Amar made his standard round of visits to Arab Argentine businesses, institutions, corresponsales and other associates.

Amar came away generally impressed by the practices of Levantine voluntary associations in the region, especially in the cities of Tucumán, Salta, and Santiago del Estero. He noted that Syrian and Lebanese associations in the North gathered regularly, and that this reinforced the sociocultural fabric of the community. He applauded their frequent gatherings for group meals and their regular celebrations of important holidays and events. He saw this consistency of intentionally created communal space as key to the long-term cohesiveness of their ethnic community and pressed readers in Buenos Aires to confront what he saw as their own shortcomings in this regard. In the capital, he lamented, "the social environment for young people . . . for our women . . . is inferior."[21] Amar's opprobrium of the porteño community reveals that he did not necessarily see Buenos Aires, undisputed Argentine mahjar population hub and print capital, as the cultural center of the diaspora. This fact adds interesting nuance to prevailing baseline assumptions of rural provincial communities as less desirable locales, less hooked into the cosmopolitan circulations of people, things, and ideas that characterized the mahjar's transnational public sphere. Mahjar historiography has traditionally privileged the metropolis of Buenos Aires and over time naturalized its primacy in the cultural landscape of the diaspora. It is important that we question this presumption.[22] Furthermore, archived mahjar press organs from across Argentina reveal that it was not just Arab Argentines from the capital who set out to tour "interior" spaces and bring ideas back to their home community. We see this same mobility in the cases of newspaper editor-owners and correspondents from elsewhere in the country.

In the case of the Argentine mahjar's oldest bilingual newspaper, we can readily observe how the flow of touring newspaper publishers and their staff also emanated from provinces located far from the federal capital. Founded in 1917, *El Eco de Oriente/Sada al-Sharq* was a long-running publication headed by its tireless editor-owner, Nallib Baaclini. Born in 1882 in Zahle in the heart of Lebanon's Beqaa Valley, Baaclini emigrated to Argentina in the waning years of the nineteenth century. After studying in Beirut, he became involved in the burgeoning Beirut press scene prior to emigrating.[23] After arriving at the Port of Buenos Aires, he migrated to San Fernando del Valle de Catamarca, the capital of Catamarca Province, where he attempted to make his way as a merchant.[24] Perhaps missing the intellectual scene, he made his way to San Miguel de Tucumán, where he established himself as an outspoken community leader at the helm of *El Eco de Oriente* and a collaborator on several other smaller publications.[25] Baaclini was in fact a close collaborator with Elías Turbay and helped to bring the first printing press to Tucumán in 1913 with the hope of convincing their colleague, writer Simón Hamati, to relocate from Buenos Aires. At any rate, Baaclini was well acquainted with porteño creative and intellectual circles, but his press tours were not merely pilgrimages to the capital. Instead, he often pressed outward toward the peripheries of the nation. Over the course of 1935, he made one such tour of Salta, Jujuy, and Santiago del Estero Provinces and another of Córdoba Province. On these tours, his daughter, Nelly Esther, herself a reporter in the employ of her father's periodical, accompanied him. They traveled long distances along the central and northwestern network of rail lines and undoubtedly withstood the intensely arid summer heat as well as the soaring altitudes in the northern provinces. They visited provincial capitals, as well as numerous small towns. In describing his peregrinations, Baaclini framed them as opportunities to "strengthen bonds and establish and reinforce friendships" (*estrechar vínculos y afianzar amistades*).[26] Throughout, he recorded information about the institutions and voluntary associations that he encountered and who often hosted him.

In Salta, Baaclini boarded the state-owned Ferrocarril Central Norte (FCN) to visit more rural rail stations and towns, such as Rosario de la Frontera about 180 kilometers southeast of the provincial capital. There, he photographed the board of directors of the local Club Sirio-Libanés and noted the names of its directors, as well as their progress toward building a headquarters for the club. Situated at the junction of two branches of the FCN, Rosario de la Frontera was home to a growing number of Arab Argentine entrepreneurs by the 1930s.[27]

Although we have traditionally looked at small clubs like that of Rosario de la Frontera as local institutions that served immediately local memberships, they were in fact more far-reaching. In the case of the Club Sirio-Libanés, members came from surrounding hamlets such as Puente de Plata, some 40 kilometers southeast along the FCN line. In sum, these small, voluntary associations were not only the common stopovers for mobile newspapermen like Baaclini; they were also points of convergence in the microregional mobilities of their memberships. For evidence of these microregional mobilities in Rosario de la Frontera, one need look no further than the slate of directors from 1935, which included Dargam Zim, a butcher from Puente de Plata.[28]

Baaclini's interest, however, did not lie solely in the institutions and associations of neighboring regions of the northwestern mahjar. He was keenly interested in amassing data about the individual Arab Argentine people in these communities. To this end, he collected mementos that would allow him to document (quite literally) the local faces of Argentina's Middle Eastern population. As he traversed the rails across Salta, Tucumán, and Santiago del Estero Provinces, he gathered more than two hundred photographic portraits of women and men that he would go on to publish the following year in a special 150-page edition of *El Eco de Oriente*.[29] When the edition went to press in 1936, it featured a "social gallery" (*Galería Social*) of these collected portraits from towns and villages spread across the region. The ladies' section featured women from General Güemes, Embarcación, Río Piedras, and Aguaray in Salta Province, alongside portraits of their counterparts in towns like Banda del Río Salí and La Trinidad in Tucumán Province, as well as Frías and Coya, Santiago del Estero Province.[30] By bringing the images of mahjar institutions, families, and, especially, individuals to the pages of his newspaper, Baaclini rendered a visual representation of the interprovincial network that connected the mahjar. Their names and their stories were thus able to gain familiarity within social circles wherever people held subscriptions to *El Eco de Oriente*. The construction of these social galleries was a common product of touring journalists and publishers.

When the brothers Rachid and Assad Rustom toured both the far northern and Patagonian regions over the course of 1943 to 1945, they engaged in a similar practice. From the road, they sent photographs and missives back to the editorial desk of the newspaper that they co-owned: *La Union Libanesa* of Buenos Aires. The descriptions of their journeys to Tucumán, Jujuy, Santiago del Estero, Córdoba, and the Patagonian national territories read as little more than endless lists of the names of all the compatriots with whom they visited, dined, or stayed the night, often accompanied by corresponding photographic snapshots from the journey.[31] In many instances, the Rustoms sought out friends and acquaintances and reaffirmed their existing connection. They also sought encounters with new people and places; like Baaclini, they pursued a balance of reinforcing old relationships and establishing new ones. Their desire for the latter was their reason for striking out on their first foray into the southern territories in 1945, which they began by taking the BAGS railway to the end of the line at Zapala in the National Territory of Neuquén.

The long lists of visits and page after page of photos from social events staged for visiting journalists can appear mundane. For this reason, they can be easy to overlook in the context of mahjar periodicals filled with splashy headlines of international news stories or bombastic debates about a range of issues. Yet it is within these galerías sociales, travel notes, and repetitive snapshots that we can take a broader view of how diasporic press organs both operated through and gave rise to cross-territorial mobilities. Press organs functioned in such a way that they depended on and encouraged the fomentation of cross-provincial networks of mahjar people and institutions. Whether these came in the form of a network of news correspondents or touring pub-

lishers with a mixed social/business agenda, the result was an increasingly visible documentation of the expansive geographic reach of the South American
mahjar, readily available to anyone who picked up a newspaper. With each
lengthy travelogue description, set of society page photos, or biography of a
Middle Eastern charitable organization, the physical and social geography of
the mahjar became more familiar to those within it. This familiarity held
the power to shrink perceived distances from one distant diasporic node to
the next. With the names and photographs of people, places, and even the
floor plans of notable Arab Argentine–owned buildings filling the pages of
mahjar press organs, readers could become acquainted or even familiar with
the diverse landscapes comprising a web of kinship, intellectual currents, and
commercial relationships that stretched across Argentina and well beyond its
national borders.

New Vantage Points

Thus far, we have made a survey of mahjar communities along distant rail lines,
followed by a study of how agents of the mahjar press moved actively among
these communities. This exploration has shed light on the primacy of movement within this diaspora—from incipient populations of Middle Eastern migrants who set their course for frontier spaces during the nation's large-scale
infrastructural expansion, to the hypermobile creators of the Fourth Estate.
This was a diaspora in flux—and not just on the part of a pioneer generation
followed by a small corps of intellectual elite newspapermen. If we peer closely
at the information contained within press organs like *El Eco de Oriente* and *La
Union Libanesa*, the reality of those mobilities begins to come through. Tucked
in the pages of these publications are evidence of everyday people who moved
routinely about the country. It was not just community leaders like Elias Amar
and Nallib Baaclini who traveled far and wide. If we take the data from *La
Gaceta Árabe* as an instructive example, the commonness of these quotidian
mobilities within the Argentine mahjar becomes obvious.

In the *Gaceta*, buried toward the back of each issue, were lists of travelers—both arrivals and departures. The main editorial desk in Buenos Aires,
as well as news correspondents all over the country, compiled these lists every
week and published them in the newspaper in lists simply titled *Viajeros*
(Travelers). In 1928, when the newspaper's director was busily touring several provinces, the *Gaceta* recorded more than a thousand other journeys in
the Viajeros sections. The recorded travelers were predominantly Arab Ar-

gentines, though some came from, or left for, the neighboring countries of Brazil, Chile, Bolivia, Paraguay, and Uruguay. Others came from, or traveled to, transoceanic destinations—France, Italy, Australia, and the United States. Several arrived directly from the Middle East—Syria and Lebanon—and many departed for the Levant as well. Of the 1,103 journeys noted, we can track down the occupations of approximately one-third (366) of the travelers.[32] They ranged from barbers, to students, to musicians, writers, and small shop owners. Most frequently we see travel by individuals of the following professions: journalists, shop owners (*tiendas y mercerías*), merchants (*comerciantes*), clergy, students, and those who worked in the textile industry. More often than not, the Viajeros lists didn't state the reasons for travel, but when they did, we gain fleeting images of the everyday mobilities of priests, shopkeepers, students, children, and others. Just under 22 percent of travel entries listed the reason for travel, with the most popular being business, family, medical needs, education, or religious trips. Much like the journalists and editors in the mahjar press world, many of the travelers in 1928 made repeated or multistop journeys. Dozens (sixty-eight in total) even referred to their travel as part of a broader *gira* related to personal or professional reasons. These included business owners like Francisco Darruich of Corrientes, who undertook a long business tour (*gira comercial*) of Corrientes Province in November, or Pedro Dahan, who arrived in San Luis Province after a *larga gira comercial* of his own the following month. Traveling clergy from the Maronite and Eastern Orthodox churches often appeared in these Viajeros lists. Among others, Maronite priest Reverend Mubarak Marun of Buenos Aires made a tour of Santiago del Estero Province to collect donations for the construction of a new school. A counterpart from the Orthodox faith, Archimandrite Ignacio Aburrus, made a similar donation-gathering tour that year as well—in his case, to raise funds for the construction of a temple. For Aburrus, this was but one of dozens of fundraising and pastoral care tours across the provinces that he made between the 1920s and 1953, when he returned permanently to Beirut due to issues of poor health.

We may not know the intricate details of many of these travelers' lives, motivations, or itineraries. In fact, in the vast majority of cases, the archival record tells us next to nothing. Nevertheless, by examining questions of travel and mobility across an aggregate of partial stories, a panorama of a diaspora in motion clearly emerges. In this manner, we flesh out a backdrop of movement that undergirded the business dealings, family networks, and spiritual pursuits of Argentina's Middle Eastern migrants and their descendants. By foregrounding this undercurrent of mobility, we gain a new vantage point from which to understand the mechanics of institutional, individual, and community projects that unfolded over the course of the twentieth century in this diasporic community. To attain this new perspective on the lived experiences of migrants who moved transregionally between the eastern Mediterranean and the Americas, we must expand the geographic scope with which we study the livelihoods that they built. A spatial approach that accounts for the connections between infrastructural development and diasporic demography is a good start. However, we also need to incorporate new archival sources and ask new questions of old sources to improve the visibility from this new vantage point. On this front, looking beyond the headlines of mahjar newspapers and digging through galerías sociales or travelers' lists is progress in that direction. This necessarily must come with a concomitant revaluation of source material rarely preserved by state or migrant institutional archives. These include sources such as the *guías de comercio*—each one a wealth of data compiled through a series of daunting travel itineraries on the part of its creator. (Brothers Wadi and Alejandro Schamún toured the provinces extensively to create their 1928 *Guía Assalam* and underwent a new set of tours in 1930 to create an updated version. Salim Constantino, their counterpart from Córdoba, and the organizer of the 1942 *Guía de Comercio Sirio Libanés*, also toured the provinces and liaised with co-nationals whom he tasked with spreading the word to more rural areas.)[33]

As sources, these business directories differ obviously and markedly from the panegyrics of community leaders printed in mahjar newspapers or circulars or the cherished prose of well-regarded intellectuals. Aside from their embossed covers and almost obsequious letters of introduction, as documents these commerce guides were at their core objects of great and immediate utility for their readers. Their function went far beyond that of the many editorials in the Arab Argentine press that clamored for solidarity within their readership. In contrast, the guías put the information in the hands of readers, opening the door for them to strike out and forge economic (or other) relationships with others in their ethnic community, whether in a small-scale local setting or on the level of long-distance interprovincial and territorial transactions. With each guide, Constantino and the Schamún brothers handed their audience a list of names, services rendered, and even directions for how to arrive at that location by rail transit.[34] Thus, the relevance and value of the guías were particular to that moment in time within the Arab Argentine populace.

These documents and their preservation were often not privileged in archival settings. Voluntary associations did not tend to preserve these guides in their curated collections of important documents and club ephemera, and state archives largely exclude them from collections of mahjar newspapers, magazines, and literature. Much like the galerías sociales of mahjar newspapers like *El Eco de Oriente*, the business directories often included visual galleries of Arab Argentine institutions, dwellings, and landscapes typical of the provincial locales featured in each guide. In doing so, they reiterated for their readers a sense of connectivity between different diasporic nodes, offering them the chance to become familiar with the human and natural geographies to which the mahjar map connected them. In this sense, the project of compiling and distributing these directories holds certain similarities to Nallib Baaclini's vast portrait-collecting project that took him rambling across the northern provinces.

This new vantage point—this centering of movement as a common thread in many diverse lived experiences of the mahjar—also points to travel and mobility as something approaching a way of being, of a culture of movement in the mahjar. It is to the intersection between culture and mobility that we will now turn for Chapter 3.

3 Art in Motion, Motion in Art

By the end of World War I, migration from the Arabic-speaking eastern Mediterranean to Latin America was already past its peak in terms of new arrivals, but there was no stop to other forms of continuous South-South circulation. During the 1920s, the first generation of individuals born on Argentine soil with Middle Eastern heritage grew—and with it their cultural, economic, and political projects. New arrivals did continue in smaller numbers, but this new generation of immigrants tended not to hail from rural peasant backgrounds as most in the first generation had. This shift in demographics is related to the vibrant cultural and intellectual scenes that flourished throughout the North and South American mahjar. Extended families, businesses, and immigrant institutions were firmly established throughout Argentina by the late 1920s. Through this social and economic entrenchment of Levantines in Latin American societies, the South American mahjar became firmly enmeshed in the circulating economy of ideas, politics, and products that constituted the public sphere of the diaspora. This new reality drew individuals who immigrated for reasons beyond the motivation of basic economic subsistence. People with political, cultural, artistic, and intellectual aspirations began to view the mahjar as a viable milieu for their projects.

This chapter tracks the stories of individuals who circulated within the Argentine mahjar (and beyond) in pursuit of artistic and cultural projects beginning in the late 1920s. Filmmakers, comedians, singers, actors, and writers moved throughout Argentina and neighboring regions of the Latin American mahjar. Their lives and professional itineraries highlight the importance of both microregional and transregional mobility in the cultural production of the diaspora. Moving from city to city, country to country, continent to continent, the success of their projects often hinged on the monetary support of Arab Argentine institutions and on the turnout of audiences from the diaspora community at large. In return for this support, artists and cultural entrepreneurs offered their benefactors and audiences the sounds, sights, and sentiments of a Middle Eastern homeland. Many of the younger generation of Arab Argentines by the late 1920s had either been born in Argentina or had arrived there as young children—leaving them with foggy or nonexistent memories of the Levant. For those with clear memories of their lives before immigration, artists promised them a sensory connection to the homeland. Cinematographers, singers, and artists forged visions, ideas, and an overall aesthetic of "the homeland" that was consumed not only across generations of Argentine Arabs but often by Argentine society at large. Thus, artists shaped an imaginary of the Middle East for both the diaspora and the host society.

In this way, the filmmakers, actors, and musicians that are the focus of this chapter served as self-appointed cultural ambassadors. They were not simply ambassadors of Middle Eastern cultural forms for a "foreign" Latin American audience. Rather, they also served as links between a broader Middle East and a widely dispersed diaspora population with heritage rooted in the Levant. Throughout the first half of the twentieth century, Argentine local and federal governments regularly recognized the importance of these citizen ambassadors in public ways. These gestures ranged from the participation of municipal officials in the documentary film projects of an Arab Argentine film company, to the deployment of an Arab Argentine "cultural ambassador" by the Perón government to the Middle East and North Africa by the 1950s. This chapter charts the intersecting cultural and political dimensions of the careers of three groups in the Argentine Arab arts scene from the 1920s through the 1950s: filmmakers, actors, and musicians. In each case, the activities of the artists, including their interactions with their audiences, shed light on the continued importance of the network of associational nodes built up over the early decades of Middle East migration to Argentina. They also attest to the interconnectedness of Middle East heritage communities across rural-urban divides and across political borders throughout the Americas. The realm of art in motion, and the theme of motion in diasporic art, is yet another way in which transregional thinking reveals two central facets of Argentina's place in a Global Middle East. First, the itineraries of these cultural producers reveal the interconnectedness of Middle Eastern, North African, and Latin American geocultural landscapes. Second, the very process of tracking the mobilities that knit together these landscapes requires us to consider the ways in which diasporic cultural production connected people and places to one another on microregional and hemispheric scales within the Americas.

By the 1920s, there existed a cosmopolitan arts scene in the Arab diaspora, with the best-known artists located in the major urban immigration hubs of the Americas. Creative scions of the diaspora included writers like Gibran Khalil Gibran and Ameen Rihani, both members of the literary society known as the New York Pen League (*al-Rābiṭah al-Qalamiyah*) from 1920 to 1932. The Pen League's counterpart in São Paulo, the Andalusian League (*al 'Usba al-Andalusiyya*) published an internationally circulated and highly regarded monthly literary journal.[1] Likewise in Buenos Aires, a group of Arab writers formed their own union, the Literary League (*al-R bi ah al-Adabiyya*), in the 1920s.[2] In all of these groups, prose writers and poets innovated Arabic literary traditions, rendering their own styles and forms to create a uniquely diasporic literature. Scholars of this diaspora literature(*adab al-mahjar*) have shown how these works in turn made their way back to the eastern Mediterranean (*mashriq*) region and were important to literary scenes in Lebanese, Syrian, and Egyptian contexts.[3] Typically studies of adab al-mahjar focus on the written word and its role in the coalescence of a transnational literary scene. The circulation of the written word certainly did define many aspects of the transnational public sphere of the diaspora, and the words of writers and poets inspired Arabs living abroad to invest in a "vision of global networks of belonging," as Jacob Berman has described it.[4] There were, however, other mediums through which diasporic artists engaged the themes of nation, homeland, immigration, and modernity. These included film, theater, and music. Prior to this study, the existence of film, music, and theater scenes in Argentina's Arab community have gone almost entirely unacknowledged in scholarly accounts of the mahjar.

The production and consumption of these genres provided Arab Argentines with opportunities to assert themselves as stakeholders in the Argentine national project while simultaneously affirming their ties to a Middle Eastern homeland. As Matthew Karush points out, "The cinema and the radio constitute important sites for the elaboration of identities, values, and aspirations which can and do become the basis for political action."[5] After all, "ordinary people are shaped by the images and meanings disseminated . . . even as they reshape those meanings for their own purposes."[6] The creators behind works of art also served as cultural links across diaspora communities and groups. Films, plays, and songs offered their audiences the chance to interpret and shape the messages and images deployed by screen, stage, and airwaves to fit their personal relationship to the idea of a Middle Eastern homeland. The process of funding and executing projects in these genres also did the work of binding Arab collectivities together across geographic, religious, and other differences.

Filmmakers

In 1927, three young Arab Argentine filmmakers came together to form the Oriente Film production company. Nabih Schamún, José Dial, and Roberto Kouri were all born in Lebanon and later immigrated to Buenos Aires. Schamún was one of eleven children from an illustrious family of politically vociferous newspaper publishers. Conversely, Dial began as a humble fruit vendor in Buenos Aires and worked his way up to becoming a well-known film director. Of Kouri, we know very little prior to his stint with Oriente Film. It is likely that he and Dial had been working together as documentary filmmakers before strategically joining forces with a member of the Buenos Aires Arab colectividad with a prominent family name and extensive connections in the diaspora's newspaper business (Schamún). It is unclear precisely how these three met one another and decided to found the company that they proudly proclaimed to be the "First Argentine-Syrian-Lebanese Cinematographic Enterprise." Regardless, their decision to do so led them to create a series of documentary films that took them on a journey across the Americas, the Atlantic, and the Mediterranean.

The trio first gained notice in the Arab Argentine press with their film *La Atracción del Oriente* (*The Attraction of the Orient*), a silent documentary film that showcased historic sites and cityscapes in the current-day territories of Syria, Lebanon, and Turkey. After shooting on location in the Middle East, Dial and Kouri took charge of the editing process in Buenos Aires while Schamún drummed up press coverage in preparation for their January 1928 debut. Before proceeding any further, it is worth noting that there are no surviving copies of the documentary films that Schamún, Dial, and Kouri produced—at least none that I have been able to ferret out of any private or public archives in Argentina where I conducted research. From a conservation and logistical perspective, film often does not have the staying power that the written word does when it comes to archives. It is more expensive to preserve, can be difficult to store, and the technology for projecting its contents is complex and can require significant upkeep. In the case of Oriente Film's work, the reels would have been barrel-sized, cumbersome, and heavy. Luckily, Arab–Latin American press organs from Argentina, Chile, and Brazil often recorded detailed descriptions of the scenes that played out on screen before Latin American audiences across the Southern Cone. Reporters fixated on the deep nostalgia evoked in dewy-eyed spectators as scenes of Beirut, Damascus, Palmyra, and Baalbek rolled across the screen, and they remarked with pride on the appearances of specific people and institutions in the documentaries. These written descriptions at least help us to grasp the vivid experience that the films created for their viewers. We can also glean information about the content of these films from the writings of the directors, who often described the production process to eager newspaper reporters.

In interviews with prominent Arabic-language and bilingual press organs, the directors advertised *La Atracción* as an opportunity to "show the progress [of] Syria and Lebanon." They wanted not only Argentines with Middle Eastern heritage to attend the films, but also other immigrant groups, as well as mainstream creole society. *La Atracción* would give their audiences a chance to know the roots of their community better so that they might appreciate its "true value," they claimed.[7] Their emphasis on showcasing the progress, potential, and value of Middle East migration to Argentina was a direct response to experiences of discrimination that they had previously faced. The filmmakers all cited their anger over racist and stereotypical portrayals of Arabs in movies as their impetus to make their own corrective films. Thus, Arab–Latin American newspapers across the Southern Cone reported on the mission of Oriente Film as one that explicitly combated discrimination against Middle Eastern immigrants in the region.

In an interview with a Santiago, Chile, newspaper in 1932, Dial attributed the inception of his film career to the moment in which he watched a film that was "biased and invidious for [the Arab Argentine] colectividad." It was this experience, he claimed, that drove him to move to Italy to study cinematography. From there, he traveled to Syria and Lebanon to film historic sites and cityscapes before returning to Argentina.[8] Similarly, Kouri recalled seeing films that "humiliated [the Arab Argentine] colony—films produced indecorously, which humiliated the *patria* with the motive of profit and in the attempt to draw spectators." As with Dial, this experience prompted him to travel to the Middle East and embark on a film project that would combat biased and inaccurate representations of their community. In Kouri's version of events, he dramatically situated the film crew as avengers for the colectividad: "So we traveled to Syria and Lebanon alone, without monetary help, and we crossed oceans, deserts, confronted revolutions, spent horrible hot days, and suffered the rigor of the freezing nights in order to film a modern film in which the typical was completely annulled along with this material prejudice."[9] With this statement, Kouri defined the work of Oriente Film as "modern," thus defining prejudice against Arab Argentines as the antithesis of modern. Drawing on the language of the civilization-versus-barbarism trope so common in intellectual and political discourse surrounding immigration in nineteenth- and early twentieth-century Argentina, Kouri continued: "Our ultimate goal [is to] demonstrate to the foreigner and whoever portrays us as half-barbarous people, that we are a grand and modern *pueblo*." Their effort to combat racist portrayals of Middle Eastern immigrants was in direct "service to the *patria*," Kouri asserted, not bothering to specify whether he referred to a Middle Eastern or Argentine *patria,* or perhaps both.

The cinematographers also viewed their audiences as collaborators in the struggle for fair representation of their ethnic community. For example, Kouri articulated his belief in a reciprocal relationship between director and audience, in which the director's role was to "serve the *patria*," while the audience "in return, would have the moral obligation to attend our showings and invite their Argentine friends with the goal of showing them the grandness of the lands of [our] ancestors."[10] Spectator and artist were bound together, in his view, by moral obligation to the colectividad. The Arab Argentine press echoed this sentiment in their coverage of the Oriente Film documentaries. In the Tucumán periodical *El Eco de Oriente*, Nallib Baaclini noted that these films had the power to produce a counternarrative to the "extravagant, grotesque, simply invented scenes that American and European producers churn out daily regarding our colectividad."[11] From the moment that Oriente Film began to appear in the diaspora press, the message from both the artists and the journalists who reported on their films was clear: documentary film was a powerful tool for calling into question the politics and economy of representation of Middle Eastern bodies and cultures. While protests against the misrepresentation of Middle Eastern peoples and cultures appeared in editorials in the Arab Argentine press, the story of Oriente Film demonstrates other ways in which some Arab Argentines (both artists and willing audience members) responded to instances of prejudice or racism that they encountered in Argentine society. Until now, we have not seen careful studies of the diverse ways in which Middle Eastern immigrants and their descendants responded to this prejudice. In the case of Oriente Film, their mission obviously resonated with audiences throughout Argentina and the Southern Cone, evidenced by their extensive touring schedule and the effusive press coverage that followed in its wake.

In this vein, a June 1928 advertisement for *La Atracción* openly billed the piece as "propaganda" for Syrian and Lebanese peoples on both sides of the Atlantic—in Argentina and in the "homeland" (*país natal*). The film crew approached Buenos Aires–based Arab press organs and made open calls to Arab Argentines living in the provinces (the "interior") to do the "truly patriotic act" of organizing a film showing.[12] The provinces responded in force. In the first half of 1928, Oriente Film debuted *La Atracción* in more than a dozen locations. Arab Argentine communities hosted showings in principal provincial capitals such as Mendoza, Córdoba, and San Juan. The cinematographers did not limit their tour to these larger cities. They also made stops in tiny towns such as Deán Funes and Cruz del Eje (Córdoba Province) and Berabevu and Sierras Bayas (Buenos Aires Province), among others. These municipalities, modest and remote, had been receiving Middle Eastern immigrants since the turn of the century, evidenced by the early formation of heritage societies and clubs in these locations. As discussed in Chapters 1 and 2, many of these small towns were in strategic proximity to important railroad hubs and stations, making them optimal locations for establishing the kinds of dry goods businesses that predominated among the first generation of Middle Eastern immigrants. Towns like Berabevu served as easy stops near rail lines where the Oriente Film crew and other artists learned to campaign for support for their artistic and intellectual projects. By the time Oriente Film arrived with *La Atracción,* many of these remote communities boasted associational nodes: voluntary organizations such as the Hogar Árabe Argentino de Berisso (established 1917), the Centro Sirio Libanés de Chacabuco (established 1923), and the Sociedad Sirio Libanesa de Deán Funes (established 1926).[13]

While these outposts of the Argentine mahjar may have been remote, they were far from isolated from the important cultural projects, political debates, and philanthropic campaigns that defined the public sphere of this heritage community. The heritage clubs and other Arab Argentine voluntary associations in these small towns did not serve merely as hospitable venues to showcase Oriente Film's reels. Schamún, Dial, and Kouri all took advantage of established gathering sites of enterprising Arab Argentines as they sought to drum up support for additional projects and institutions. For example, while touring the provinces, Schamún took the opportunity to recruit new subscribers to *Assalam*, the Schamún family's Arabic-language newspaper and press.[14] In other instances, they used film showings to build support for projects such as the construction of the Hospital Sirio-Libanés located in Buenos Aires but funded in large part by decades of fundraising in every province and national territory. While the Oriente Film crew did not make direct statements to this effect, it is likely that their time touring the provinces and meeting compatriots across the country had an impact on the direction of the subsequent projects that they chose to pursue. After their initial foray into film with *La Atracción*, they turned to the diaspora as the subject matter for a series of documentaries.

By the end of 1928, Oriente Film was in full swing with their next project, *Los Sirios y Libaneses en las Américas* (Syrians and Lebanese in the Americas.) This new endeavor would become a documentary chronicling the lives and work of Middle Eastern immigrants and their descendants in Argentina, Brazil, Chile, and Uruguay. Nearly a decade after the inception of their first project, updates on Oriente Film's work as chroniclers of the Middle Eastern community in the Americas appeared frequently in both ethnic and national press organs across the Southern Cone. In the first phase of this new project, they traveled from province to province in Argentina, filming scenes at Middle Eastern voluntary associations, religious institutions, and prominent businesses owned by members of the colectividad. They continued to use film showings of *La Atracción* as fundraisers to bolster the *Sirios y Libaneses* project. From 1928 to 1929, they shot footage of their co-nationals and sat for interviews with local media in the provinces of Buenos Aires, Rosario, Santa Fe, Córdoba, Mendoza, San Juan, Tucumán, and Salta.

As provincial news outlets published updates on the film crew's progress, they often concluded with congratulatory statements about the cultural mission of the cinematographers, concluding in one case that the *Sirios y Libanéses* documentary would "showcase the greatest accomplishments of [our] community not only to citizens of the Americas, but also to those in Syrian and Lebanese homelands."[15] The portrayal of industrious Arab Argentines would also serve as a model for emulation by other immigrant collectivities, asserted Schamún in a 1929 interview.[16] Throughout their travels, the associational nodes and individuals who hosted Oriente Film took them seriously and treated them as prestigious visitors. They acted as local guides and facilitators, aiding filmmakers in gaining access to interviews with powerful economic and political figures on both the municipal and national scene while on tour. In many cases, these individuals made cameo appearances in their films. This became an important feature of the *Sirios y Libaneses* project, especially after audio technology became available, allowing them to move beyond the constraints of silent film by the early 1930s. Police chiefs, governors, municipal superintendents, and even Presidents Getúlio Vargas (Brazil, 1930–1945, 1951–1954), Gabriel Terra (Uruguay, 1931–1938), and José F. Uriburu (Argentina, 1930–1932) attended showings of the documentaries, and in many cases they contributed recorded interviews.[17] Clearly members of the Arab Argentine community, as well as Argentine authorities, recognized Oriente Film's work as important and worthy of collaboration. The film crew's brushes with fame and powerful political icons drew the attention of the press in the Middle East as well.[18]

Filming Arab Argentine communities soon led to forays into Brazil, Uruguay, and Chile to undertake the same task. As the members of Oriente Film worked with Middle Eastern communities in the wider Southern Cone region, they began to articulate a new narrative about their perceived mission. By the early 1930s, the cinematographers saw their body of work not merely as a set of films but as an "archive." They referred to the Argentine, Chilean, Uruguayan, and Brazilian footage of Middle Eastern diaspora communities as the "official archive of the Arab collectivity."[19] In their eyes, this was an opportunity to correct the historical record's portrayal of their community by exhibiting the life and work of actual Arab Latin Americans rather than orientalized abstractions and racist stereotypes. Perhaps imbued with a sense of authority after proclaiming themselves "archivists" of the colectividad, the filmmakers began to weigh in on more explicitly political and controversial issues that were already topics of debate within the diaspora's public sphere. For instance, Schamún returned to Buenos Aires with strong opinions about the preservation of the Arabic language in the diaspora after filming portions of *Sirios y Libaneses* in various Brazilian cities. Reflecting on his experience in Brazil, Schamún announced that "Arabic is the language of commercial transactions and family matters there." [20] He claimed that ninety percent of Arab-Brazilian children spoke "perfect Arabic and go to [Arabic] language school." In this case, his interviewer responded that he must surely be exaggerating (and most likely he was), but Schamún resolutely denied it.[21]

In a letter that Schamún penned while in Brazil, he condemned his breth-
ren who wished to "pass" as Euro-Argentines:

In the streets, in the cinemas, in the theaters, in the very houses of co-national
families, there in Buenos Aires, the whole world appeared to forget their own
language. . . . If anyone attempted to converse in a raised voice, in the language
of their fathers, in their very language . . . shhh. Don't speak so loud, what will
people say!! It is a bit of shame that we feel upon listening, upon speaking our
language, and we fear that a neighbor, a lady upon whom we want to make a
good impression with our figure, upon hearing us speak a foreign language, will
disvalue us.[22]

Here the author rails against the lack of a unified front against social pressure
to suppress outward cultural markers of Middle Eastern heritage, such as the
Arabic language. His concerns indicate that overall, Schamún believed that
Arab Argentines could maintain their Middle Eastern identity while being
fully embedded in the march toward Argentine progress and modernity. Their
Middle Eastern heritage and this national project were not contradictory, he
insisted. This exemplified the ways in which the experience of travel between
regions of the Latin American mahjar influenced one Arab Argentine artist
and public figure to revise his views on his local heritage community—their
values, practices, and future as a cohesive colectividad.

The process and experience of travel was a central theme in the adab al-
mahjar. The tendency to focus on travel writing and modes of transportation
is what Leyla Dakhli refers to as the "seal of movement." For example, this
"seal" appears in the texts of early twentieth-century authors such as Amin
Rihani and Khalil Gibran, pillars of the North American mahjar intellectual
scene.[23] In the case of Oriente Film, its members frequently paused to publicly reflect on their journeys through South America, commenting on their
experience of movement and travel. This repeated attention to the dynamics
and modes of travel connects the work of the Oriente Film crew to the transnational literary genre of adab al-mahjar. During their trips from one country, province, or heritage society to the next, the members of Oriente Film
took time to reflect on the journey itself—on the experience of movement
and travel.

This dynamic is especially strong in a series of a dozen letters that Schamún
wrote to the Arab Argentine periodical *La Gaceta Árabe* while filming *Los
Sirios y Libaneses* from 1928 to 1929. In Brazil, he paid special attention to the

conditions of the train cars that carried them from Santos to São Paulo, noting that "the train cars are numerous, and in each one there is a determined
number of seats. Also, the seats are numbered in such a way that each passenger has his own seat, [guaranteed] until he reaches his final destination." He
even went on to compare the technology of Brazilian trains to that of trains
that run from Beirut to Dar el Baider, Lebanon, with the conclusion that the
Brazilian system was "more effective and positive." Aside from the cheaper
ticket prices, they were, however, "inferior to Argentine trains in every sense,"
he opined.[24] In fact, a great deal of the travel narrative that Schamún penned
during his time filming in Brazil consists of descriptions of the journey and
the trains, placing a great deal of importance on the methods and time spent
traveling from one location to the next. His emphasis on the technology of the
train suggests that it was clearly a meaningful mobile space in his eyes. His observations of the train travel rivaled the attention that he directed toward the
stops along his route where he shot the documentary. This attentiveness to the
experience of mobility—sometimes at the expense of actual places or human
encounters—makes sense in the context of a perspective that sees movement
as the bedrock of this diaspora community rather than stasis. In the case of
Oriente Film, the practice and experience of mobility was integral to the work
that they did as archivists of Middle Eastern migration to South America.

Just as they began to publicly assume the role of archivists for South
America's mahjar, the Oriente Film enterprise underwent deep changes:
Nabih Schamún died and Kouri decided to return to Lebanon. Schamún died
suddenly in April 1930, before seeing the completion of the *Sirios y Libaneses*
documentary. This elicited dramatic expressions of mourning among Arab
Argentine *porteños*.[25] These included an announcement from the Club Atlé-
tico Sirio-Libanés, which held their next six board meetings with all members
standing up as a gesture of their sorrow and respect.[26] It was Kouri's ambitions as a cinematographer and chronicler of the diaspora that led him to leave
Argentina. In 1931, he set off on a cinematic tour of "all of the American territory, Paris, and Cairo," where he shot footage for his dream of a master documentary of the global Arab diaspora.[27] For Kouri, any attempt to construct
a record—he and his compatriots conceptualized it as an archive—of Arabic
speakers in Argentina would necessarily have to locate Argentina within a
global map of mahjar communities. Kouri recorded footage for his expanded
documentary project as he traveled northward, documenting scenes of the
mahjar in Chile, Ecuador, Mexico, and the United States. From the United

States, he returned to the Middle East and opened a film production studio in Beirut in time to participate in Lebanon's Golden Age of cinema that took off in the 1940s.[28] In Kouri's case, we see an artist who integrated into the Lebanese film industry after laying the foundation of his career in the diaspora. While the influence of Arabs in the diaspora on Middle Eastern literary forms has been well established, the ways in which this influence extended to other mediums in the expanded context of adab al-mahjar, including the visual arts, merits further study.

José Dial was the only one of the three original members of Oriente Film who remained at work in Latin America over the long term. Despite the loss and relocation of his collaborators, his film career flourished. By 1940, he completed the initial documentary project on Middle Eastern heritage communities in Argentina, Brazil, Uruguay, and Chile. He also began to import Arabic-language cinema hits from Egypt and gave screenings for Argentine audiences.[29] Having gained recognition for his filmmaking, he started to receive requests for commissioned documentaries from powerful firms in the Arab South American business world. For one of these commissioned films, he temporarily relocated to Chile to film a documentary on the Yarur textile factory.

Established in 1937, the Yarur textile factory was Chile's first modern cotton mill. Owned by Juan Yarur, a Palestinian immigrant to Santiago, the mill was part of a larger textile empire owned by the Yarur and Said families that stretched from Chile to Bolivia and Peru.[30] Dial's film recorded the entirety of the mill's processing technology, showcasing the machinery responsible for the transformation of raw cotton into fine silk.[31] Immigration historians have noted that the adoption of modern technologies and products often served as an avenue by which immigrants could facilitate their integration into the host society and stake claims on national modernization projects.[32] In this regard, we can see Dial's film as tied into efforts made by members of the wider South American Arab diaspora to promote their role in the economic and technological progress of the region in the years following the global economic depression. Besides the Yarur mill, Dial's other documentaries examined various private industrialists in Argentina and a film about Arab businessmen in Chile's burgeoning *salitre* (sodium nitrate) economy. Throughout the 1930s, he also continued to return to the Middle East, filming updated documentaries on politics and society in Syrian, Lebanese, and Palestinian contexts.[33]

Dial's use of documentary film to record the relationship between South

American Arabs and national progress made him a desirable commodity in elite circles of the Argentine, Chilean, and Brazilian mahjar. By all press accounts, audiences eagerly consumed these cinematic renderings of an idealized uplift narrative that affirmed for its viewers a seamless transition from immigrants into innovators. The popularity of this uplift narrative likely helped to accord Dial a certain degree of authority in discussing the overall "progress" of mahjar Arabs in other regions of Latin America beyond Argentina. Despite not being a Chilean, in 1940 he was invited to Santiago to dissertate at length in Chile as part of a grander panorama of "Arab contributions to América"; his speech was titled "General Progress of the Colectividad"[34] Thus, documentary film was a way for Arabs in the diaspora to build connections and affirm mutual values across national borders in South America. Dial's local porteño mahjar community clearly saw this network building as an important project, as evidenced by a gala that they organized in his honor in 1941. Leaders of the most powerful Arab Argentine voluntary and financial organizations, Moisés Azize of the Patronato Sírio Libanés, and Elías Teubal of the Banco Sirio Libanés, organized the event to "recognize [Dial's] work for the colectividad."[35] In sum, Arab Argentines saw transnational film projects as valuable manifestations of their part in the Pan-American mahjar's contribution of economic, intellectual, and cultural capital to their Latin American host nations. There are also indications that Middle Eastern political authorities saw the cinema as a viable way for bolstering Middle East–Latin America relationships.

By 1947, filming was underway for yet another documentary by Dial, but this one was not commissioned by Latin American backers. In this case, Dial worked in conjunction with authorities from various Middle Eastern countries to document the diplomatic relationships between Latin America and the Middle East. This project represented yet another cinematic enterprise that unfolded transnationally across the South American mahjar. In April 1947, diplomatic envoys and ambassadors from Lebanon, Saudi Arabia, and Egypt arrived in Chile to attend a formal dinner hosted by recently elected President Gabriel González Videla in Santiago's La Moneda presidential palace. Following the event, Ambassadors Sheikh Asad Mansur al-Faqih of Saudi Arabia and Wagih Rustom Beik of Egypt, as well as Consul Canaán Apsé of Lebanon, invited José Dial to travel to Santiago and meet with them. They voiced support for his documentary project on Middle Eastern diplomacy to Latin America, and Dial updated them on the progress of this venture. The Arab

Chilean press picked up the story and reported that the documentary would be a full-length bilingual (Arabic and Spanish) feature that highlighted the relationships between Middle Eastern diplomatic representations and mahjar businesses, intellectuals, and institutions. Santiago news organ *La Reforma* concluded that "this film will allow us to admire the progress attained . . . by the Arab colony, composed of Syrians, Palestinians, Lebanese, Egyptians, and Transjordanians." The film would also include panoramic vistas of Latin American backdrops, with the intention of introducing Middle Eastern audiences to the landscapes of Arab diaspora host countries. Dial planned to take the completed documentary on tour through South America and also the United States, demonstrating once again that he conceived of his audience as spanning a broader Arab América.[36]

While we do not have archival evidence proving the extent to which Dial was able to undertake this ultimate American tour, the production of this documentary nevertheless represents the apex of the intersection between his film career and the political links that connected Argentina's Arabs with other regions of the diaspora, as well as the Middle East. Altogether, the history of the Oriente Film crew pushes us to reconsider our perspective and scope when it comes to studying cultural production in the Arab diaspora. The production of these films reveals the continuous intersection that artists and intellectuals had with the circulating ideas, politics, and economies of the mahjar's larger public sphere. However, the story of Oriente Film is not merely one of movies, as the final sections of this chapter make clear. The exhibitions of documentaries like *La Atracción de Oriente* and *Los Sirios y Libaneses en las Américas* were events that included artists from other genres beyond the film scene, including poetry, music, and stage acting. By using the examples of musical and theater performers, the following sections illuminate Oriente Film as a polestar for the energies and creativities of an Arab Argentine arts world that maintained strong connections with the Arabic-speaking eastern Mediterranean. Thus, together, Arab Argentine cinematographers, comedians, and musicians brought the sights and sounds of the Middle East to the distant and disparate limbs of the diaspora in Latin America. In the process, they drew Argentina into the international dialogues about culture, values, and political consciousness that were at play in the Middle East and elsewhere in the diaspora. Their stories are evidence that it was not just the typically acknowledged´ intellectual vanguard of journalists, religious leaders, and political activists who drove the political and cultural dialogues of the mahjar's public sphere.

Stage and Sound

Before the advent of movies with sound, the Oriente Film documentaries required live soundtracks. Schamún, Kouri, and Dial brought in live orchestras to
do this and hired other artists to entertain audience members before and after
each screening. Even after Dial adopted sound technology by the early 1930s,
he maintained the practice of framing each screening with music, poetry, and
stage acts. Delineating the web of actors and musicians who performed as part
of the Oriente Film screenings reveals an artistic community that circulated
among the Levant, Egypt, and the Americas. The work of literary scholars such
as Dakhli shows that this mobility was central to the mahjar's literary scene; for
example, Arab American author Amin Rihani openly viewed travel as "the duty
of the intellectual."[37] This was also the case for the visual and performing arts in
the mahjar. It is important to understand the mechanics by which these artistic
performances circulated in the mahjar, because these mediums were accessible
to and consumed by wide audiences beyond the literate elite and middle classes.
Musical performances in particular—often disseminated by radio shows in addition to live theater performances—had the ability to capture the imagination
or evoke nostalgia among the mahjar's working class and remote rural populations. Music, dance, or jokes from comedic performances, more so than the
great poetry and prose works of the mahjar, could (and were encouraged to) be
reproduced in the homes of Arab Argentine families throughout the provinces
and across the socioeconomic spectrum. While adab al mahjar, as defined by its
literary genres, plays a looming role in the cultural legacy of the diaspora, it is
the broader adab al mahjar that also includes these other mediums that better
defines the regular consumption of cultural production for Arab Argentines
and other Arab Americans. Movies, music, and stage performances rendered
an audiovisual aesthetic of the homeland that Arab Argentines could often relate to across class, religious, political, or regional heritage differences. It was
in these moments of performance and consumption that the imagined community of the mahjar crystallized most visibly and in contrast with venues in
which fracture and local contingency were not uncommon.

One of the chief collaborators in the Oriente Film screenings was the comedic actor Gibran Trabulsi. He was already well known by the late 1920s
to Argentine mahjar audiences, and so the film crew had to shell out "many
thousands of pesos" to hire him. They clearly believed that he was worth the
investment—Schamún expressed his hope that the actor's ability to make

people laugh would help viewers forget about their economic woes while watching the show.[38] It was a valid concern: Oriente Film began touring with Trabulsi just as Argentine citizens began to feel the ripples of the world market crash. The ambitious film entrepreneurs would have had no small interest in an audience unfettered by the preoccupation of financial troubles. The continuation of their projects depended on ticket sales and willing investors from their Argentine, Brazilian, Chilean, and Uruguayan audiences. Luckily, Trabulsi appeared enthusiastic to collaborate.

Like the Oriente Film crew, Trabulsi engaged with his craft via an intensive travel regimen. Beginning in the mid-1920s, he traveled thousands of kilometers, often in the company of a Middle Eastern theater troupe and a rotating cast of musicians. Between November 1929 and 1930 alone, he covered nearly 5,000 kilometers with stops in Córdoba, Tucumán, San Luis, Mendoza, and San Juan. In 1931, he embarked on another tour that spanned the width of the country from the small town of Colonia Alvear in Mendoza Province, through San Juan, and back to Buenos Aires, all by rail.[39] In 1923 he made a foray into Brazil before returning for another *tournée* of the Argentine provinces.[40] By 1937 he was back in Brazil for a second tour (see Map 4).[41]

Trabulsi's performances can best be characterized as variety shows. He often traveled with a sizable troupe of actors who presented comedic skits and short plays that he penned himself. The cornerstone of each show was an appearance by Trabulsi under his stage persona of "Chic Chic Bey." As Chic Chic, he engaged in burlesquely exaggerated satirical monologues, word play and Arabic-language puns, and slapstick antics. Mahjar press organs routinely reviewed his shows, and some treated Chic Chic Bey's performances as more than frivolous vaudevillian humor, despite Trabulsi's facetiousness. In 1932, when many Argentine families and business owners were feeling the strain of the global market crash, a review in *La Gaceta Árabe* extolled the health benefits of attending Trabulsi's shows: "Laughter removes sorrows, comforts the spirit, calms rancor, and reconciles everything else . . . all of [these benefits] you will obtain in copious amounts from the art of Trabulsi," for he is a "great doctor of the soul."[42] By lauding his talents in such a manner, this review presented Trabulsi's art as playing an important social role: his work raised morale as many Arab Argentines struggled through economic hardship and xenophobic backlash. When Trabulsi announced in 1933 that he planned to stop touring, another *Gaceta Árabe* journalist excoriated him in an editorial titled, "What's Wrong with Our Friend Trabulsi?"[43] Attacking

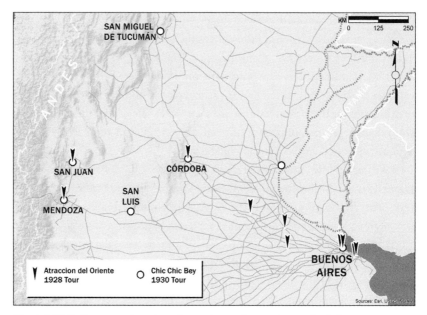

Map 4. Middle Eastern cultural producers in motion, 1928–1930. Artistic tours undertaken by Oriente Film Company and Chic Chic Bey. Data source: La Gaceta Árabe (Hemeroteca, Biblioteca Nacional, Buenos Aires), 1928–1931.

Trabulsi's move to stop touring, the editorial stated that Trabulsi was quitting the time-honored strategy of economic success through mobility that was the bedrock of their colectividad (and the mahjar globally). Perhaps in response to protests such as this one, or perhaps because Trabulsi never intended to quit touring in 1933, Chic Chic remained on the road into the early 1940s. He used the fame that he gained and the social connections that he built in his early provincial tours with Oriente Film and invited other artists to join him.

It seems that both the Oriente Film crew and observers such as the reviewer from the *Gaceta* recognized the ability of a good comedic performance to boost an audience's morale. Historical studies of immigrant communities tend to focus on the institutional mechanisms for providing the community with services such as medical care or financial aid. These institutions were no doubt of paramount importance in the mahjar, but focusing on them exclusively comes at the expense of recognizing other venues and actors who provided important, if less tangible, services to Middle Eastern immigrants and their descendants. Movies, music, and comedy offered viewers an emotional outlet—a respite from daily stress or an invitation to bask in nostalgia for the sights and sounds of the homeland. Trabulsi himself assured the editors of *La Gaceta Árabe* that he found his tours to be not only lucrative but also "morally satisfying."[44] Here, Trabulsi's reflections on his tour echoed the language used by the Oriente Film crew, who repeatedly insisted that the greatest reward from their work was the moral rather than material gain. These artists insisted that their mission had both cultural and moral value beyond the commercial success that they also sought. They clearly saw themselves as the purveyors of an important service for their conationals.

While Trabulsi's peripatetic career signals the important role that artists played in the emotional panorama of the Argentine mahjar, the origin of his "Chic Chic Bey" sobriquet belies the transnational links between Argentina and other regions of the global Arab diaspora, as well as the diaspora's Ottoman past. "Chic Chic" was not an original invention by Trabulsi; it is a character whose appearance we can trace back to the Ottoman revolutionary press of 1908 to 1911. The year 1908 marked the fall of Sultan Abdul Hamid, the thirty-fourth sultan of the Ottoman Empire, who ruled autocratically until his deposition by the Young Turk Revolution that culminated on April 27, 1909. Along with Abdul Hamid fell the gag of censorship in the Ottoman press. Palmira Brummett notes that as a result, "the revolution in thought that had precipitated the revolution of arms at last found its way into print."[45] Satire, often expressed through cartoons, became a vehicle for expressing pointed critiques of the revolution and the threat of European imperialism. It was in this milieu that the character of Chic Bey first appeared as a satirical cartoon in the Ottoman press. Chic Bey, Brummett notes, "was a suave, fashionable seeker of comfort, a weakling who needed to imitate his rivals rather than challenging them in combat." Characteristically clad in European fashion, Chic Bey "personified the threat of European cultural hegemony." Thus, he was a cartoon rendered as an anti-imperialist critique, the satirists behind the pen warning readers against the ways in which European fashion "subjected the mind and body." [46] In sum, Chic played the figure of a dandy and was a "burlesque [depiction] of the western-struck male" notes Deniz Kandiyoti.[47] The next iteration of Chic Bey came with a set of stage performances that also preceded Trabulsi's assumption of the moniker.

Shortly after Chic Bey began to appear in the Ottoman satirical press, Egyptian actor Naguib el-Rihani brought this persona to his stage act, dubbing himself "Kish Kish Bey." El-Rihani was the father of Egyptian comedy, often referred to as "The Laughing Philosopher" (*al-filusuf al-dahik*). He was known for performing versions of European comedic and theatrical works, but adapting them to a Middle Eastern cultural context as opposed to pure mimesis of the European model.[48] El-Rihani's performances as Kish Kish Bey constitute part of a stylistic evolution in the Arab world's comedy scene from improvisational comedic skits (*fasl mudhik*) popular at the turn of the century, to socially and politically relevant satire-based comedy. This process of reinterpreting Western cultural productions through Eastern cultural milieus was a central theme in the *Nahda*–Arab Renaissance, or modernist awakening—movement. Across the Arabic-speaking world, including mahjar communities in the Americas, comedians adapted Kish Kish Bey to suit their own cultural contexts. This was sometimes to the chagrin of the original Kish Kish (el-Rihani), who went so far as to fret publicly about comedic troupes that routinely "copied his ideas."[49] El-Rihani's Kish Kish Bey character was a turn-of-the-century feudal mayor dealing hilariously with his life after being transplanted into the big city of Cairo. His was a satirical performance that hinged on the tensions between urban versus rural life and culture, as well as other dynamics of early twentieth-century Egyptian society. Rather than a carbon copy of the Chic Bey cartoon's satirical critique, his was an adaptation to a contemporary reality that theater audiences could presumably recognize.

Thanks to his portrayal of characters like Kish Kish Bey, El-Rihani was a star of Cairo's vaudeville theater and popular movie actor when he married the young actress Badia Masabni. Masabni, born in Syria, had emigrated to Buenos Aires with her family as a child and then to Cairo as a teen. For the newlyweds' year-long honeymoon, they returned to Masabni's childhood home and proceeded to tour throughout South America before returning to Egypt, where Masabni would become a dance star and owner of several famous nightclubs. Throughout their traveling honeymoon, they staged shows and performances, while mahjar communities in Brazil, Uruguay, and Argentina hosted the performers in major urban centers such as Rio de Janeiro, São Paulo, Santos, Montevideo, and Buenos Aires. They most likely appeared in smaller provincial cities and towns as well along the way, according to Masabni's claim that "we didn't leave out any place. We did great work and Naguib was successful. So was I."[50] It was during the Buenos Aires leg of their tour that the story of the honeymooning couple became entwined in the artistic and intellectual projects of various members of the Argentine mahjar community.

Gibran Trabulsi spent some time touring with the newlyweds in 1925. (They most likely made his acquaintance while on the road.) When the couple departed for Egypt, Trabulsi continued to tour, assembling his own troupe of actors who followed him across the country. He proceeded to adopt the comic persona of Chic Chic Bey, performing comedic sketches, pantomime, and satirical monologues in theaters, cinemas, and social clubs before being signed by Oriente Film. His moniker was, of course, a spin on Rihani's "Kish Kish," but this time the satirical figure was adapted for Arab South American audiences. When announcing Trabulsi's upcoming appearances in local theaters, the Arab Argentine press would occasionally even render "Chic Chic" as "Kish Kish." Tracing the genealogy of this fictional character from the Ottoman revolutionary press to the Argentine stage allows us to witness the chain of artistic transmission and innovation that stretched from the Middle East to Latin America from the late nineteenth century onward.

The story of Chic Chic Bey encapsulates multiple overlapping layers of mobility across international borders, provinces, and continents. At the scale of the family unit, we see Badia Masabni's history of movement from Syria, to Argentina, to Egypt over the course of a decade. It was this multisite circular migration from the Arabic-speaking eastern Mediterranean to South America and back that ended up connecting Masabni with the burgeoning arts scene in Cairo. When el-Rihani married Masabni, he became involved in this circuit as well, as did his artistic influence and personas, which lived on through the hypermobile artist Gibran Trabulsi. Trabulsi brought his craft to a plethora of audiences across South America and along the way attracted artistic collaborators from both South America and the Middle East who would join him for these ambitious tours, thus retracing (and forging their own) circuits of mobility that would bring together moral and material audience support . It is this phenomenon of overlapping layers of mobility that defined the development of cultural production in the Argentine mahjar. Although this chapter has focused on the life and work of screen and stage artists, these individuals do not represent unique examples of these overlapping layers of mobile people and ideas. These patterns characterized the diaspora's musical scene as well. The musical history of the mahjar indeed merits an in-depth study on its own terms. But for now, a brief examination of one Arab Argentine musician reveals the same triangulation of movement between Latin American and eastern Mediterranean geographies.

One musician who moved between these geographies was tenor singer Selim Zeitune, who toured both independently and alongside Trabulsi from the 1920s to 1940s.[51] His career also represents a web of connections between artistic communities in Argentina (and other Southern Cone nations), the Levant, and Egypt. Zeitune specialized in Arabic-language opera and gave performances in Argentina, Brazil, and Chile before returning to Egypt for further musical training by the end of the 1930s. The accolades that he garnered through showcasing his talent along his South American tour circuits likely enabled him to secure a spot as the pupil of the most prolific Egyptian composer of his era: Abdel Wahab. Wahab, born in Cairo in 1907, was an extremely popular composer, musician, actor, and singer who innovated traditional Arabic musical forms by introducing Western rhythms.[52] Inspired by time spent in Paris, Wahab's modernist experimentation with musical forms reflected his interaction with other musical styles, including Argentine tango music.

Tango had become all the rage in the vibrant Parisian arts scene by the first decade of the twentieth century, and Wahab brought some of its rhythms and instrumentation to the musical scores that he began to create. Mahjar audiences in both North and South America became enamored with Wahab's signature sound after he produced and starred in the musical film *The White Rose* (*Ward El Bayda*) in 1934. Entrepreneurs and cinema buffs such as José Dial orchestrated the importation of the film to the Americas. For decades following this debut, Arab American audiences remained enthralled by Wahab's talents. Mahjar elites went out of their way to meet Wahab if they were traveling to Egypt, and they hired his vocal students to perform at important family and community events.[53] Once again, we witness intersections, and movement, between the art worlds of the Argentine mahjar and the Levant, with Egypt (especially Cairo) often serving as a key triangulation point and space of convergence for artistic talent or innovation.

When the Oriente Film crew reached the capital city of Santa Fe province while on a 1932 national tour, they showcased an updated version of their popular documentary *La Atracción del Oriente*. Their new version, titled *La Canción del Oriente* (*The Song of the Orient*), included a musical score and footage of Latin American landscapes interspersed with Middle Eastern ones. Accompanying the panoramas of Syrian and Lebanese cities, countrysides, and historic sites were the voices and melodies of Cairo's musical icons Abdel Wahab, and Oum Kalthoum, the latter lovingly dubbed "The Star of the East" by generations of adoring fans.[54] That night, the audience at Santa Fe's Empire Theatre watched as landscapes of Argentina, Brazil, Uruguay, and Chile bled seamlessly into scenes from the Levant, all the while backed by an Egyptian soundtrack. This image conveys the very core of a dynamic that the work of many Arab Argentine artists had in common by the 1920s and would characterize the development and dissemination of cultural production in the South American region of the Arab diaspora in the decades that followed. These individuals refused a compartmentalization of space and nationality, opting instead for fluidity and connectivity between South American, Levantine, and Pan-Arab identities. The main goal behind their highly mobile lifestyles was to draw their network of audiences and benefactors closer together to define their ethnic community by its membership in—and importance to—a greater diaspora and to stake a claim on their host country as productive citizens. This mobility offered them new perspectives on cultural forms, styles, and ways of expressing a relationship to the homeland as a place, set of values, or aesthetic forms.

News coverage of Middle Eastern artistic performances printed in the Arab Argentine press made clear that many Arab Argentines saw musical and visual arts as playing an important role in their community. Time and again reviewers gave descriptions of the "authentic" Arab orchestras that played the musical score for Oriente Film documentaries, praising their ability to transport an audience to the Arab world. Art often represented a universal language with which mahjar communities could communicate the "beauty of those lands and people" to Argentine audiences. Art had the ability to create a counternarrative to the misrepresentations of Middle Eastern people and cultures that were so common in mainstream popular culture in Argentina (and the American hemisphere in general).[55] In addition, artistic projects were often outside the regulatory goals of the state in a way that contrasts other aspects of the immigration boom era during which governments observed unprecedented global levels of human mobility. There were of course exceptions—for example, British authorities denied José Dial access to film in Palestine—but in general, the artists covered in this chapter moved freely through the Americas, Levant, and Egypt in pursuit of their craft. This did not mean that authorities did not take notice of their activities. This was clearly the case when members of the Argentine government—from municipal functionaries to federal officials—took the time to give interviews for Oriente Film documentaries or attend screenings of the film.

The film screenings and theatrical performances highlighted in this chapter were spaces where Arab Argentines came together to watch movies, laugh, or feel collective nostalgia toward a homeland that they may or may not have ever experienced in person. However, these events were also spaces of exhibition, where Argentines outside the Arab colectividad were invited to witness footage of the Middle East and its peoples or admire the contributions of Middle Eastern immigrants and their descendants to South American economies and cultures. After all, the artistic material produced by artists like Dial or Trabulsi was not merely for an Arab South American audience. Especially in the case of his collaboration with Oriente Film, these performances were meant to showcase aspects of Middle Eastern culture, landscape, and architecture to a broad audience of South Americans from across a spectrum of identities. That local and federal officials attended these events and national press organs took notice indicated that Argentine authorities recognized these artistic events as important to the cities and towns where they took place. In this light, the contents of a Chic Chic Bey or Oriente Film performance marked the leisure-time consumption of Argentine audiences beyond merely the Arab Argentine community in many cases.

Official interest in the activities of these artists was also apparent in the other direction: from Arab governments toward Arab Argentine artists. This was obvious when Arab diplomatic corps members from various states expressly sought out an Arab Argentine filmmaker in the hopes that he would create a visual archive of their engagement with Latin American Arab populations and their host country governments. In Argentina, Perón's administration, which came to power in 1946, took a keen interest in the possibility of cultural production as an avenue for building international ties with the Arab region. Perón even deployed a cultural attaché (*agregado cultural*) as part of Argentina's formal diplomatic mission to Lebanon, Syria, and Egypt in 1951. In 1955, Perón extended the duties of the cultural attaché to the Kingdom of Saudi Arabia. The attaché he selected was Malatios Koury, a Syrian Argentine writer and translator whose work appeared frequently in the literature and arts section of Arab Argentine press organs from the late 1930s onward. Although Koury was not involved in the visual and performing arts, as were the subjects in this chapter, he nonetheless had in common with them the role of cultural ambassador. He was officially sanctioned to play this role by the Argentine government as of 1951, whereas individuals such as the artists who fill this chapter assumed this role informally as they moved among Latin American geographies, the Levant, and Egypt from the 1920s onward. The physical routes of their journeys traced the cultural, intellectual, and political currents that bound Argentina's diaspora, and the nation more broadly, together with the Arabic-speaking eastern Mediterranean with increasing intensity in the first half of the twentieth century.

Altogether, this contingent of highly mobile artists and performers suggests the need to reconsider our perspective and scope of study when dealing with Middle Eastern communities in Argentina. At the very least, we cannot continue to treat mahjar communities scattered across Argentina as isolated data points on a map. Focusing on the mobile careers of individuals like Dial, Trabulsi, or Zeitune renders visible the ways in which many Arab Argentines relied on a lattice of contacts, collaborators, and willing audiences that penetrated the most remote regions of the country and often extended across American borders.

Scholars often focus on the way in which a host country can develop a relationship with the sending country of a given immigrant community, but this chapter challenges us to think beyond such a bidirectional relationship. In the case of Argentina, its Levantine diaspora community built relationships and responded to artistic, cultural, and political influences across a broader Middle Eastern and North African region. Thus, the story of an Arab Argentine opera singer or filmmaker is really one of how the cultural and intellectual history of this diaspora population cannot be contained in the national borders of its primary host country. Instead, it is a history that spans the eastern Mediterranean and Southern Cone alike. Using this tendency toward transnational mobility and exchange as a base unit of analysis is the first step toward attaining a clear picture of how this ethnic group simultaneously navigated Argentine society and sought to make an impact on the mahjar's transnational public sphere. In many ways, the history of other groups, such as highly mobile Arab Argentine journalists or enterprising philanthropists, echoes the dynamics of the Arab Argentine art world. It is to this latter group, specifically Arab Argentine women who mobilized as philanthropic advocates, that we shift our attention in the next chapter.

4   Moving Money, Mobilizing Networks

As the twentieth century unfolded, Argentina's immigrant colectividades inscribed themselves ever more visibly on the nation's landscape. German, Italian, Spanish, Japanese, and many other groups opened schools and hospitals in the name of their colectividad. Heritage associations buzzed with plans to erect monuments to their immigrant roots or lobbied for the naming of city streets or plazas after their colectividad (Plaza Italia, Avenida República Árabe Siria, and so on).[1] While some of these projects never came to fruition, many others did, and the Argentine landscape became more and more a reflection of its history of mass migration. Some of the most prominent organizations that coalesced to propel building projects or take charge of lobbies were ethnic voluntary organizations that fell under the umbrella of "beneficence associations" (*asociaciones de beneficencia*). These charitable associations did everything from orchestrating bread lines, to providing burial services, to disbursing funds to destitute individuals who wished to repatriate to their homeland. In the mahjar press, the development of these organizations received prominent treatment. It was common to find portraits of those who served as board members featured prominently in *galerías sociales*, or open letters from the executive officers published with fanfare in the pages of *La Gaceta Árabe, El Eco de Oriente, La Union Libanesa*, and other periodicals. In some cases, beneficence organizations even ran their own periodicals and radio shows, further entwining the mechanics of these groups with that of the ethnic press.

This chapter examines the activities of some of these beneficence associations, and the ways that they practiced institutionalized charity.[2] Specifically, it examines the role of women in these organizations and the fundraising networks that they cultivated. This provides us with insight into the ways that, much like the ethnic press and roving cultural producers of the previous chapters, beneficencia also linked rural and urban nodes of this diaspora community. In addition, the study of these organizations allows us to examine the realm of women's work and the gendered dynamics of philanthropy in the Argentine mahjar. Through the analysis of periodicals and financial records from philanthropic campaigns, we can map a network of intercommunicating Arab Argentines from the federal capital to remote outposts of unincorporated national territories. Furthermore, we can begin to track how the women in this intraregional web of connection strategically hooked into the mahjar's public sphere of politics, anti-imperial ideologies, and remittance economies. In tracking these ties, we also better approximate a gendered perspective of Arab women's work and the ways in which it bound mahjar geographies together. Much like other realms of mobility in this book, the geography within which these philanthropic relationships arose was not delimited strictly by a question of a singular homeland–host country exchanges. It was in fact much more expansive than the translocal connections that the existence of hometown associations might intimate, and more expansive than traditional conceptions of transnational relations have previously suggested. Organized philanthropy created networks of fundraising and giving that spilled across national borders in both the Americas and the wider Mediterranean region.

Implementing this transregional perspective is important because in the fields of mahjar and Argentine historiography, the city, traditionally conceived of as the epicenter of institutionalized philanthropy, is often rendered in opposition to the "interior" in a way that marginalizes individuals whose livelihoods are staked in the movement between these spaces. As women in an immigrant minority group, the subjects of this chapter are often doubly marginalized by official histories or scholarly accounts.[3] By contrast, this chapter highlights three distinct facets of Arab women's involvement in the economy and politics of both their diaspora community and the diasporic homeland. First, it examines their role in the construction of ethnic institutions, with a focus on the example of the Hospital Sirio Libanés (established 1937) of Buenos Aires. Second, it discusses the role of these women in fostering cultural production within their ethnic community through hosting radio programs and cultivating venues for Arab Argentine artistic performances. Finally, it attends to transnational beneficence projects undertaken by Arab Argentine women in order to demonstrate that many of these organizations operated across multiple geographic planes in their philanthropic work. Along with these campaigns came a certain level of prestige for the Arab Argentine women at the helm, and it in turn provided them with the ability to subtly engage transregionally with political events across the broader Middle East. In applying the same lens of mobility to these beneficencia institutions as we have to the settlement patterns, press organs, and cultural production of the colectividad, we can push back on the idea of institutions as entities that arise from and serve fixed locations. In turn, this leads us to extend our vision of Argentina as a nation of immigrants into spaces previously excluded from scholarly conversations about ethnic diasporas in the Southern Cone.

Institutions as Associational Nodes

The subject of institutionalized charity is yet another topic that benefits from its contextualization in a landscape of the mahjar's associational nodes. These nodes served as gravitational centers in mahjar communities, especially those far from larger diasporic hubs such as Buenos Aires, Córdoba, and Tucumán. As Chapter 2 explored briefly in the case of the Club Sirio Libanés de Rosario de la Frontera in rural Salta Province, these clubs often convened members and leadership from broader geographic areas than their seemingly local-oriented names might suggest. In other words, they represented points at which migrant mobilities tended to converge, overlap, or begin. This was the case for both intraregional and international movement. Traditionally, migrant institutions such as those we explore here have occupied a central focus in the study of immigrant communities in Latin America. For that matter, contemporary scholarship still tends to favor the centrality of the institution in the analysis of immigrant community building over time.[4]

This chapter builds on this tradition and brings new attention to both the specific role of women and the mechanics of rural-urban relationships among ethnic diaspora communities that participate in transnational networks. All too often, when we construe the process of community building, it is as a process that takes place in spaces that house critical masses of people. However, this chapter sheds light on the fact that in the mahjar, the engine for community building existed in a sense everywhere. When we think about the events and projects that constitute the practices of community building in the mahjar, the role of these associational nodes looms large. They set the rhythm for communal celebrations of holidays, served as venues for artistic and cultural performances, and were powerful engines with the ability to rapidly mobilize aid if the need arose. In these contexts, associational nodes were central to local milieus, while simultaneously maintaining an ability to engage transnationally with political and economic panoramas of the homeland. The case studies of women's philanthropic organizations that follow reflect this simultaneity and reveal the ways in which associational nodes linked diasporic denizens of diverse regions of a single host country. They also gender our perception of some of the most prominent institutional projects that arose from this network.

Moving toward a gendered recalibration of our perspective on mahjar history allows us to question some of the foundational narratives about the diaspora. Notably, it allows us to critically question the frequent framing of Arab American communities as a consequence of an ineffable enterprising spirit (*espíritu emprendedor*). Beginning in the early twentieth century, mahjar journalists, intellectuals, and business owners across the Americas firmly ascribed to the notion that this spirit drove their community. The enterprising spirit is a trope that appears in the foundational myths of many immigrant community, national, and family histories—a combination between bootstrapping and innate financial shrewdness that allowed forebears to prosper in América. Unsurprisingly, this trope appeared frequently in the early historiography of the Argentine mahjar—for example, in the article about Julián Echivalle, the pioneering Lebanese landowner in Salta province whom we met in Chapter 2. This is only logical, seeing as the very mahjar organizations and press organs that publicized this foundational narrative of the enterprising spirit were themselves the very institutions that generated and encouraged scholarship on this group's history. Even contemporary accounts, both journalistic and scholarly, lean on this trope in their treatment of early Middle Eastern migrants in the Americas.[5] Left unexamined, however, this trope is problematic. Principally, the notion of the enterprising spirit is an implicitly gendered set of qualities used most often to account for the business acumen of men. It is a framework that applauds the idea of collective advancement as measured by perceptions of political, social, and economic insertion, yet it tends to obscure the role of half the community—of women—in these various projects. The following case studies offer an alternative vision of the sort of political and financial perspicacity that drove the advancement of community-building projects by centering the narrative on women's work.

If men managed the majority of the Argentine mahjar's purchase power in traditional markets through their predominance as business owners, professionals, and even industrial magnates, women presided over the emerging sphere of institutional charity over the first several decades of the twentieth century. In the dozens of associational nodes that dotted the Argentine landscape, men served on the boards of numerous mutual aid societies, social clubs, and heritage organizations, but by the late 1920s, the most widely reported religious and lay organizations filling the pages of Arab-owned newspapers were women's organizations. Many middle- and upper-class women made prominent careers of philanthropy and proved adroit at leveraging their social capital to gain financial support for their projects. They interfaced with an array of donors and collaborators—rich and humble, urban and rural, across religious denominations. Analysis of some of the most prominent beneficencia campaigns from the 1920s through the 1940s reveals that Arab Argentine women played a critical role in the wealth and welfare of their colectividad. This analysis also leads us toward a more globalized vision of the wider web of immigrant philanthropy and humanitarian aid in Argentina in the twentieth century.[6]

Women and the Construction of Ethnic Institutions

To shed light on the interprovincial scale of beneficence projects undertaken by various female-run Arab Argentine associations in the twentieth century, it is instructive to examine one of the longest-running secular institutions in the Arab Argentine community: the Hospital Sirio Libanés. One can still visit this medical facility today at its original location in the northwestern Villa Devoto neighborhood of the federal capital. Evidence of numerous additions and efforts to modernize its medical facilities are visible from the street. Inside, however, the tiled courtyard and the converted mansion that housed the original physicians' offices and dispensary remain perfectly intact. What is not immediately visible to the twenty-first-century visitor, however, is that this physical space embodies the protracted effort of thousands of donors and organizers throughout the better part of the twentieth century. What began as a small, voluntary association transformed into a large-scale community project over the course of just a few decades and continues to function today.

Though it was established formally in 1937, the dream of a hospital that would serve the colectividad dates back twenty years before that. It was in 1917 that a group of Arab Argentine women came together to discuss the need for better medical service for their community and began to envision themselves as the ones who would advocate for this community resource. They subsequently formed a secular association, the Society of Merciful Works (Sociedad de Obras de Misericordia). While they certainly were not the first voluntary association to form in the mahjar (others in the Americas date back to the 1880s), they were one of the earlier associations whose mission was to openly provide service to individuals beyond monthly dues-paying membership. This was, in other words, what sociologists and historians of migration often refer to as an instrumental association—one whose goals are to serve a population broader than its formal membership roster.[7] The hospital was the product of but one of many female-led instrumental associations that coalesced from the 1910s through the 1930s in many provinces. Several of these were lay organizations, such as the Sociedad Zaharat-el-Ihsan of Corrientes Province, which formed in 1929 with the objective of building a school. Other instrumental associations maintained close ties to religious institutions, such as the array of institutions tied to Orthodox churches across the country. Among many others, these included the Sociedad de Beneficencia Nur el Ifaf and the Asociación Femenina Sirio Ortodoxa of Buenos Aires, the Sociedad An-Nahadat El Charkiat of Tucumán, and the Sociedad de Beneficencia de Damas Sirio Libanesas Ortodoxas of Salta. Over the years, the philanthropic activities of these groups resulted in South-South circuits of charitable remittances that geographically mimicked the South-South migratory circuits that gave rise to the mahjar.

Although their impetus for organizing was the establishment of a local hospital, in its first incarnation, the Society of Merciful Works was principally a place for international humanitarian aid coupled with itinerant individualized services (e.g., door-to-door clothing donations, care for the sick). The women who sat on its board of directors focused their fundraising events on generating donations to remit to disadvantaged populations in the Middle East, in addition to assorted smaller drives to provide short-term relief to recently arrived migrants in need of services. On several occasions, they collaborated with another Buenos Aires–based instrumental association, the Central Committee for Aid to Syria and Lebanon (Comité Central de Ayuda a Siria y Líbano), to raise money for causes such as the Tuberculosis Hospital of Beirut. International philanthropy was already a path well trodden by other Arab Argentine instrumental associations, and perhaps this accounts in part for the Society of Merciful Works' early participation in these South-South charitable remittance circuits. When the society decided to renew its commitment to a centralized local project that would serve the diaspora community rather than the homeland, they also shifted their focus to building interprovincial, rather than international, networks of donors.

By 1923, the vision of domestic medical services for Arab immigrants and their progeny in Argentina once again became the group's main focus, and the board of directors renamed the organization the "Pro-Hospital Syrian Lebanese Beneficence Association" (PSLBA; Asociación Pro Hospital Sirio Libanés). They ratified official statutes, and by 1927 the municipal government legally recognized them, granting them personería juridica, as a charitable organization with the express mission of building a hospital.[8] The women set their sights on purchasing a villa situated on almost an acre and a half of land on the outskirts of Buenos Aires. Once occupied by a wealthy family, the home was spacious and well appointed, and the parcel of land would provide ample space for building new wings for the future clinic as the operation grew. The sale price was 140,000 pesos, and the PSLBA quickly set to the task of raising money toward a down payment and initial mortgage installments (see Figure 6).[9] Their methodology for raising this prodigious sum relied on inspiring Arab Argentines across the nation to buy in to the functional and symbolic importance of the larger hospital project. In order to do this, the Pro-Hospital group ran a savvy fundraising campaign based on the notion of collective ownership of a community resource.

The women of the PSLBA offered donors the opportunity to become "member owners" of the new institution. They calculated the property area to be approximately 7,100 square *varas* of land (the *vara* being the customary measurement unit for measuring Spanish properties and land grants since the nineteenth century), and then proceeded to announce the Grand Varas Sale (*Gran Venta de Varas*) of 1935. Each vara would be "sold" for the accessible price of 30 pesos, and in return, the "buyer" would receive a certificate stating the buyer's status as an honorary member of the PSLBA, as well as a title declaring ownership of a piece of the land from the hospital grounds. This symbolic bequeathing of ownership to donors aligned with the overall rhetoric of their campaign, which often described their project as, above all, "Collective: By the People and for the People." This language appeared time and again in speeches at fundraising events and in open letters to the press.[10]

During the Grand Varas Sale, which stretched from 1935 into 1936, individuals from across the provinces chipped in 30 pesos each and in turn became member owners of the future hospital. The first round of varas donations went exceedingly well. In 1935 the PSLBA was able to make its first 35,000

Figure 6. Hospital Sirio Libanés fundraiser, ca. 1940. Pictured women of the PSLBA dressed up for an evening fundraising event. Source: Asociación de Beneficencia del Hospital Sirio Libanés, Buenos Aires, Argentina. Reprinted with permission.

peso mortgage payment a full three months prior to its due date and, on top of that, saved 13,000 pesos to be used toward the second mortgage payment.[11] The capital for these payments came from nearly 1,600 varas "purchases" that rolled in from across the country. By 1937, the PSLBA was running its own newspaper, *La Voz del Hospital*, which became a platform for promoting fundraisers such as the varas sale. In February 1937, a special edition of *La Voz* announced that the rest of the mortgage was officially paid off. On the cover of the special issue featured a copy of the notarized property title in their name before launching into a long letter of thanks and congratulation. PSLBA president Wacila de Adre and secretary Estela Chacar de Chacar attributed their success to the funds that poured in from provincial donors. They announced that five thousand individuals contributed to the completion of their mortgage payments. With this many donors, the PSLBA not only paid off the mortgage, renovated the property, and equipped it as a medical facility, but also ended up with a surplus of 10,000 pesos cash and 11,000 pesos worth of stocks in their account. Relentless, they immediately began soliciting donations for the construction of an entire new wing, named the "Monoblock," that was to be constructed adjacent to the existing hospital building.[12]

Beyond the enthusiastic rhetoric of the organization's leadership, a quantitative breakdown of the data from PSLBA fundraisers confirms the important role played by a geographically broad donor base. Taking the varas sale fund drive as an example, we learn that donations came in from the length and breadth of the country. Of the 1,583 Varas sold in 1936, relatively few (just over 4 percent) came from individual donors or institutions near the physical site of the hospital in Villa Devoto. Another 18 percent came in from donors in surrounding (though still quite distant in many cases) locations in Buenos Aires Province. The other 78 percent of the sales (1,235 varas) took place across nineteen provinces and territories. These remaining donations came in from 211 cities, towns, villages, and rail stations. The list of provinces and national territories that contributed to the project is in fact so extensive that it is much more succinct to name the handful of territories that did not contribute to the varas sale (Formosa, Santa Cruz, and Tierra del Fuego).

Donation records also reveal that those in rural areas were often high per capita contributors to projects like the Monoblock construction and varas sale. If we look at the province of Buenos Aires as an example, it is clear that larger aggregations of donors did not always coincide with that province's geography of urban hubs. PSLBA records of 1936 varas sales across seventy-one provincial municipalities list the two largest cities, La Plata and Mar del Plata, as having eight donors in the case of the latter and only two in the case of the former. There were significant populations of Arab Argentines living in both locations, as indicated by the presence of associational nodes and dozens of self-registered entries in both the 1927 and 1942 Syrian-Lebanese business directories. This dynamic is even more pronounced in Junín and Pergamino, where no donors are recorded. Both of these locations were host to growing Middle Eastern diaspora populations in the 1930s and several associational nodes. Well-to-do intellectuals from Buenos Aires such as newspaper owner Elias Amar even went out of their way to make networking visits to Pergamino and Junín in the same era that the PSLBA was actively fundraising. Because PSLBA did not publish records from every fundraiser that they did, it is of course possible that archival records of collaboration from places like La Plata, Mar del Plata, Pergamino, and Junín became lost in the shuffle. This possibility aside, it is nevertheless an important indicator that we should not naturalize connections between diasporic population density and propensity to participate in nonlocal community building projects. These records also show unequivocally that there were relatively high participation rates of Arab Argentines located in extremely rural areas of very low population density—diasporic or otherwise. In a sample of fifteen locales in Buenos Aires Province, ranging from larger cities to tiny rail line outposts, the presence of donors in remote areas is clear (See Table 1). The village of Indio Rico is one example. Far from a burgeoning hub of mahjar population, institutions, and business (like Junín or Pergamino), Indio Rico was essentially a railroad station around which a small village grew starting in the late 1920s. By 1942, a few Arab Argentines registered as tienda and almacén owners in that year's *Guía de Comercio*. Despite its few inhabitants and overall remoteness, the village boasted six donors in 1936—four of whom mustered a 1 vara donation of 30 pesos. The remaining two went in on a vara purchase jointly, combining their funds to reach the 30 peso mark. In return, these donors—Felipe Kemel, Salvador Moreno, José Dacruh, Emilio Abdalah, and Pedro and Felipe Melken—each received a certificate stating their "ownership" of a piece of the soon-to-be-built Hospital Sirio Libanés more than 500 kilometers away. We can observe similar dynamics of consistent donations from small to medium-sized towns in the provinces that appear to have had small Arab Argentine populations such as General Pinto, Lobería, Cañada Seca, and Castelli.

Examples like the town of Indio Rico demonstrate that philanthropy was not solely the purview of urban Arab Argentines proximal to the exclusive circles of charitable organizations. Previously, historians have analyzed these organizations as places in which the performance of beneficence was as much an altruistic act as a status symbol for women across the ethnic and religious spectrum in twentieth-century Argentine society.[13] And this was undoubtedly the case for Arab Argentine women such as those on the PSLBA board of directors—much as it was for Southern European Catholic Argentine women, Jewish Argentine women, and many others.[14] However, in the case of the Arab Argentine community, the Hospital Sirio Libanés's fundraising records allow us to move beyond exclusively focusing on the women at the helm of a major philanthropic project. In addition, fundraising records enable us to excavate information about who these women targeted as an audience (that is, their business rationale). These records also shed light on the question of the composition of the population of supporters who monetarily fueled the PSLBA women's philanthropic engine.

From the beginning of their campaign to build the hospital, the PSLBA

Location	Individuals Registered in Guía, 1927	Individuals Registered in Guía, 1942	Number of Varas Donors, 1936
Tres Arroyos	38	72	39
Bahía Blanca	37	27	30
Olavarría	8	5	13
Gral. Pinto	7	7	11
Zárate	16	0	10
Tandil	30	18	9
Lobería	6	9	9
Gral. Madariaga	20	5	8
Saladillo	22	5	7
Mar del Plata	39	66	7
Cañada Seca	7	5	7
Castelli	7	7	6
Campana	10	5	6
Indio Rico	0	3	6
La Plata	66	59	2
Pergamino	51	128	0
Junín	56	92	0

Table 1. PSLBA Varas Sale Donations, Buenos Aires Province, 1936.
Data source: Wacila J. de Adre and Estela Ch. de Chacar, "Asociación de Beneficencia Pro-Hospital Sirio-Libanés: Origen, Fundación y su Obra hasta el Presente," La Voz del Hospital (Hemeroteca, Biblioteca Nacional, Buenos Aires), February 1937, 1–4; and Syrian-Lebanese business directories from 1927 and 1942.

pointedly appealed to Arab Argentines on a national scale rather than focusing on the local Buenos Aires community. They employed a system of "honorary delegates"—women and men throughout the provinces and national territories (as well as neighboring countries) whom they tasked with spreading the word about fundraising drives such as the varas sale. Honorary delegates also acted as liaisons to remote provincial geographies of the mahjar (like Indio Rico and other locations yet farther afield). The official job description of an honorary delegate was to "traverse their surrounding towns, visit co-nationals, and get them interested in the project" on a volunteer basis, paying out of pocket for their travel expenses.[15] The PSLBA also paid a modest salary to a small corps of employees whose sole purpose was to travel through-out the country, drum up enthusiasm among the honorary delegates, and col-lect funds already raised by these delegates. From a fundraising standpoint, it was an extremely effective system. The intricacies of the delegate system also provide insight into yet another way in which philanthropic projects in the nation's capital could be intimately tied to rural efforts and provincial buy-in to sentiments of collective ownership. Furthermore, careful study of the fundraising data revises notions of philanthropy and charitable giving as strictly the purview of the more privileged sectors of Arab Argentine society. It is the mechanics of this delegate system, and the fiscal results that it yielded, to which we now turn.

Between 1935 and 1946, the number of honorary delegates recruited by the PSLBA and their small corps of traveling employees increased steadily from 215 in 1935, to 340 in 1937, to 400 by 1946 (see Map 5).[16] To become a delegate represented a chance for Arab Argentines living in remote rural spaces or cit-ies with minuscule percentages of Middle Eastern immigrants to gain visibil-ity and assert membership in the broader Argentine mahjar. The PSLBA saw to it that collaborators received accolades for their contribution in print and over the airwaves. From the outset of the varas sale campaign in 1935, the dis-tinguished president and founding member of PSLBA, Estela Chacar de Cha-car, dutifully read long lists of delegate and donor names on her weekly radio show, *The Voice of the Hospital* (*La Voz del Hospital*). Every three months, the board of directors published a news bulletin that listed names and locations of donors and delegates alongside updates on hospital fundraising and con-struction progress. The PSLBA's commitment to regularly publishing infor-mation about collaborators in their newsletter allows a detailed accounting of the provenance of the capital that went into this major institutional project. These records attest to the fact that their delegate system was highly efficient and that it generated a nationwide effort to build the Hospital Sirio Libanés.

In preparation for on-the-ground fundraising campaigns, PSLBA strate-gically employed the airwaves to cultivate investment in the hospital project across the provinces. In 1934 they decided to allocate 150 pesos from their monthly budget to short segments and advertisements on two bilingual shows. After six months of regular advertising on the radio programs *Arab Voice* (*Voz Árabe*) and *Syrian-Lebanese Hour* (*Hora Sirio-Libanesa*), the PSLBA elected to invest in their own radio program, *Voz del Hospital*. The show aired every Sunday on the L.R.9 Radio Fenix Broadcasting station for thirty min-

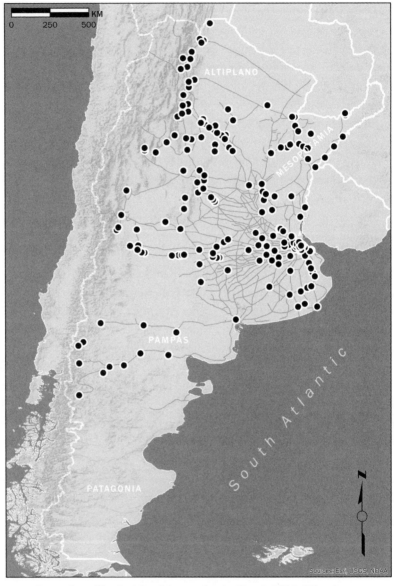

Map 5. Expansion of fundraising delegates for the Hospital Sirio Libanés, 1937 (left) to 1947 (right). Data source: La Voz del Hospital, Hemeroteca, Biblioteca Nacional, Buenos Aires), 1937–1947.

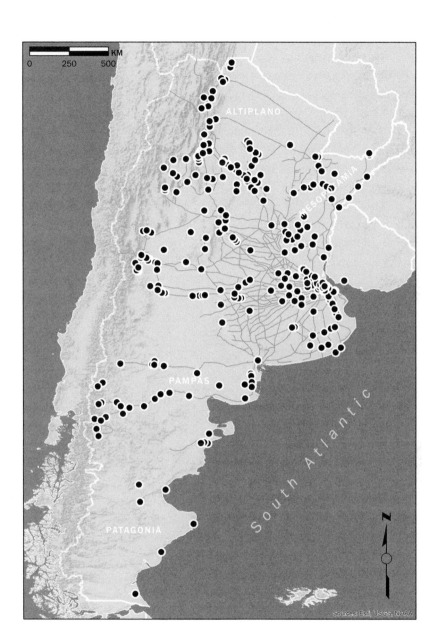

utes.[17] Then radio stations in the provinces rebroadcast these transmissions on local stations, such as Radio Callao in Tucumán.[18] Thus, many provincial Arab Argentines would have been familiar with the hospital project before the PSBLA's fundraising corps and honorary delegates began mobilizing throughout the country. Because their radio show also acted as a space for hosting Arab Latin American and Middle Eastern musical performances, this may have helped Arab Argentine listeners associate the project with a cultural mission from the outset. They hosted performances by artists such as those examined in Chapter 3—for example, comedian Gibran Trabulsi, opera singer Selim Zeitun, the Oriente Film crew, and the band Los Orientales. Audiences from multiple provinces tuned in to PSLBA's radio show and became part of this ethnic space.

Meanwhile, honorary delegates across the provinces and throughout neighboring South American nations used their local knowledge to guide paid fundraising officials sent out from the federal capital. Individuals such as wool salesman Mariano Abdenur guided Buenos Aires–based fundraising employee Jorge Dial through the Argentine-Bolivian border region immediately surrounding the town of La Quiaca, where they secured twenty-six donations to the hospital that totaled 350 pesos.[19] In the Río Negro Territory, grocer José Sede and his brothers guided Dial to the small Patagonian village of Maquinchao, where they helped facilitate his contact with twenty-one donors for a total of 877 pesos. The Maquinchao donation was actually a substantial contribution in comparison to much larger provincial capitals such as Mendoza (2,138 pesos), San Luis (594 pesos), and San Juan (1,942 pesos), which boasted wealthy circles of elites and active voluntary associations whose sizable contributions bolstered their city's donation quotas.[20] With a population of 12,382 people in the entire department of 25 de Mayo surrounding Maquinchao, it was a backwater in comparison to cities like Mendoza, whose core capital area alone boasted 97,476 people that year.[21] Much like Indio Rico and the other Buenos Aires provincial towns noted earlier, Maquinchao is emblematic of dozens of small towns across Argentina whose contributions to the hospital far exceeded what might be expected because of their small size. Arab Argentine residents of tiny towns like La Quiaca and Maquinchao were generally not wealthy; they ran small grocery or dry goods stores or fruit stands. They were mechanics, hairdressers, leatherworkers, butchers, bakers, and small-scale farmers.[22] In fact, the fundraising records from PSLBA provide a rare window into the ways that Arab Argentines with modest incomes chose to spend their money every month. Their participation in the hospital project also gives clues as to the value that they placed on participating in projects for institutions that they would likely never visit themselves yet clearly held symbolic meaning for them as part of the wider mahjar.

The women of PSLBA recognized donations from these compatriots in small, rural communities as the backbone of their fiscal success. Time and again, they framed their project as one whose true engine was the solidarity of Arab Argentines in the provinces—whether they were donors, honorary delegates, or humble families donating a single peso per month. Even those who donated a peso per month were given the recognition of having their names read aloud on the radio or printed in the newsletter. "What started out as a project endorsed by a small group of people is now fed by the zeal of thousands of co-nationals from all corners of the country. . . . Everyone contributed their grain of sand," wrote PSLBA president Wacila de Adre and general secretary Estela Chacar de Chacar in an enthusiastic letter that they penned jointly after making their first mortgage payment. "They are columns of gold that majestically sustain our vision, true pillars of our institution" they gushed to the readers of La Voz del Hospital in 1935.[23] When it came time to finally break ground on the new hospital building in 1937, they made sure that representatives from their legion of honorary delegates were present at the inaugural ceremony. On the day of the groundbreaking, the women of PSLBA nervously prepared for the event beneath a seemingly ceaseless downpour of torrential rain. But by the afternoon, the sky cleared, and a crowd amassed; some reports even put the number of attendees at close to ten thousand. Delegates from the provinces were present to bear witness to the festivities, with onlookers so eager to get a better view that some even climbed nearby trees (see Figure 7).[24]

That the PSLBA invested in cultivating lasting ties between this Buenos Aires institution and its rural donors is also evident in the services they offered to members who purchased varas or donated a monthly quota. In exchange for monetary support, the PSLBA determined that the Hospital Sirio Libanés would offer special medical services to donors located in remote provinces and unlikely to travel to Buenos Aires due to the long journey or limited financial means, or both. These included rosters of laboratory analyses of blood, urine, spit, and fecal matter. Advertisements in La Voz del Hospital encouraged readers to mail in their first sample for free analysis, as a perk of being a member owner of the institution. Over the years, they expanded

Figure 7. Hospital Sirio Libanés groundbreaking ceremony, 1937. Source: Asociación de Beneficencia del Hospital Sirio Libanés, Buenos Aires, Argentina. Reprinted with permission.

the range of tests offered as medical technology advanced, but the prices remained consistent at between 2 and 5 pesos per test throughout the 1940s. In other words, they kept prices accessible to humble donors such as grocers, butchers, or fruit sellers in distant regions like Patagonia or the Chaco.[25]

The extension of their laboratory services to mahjar communities in the provinces was much more than a gimmick to encourage further donations. The provision of these services must be situated in the context of the Hospital Sirio Libanés as a nationwide project within the Arab Argentine community. In this context, it follows logically that the board of directors would create a roster of medical services available to members in geographically remote locations. Long-distance analyses of blood and other bodily fluids brought the hospital's medical care to Indio Rico, La Quiaca, Maquinchao, and beyond. Members who elected to participate in these fluid analyses and biopsy services in turn mailed small pieces of their physical constitution—knowing that even if they never made the journey to Buenos Aires, their cells still occupied petri dishes and test tubes in the hospital's laboratory. In a sense, albeit on the smallest possible scale—despite the hundreds or thousands of kilometers separating their hometown from Buenos Aires—their bodies were handled with care by medical professionals from their ethnic community (see Figure 8). At

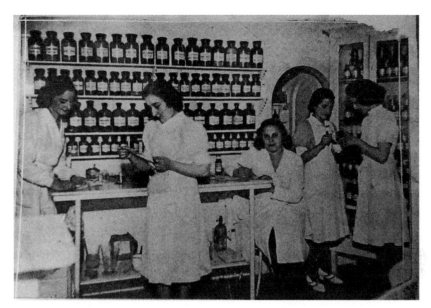

Figure 8. Hospital Sirio Libanés pharmacy staff, ca. 1940. Source: Asociación de Beneficencia del Hospital Sirio Libanés, Buenos Aires, Argentina. Reprinted with permission.

a time when the Arab Argentine press often printed heated debates about the need for unity of purpose across the diverse communities and institutions that constituted the mahjar map, the women of PSLBA constructed a robust economic network of donors throughout the Southern Cone region. At a more metaphorical level, their mail-order medical services literally pumped the circulation of Arab Argentine blood throughout the nation.

Women's Organizations and the Creation of Cultural Space

Arab Argentine women's work in the realm of philanthropic organizations often played the multifaceted role of promoting and preserving cultural production within their ethnic community. In the first half of the twentieth century, many of these women's groups used the power and status that they accrued through these campaigns in order to promote and preserve Arabic art, literature, music, and language within the diaspora. Whereas numerous editorials by male journalists ranted about the importance of preserving Arabic cultural forms and language, women's beneficence organizations from Tucumán to Mendoza to Misiones did the fundraising work to open schools and act as patrons of the arts.

Similar to women's groups in other immigrant colonies, Arab Argentine women became involved in efforts to preserve their community's heritage language—in this case, Arabic.[26] In the early twentieth century, the Argentine landscape was dotted with immigrant institutions dedicated to preserving ties to the homeland through language instruction—German, Italian, and Yiddish, for example. By the late 1920s, Argentina's mahjar press regularly reported on the activities of numerous beneficence organizations run by women throughout the country who had the common goal of constructing a school where the children of the colectividad could learn Arabic. Women founded beneficence organizations in order to raise funds and gain the moral support of their communities in their efforts to open schools in Buenos Aires (established 1916), San Juan (established 1919), Santiago del Estero (established 1926), Tucumán (established 1926 and 1929), Entre Ríos (established circa 1929), Salta (established 1930), and Corrientes (established 1931) Provinces. While editorials in mahjar press organs often commented on (and at times ranted about) the importance of maintaining the Arabic language in their ethnic community, beneficence groups tackled the issue in a pragmatic way.

In one instance, the women of Sociedad Zaharat-el-Ihsan of Corrientes Province sought to open an Arabic-language school in the city of Paraná "for the descendants of Arabs in Argentina." Their mission statement articulated the cultural goals that the organization embodied. In 1929, they reported that they wished to create "a totally laic environment that would conform to the official educational standards and guidelines of the Argentine Republic but also including Arabic language and history in order to forge in the spirit of these children love for their race and respect for the homeland [patria] of their progenitors."[27] Thus, in a very direct way, these women positioned themselves as custodians of Arabic language and history. In other cases, women's organizations worked to preserve and promote Arab artistic and cultural production. Similar to the PSLBA's Voice of the Hospital radio program that provided airtime for traveling Middle Eastern and Arab Latin American musicians, many women's organizations acted as hosts for traveling artists and musicians. In the 1920s and 1930s, the mahjar press reported on several events sponsored by women's groups in the provinces and neighboring Southern Cone nations to showcase the work of traveling artists, musicians, and intellectuals. When cinematographer José Dial of Oriente Film traveled to Santiago, Chile, in 1932, it was the Ladies Auxiliary of the Syrian Palestinian Club (Club Sirio Palestino) that hosted the filmmaker and his crew of young artists as their guests of honor. Dial gratefully thanked the Club de Damas for their hospitality, acknowledging they went out of their way to be gracious hosts despite what he referred to as the "latent economic crisis" that Chile was experiencing during that time. "The Ladies Auxiliary is a patrician social institution, similar in importance to the Jockey Club of Buenos Aires, with the only difference being that it is a club only for women, distinguished by its excellence," reported Dial on his return to Argentina.[28]

In Buenos Aires, the Women's Syrian Orthodox Association (*Asociación Femenina Sirio Ortodoxa*, AFSO) chose to sponsor and promote the work of prominent Lebanese playwright Najib al-Haddad, a member of the Nahda cultural movement of the late nineteenth- and early twentieth-century mashriq. The production chosen by the AFSO, titled *Hamdan*, exemplified al-Haddad's method of breaking the mold of traditional Arabic literary forms and sat squarely in a Nahda cultural renaissance canon characterized by an innovation of lyrical and poetic reform. In this case, we see an Arab Argentine women's organization acting as cultural interlocutor between an artistic-cultural movement of the mashriq and the Latin American mahjar.

In anticipation of the debut of the play, women from the AFSO sold tickets in Middle Eastern–owned storefronts throughout the city, advertising the charity projects that they were engaged in alongside logistical information about ticket sales.[29] On the night of *Hamdan*'s debut, the AFSO hired the Lebanese journalist Rafael Lahoud to provide the opening act for the play. In his introductory act, Lahoud sang passionately "in favor of independence of the Arab States, exhorting all Arabs to unite in order to achieve this ideal," reported the press afterward.[30] In choosing this play and this opening message, the AFSO was clearly participating in both the cultural ripples of the Nahda in the diaspora and rising twentieth-century discourses of anti-imperialism and self-determination that took shape during the 1920s to 1940s period of European mandate control in the Levant. It would appear that the women who organized this event conscientiously placed themselves well within the realm of charity and the arts—arenas of public action that were palatable to elite and middle-class gender norms. From within that arena, however, they made calculated political statements and unambiguously associated themselves with Middle Eastern intellectual currents. If the PSLBA used the notoriety of their fundraising events and their radio transmissions to create space for Arab cultural production, the women of the AFSO went a step further and used their sponsorship of al-Haddad's play as a platform to engage with timely political debates surrounding nationalism and political sovereignty.

While Arab Argentine women did not often contribute overtly political diatribes to the ethnic press (as did their male counterparts), they found alternative ways to position themselves politically through what Donna Guy refers to as the "performance of charity."[31] This performance allowed groups such as the AFSO and PSLBA to accrue social capital; after all, these organizations "worked for free but demanded respect" as Guy notes in her study of the Argentine welfare state.[32] Arab Argentine women took advantage of the respectability that they gained from these campaigns and good works and relied on it in order to exert pressure on their co-nationals to collaborate financially or participate in the fray of intellectual and political debates in their community. In the wider context of female philanthropy, Arab Argentine women deployed strategies to accrue patronage and social status that were strikingly similar to those of not only Euro Argentine women, but also philanthropists in Europe, the Middle East, and North Africa.[33] Archival material from organizations such as the PSLBA and AFSO provides evidence of Arab Argentine women as powerful, often politicized philanthropists in their communities. Beyond local projects, some of these philanthropic organizations leveraged the respect and financial networks that they built within the national context of beneficence work in order to simultaneously operate on a transnational scale. This perspective brings new dimensions to current historiography of the trans-American landscape of the mahjar and its connections to a globalized landscape of philanthropy and political activism.

Beyond the Provinces: Transnational Beneficence

Groups such as PSLBA and AFSO were experts at activating the interprovincial network of associational nodes and individual donors in order to fund institutional projects or generate funds to ameliorate the plight of needy Argentines, Arab and non-Arab alike. Having given examples of their contributions to bolstering an interprovincial network of Arab Argentines, as well as their efforts to create and preserve cultural production in the mahjar, this section looks at their ability to operate philanthropic projects on a transnational scale. In this light, we are able to view women's work as another dimension of the mahjar's transnational public sphere.

In many cases, the women of Arab Argentine beneficence organizations did not confine the scope of their projects within national, or even continental, borders. Sometimes they remitted money in a one-time donation, such as the AFSO's 1922 donation of 50,000 pesos to Russians suffering the Povolzhye famine, or their 1923 donation of 4,000 pesos to victims of the Japanese Great Kantō Earthquake and Tsunami.[34] But in many cases, the aid and correspondence was ongoing. An examination of the range of projects that groups such as the PSLBA and AFSO undertook makes it obvious that these groups' members were also deeply concerned with long-term political and social panoramas in the Middle East. While the premise for their donations was almost always the provision of aid in the aftermath of natural disasters, groups such as the AFSO used the arena of charity as an avenue for making contact with key political actors in the Middle East. A notable instance of this sort of politicized performance of charity came after a string of seismic activity rattled the southern Syrian region including Mandatory Palestinian and Transjordan in July 1927. In the months following the deadly quake, women from the AFSO collected donations for the victims of the disaster and sent a check for 1,000 pesos to the Ottoman Bank of Cairo. In an open letter sent to numerous Arab Argentine press organs, the president and secretary of the AFSO, respectively, Nagibe Abud and Zahia Farah, announced that they had sent the money directly to Prince Michel Lotfallah, along with instructions on exactly how the aid money should be disbursed.

The fact that they elected to advertise their choice of Lotfallah as the courier of their check from Cairo to its final destination in Mandatory Palestine is significant. In the AFSO's open letter describing their donation to the "destitute victims" (*damnificados*) in the southern region of the Levant, they reported that Lotfallah was the president of the "Pro-Palestine Victims Aid Commission."[35] By announcing to the public that they were corresponding with (and sending money to) the director of another beneficence organization, they stayed well within a gender-normative realm of acceptable conduct.[36] They framed their communication with Lotfallah as simply correspondence between one philanthropic organization and another. What they left out of their communiqué (but was well known to any Arab Argentine marginally interested in the mashriq's current events) was Lotfallah's role as a key agitator on the post–World War I geopolitical stage.

Deeply concerned with the nebulousness of their trajectory toward national sovereignty as laid out in the Covenant of the League of Nations, numerous Syrians organized oppositional political parties while in exile in North Africa and Europe. Lotfallah was one such organizer, and acted as president of the Syrian Unity Party, which operated out of Cairo. Even before the League of Nations drafted the final version of their covenant, Lotfallah had vigorously lobbied for Syrian independence. In a January 1919 letter to French statesman and chair of the Paris Peace Conference, Georges Clémenceau, he wrote, "The Syrian Unity Party, which represents the absolute majority of Syrians residing in Egypt and abroad, without the distinction of religion or sect, solicits from the Peace Conference the recognition of complete and effective independence for Syria." Lotfallah then proceeded to outline a four-prong plan for the immediate concession of sovereignty.[37] Two years later, Lotfallah acted as the president of the Syro-Palestinian Congress that took place in Geneva. That meeting represented one of the earliest internationally recognized attempts at challenging the French and British Mandate systems in the Middle East. During the Congress, participants demanded independence and national rule for Syria, Lebanon, and Palestine, insisting on the concession of effective sovereignty in terms that echoed Lotfallah's 1919 cable to Clémenceau.

In both Lotfallah's letter, and the grievances presented by members of the Syro-Palestinian Congress to the League of Nations, their prominent references to the multitude of Arabs living outside Syria in the diaspora were a common thread. In the first line of Lotfallah's words to Clémenceau, he was quick to assert that he spoke not only for Syrians living in exile in Egypt but also for Syrians living "abroad." When the *New York Times* published an update on the grievances that Lotfallah and his compatriots voiced to the League of Nations in 1921, the reporter made special mention of George Youssef Salem, another member of the Congress. Salem claimed to "represent 250,000 Syrians in the United States, who, he [said], all want Syria to be entirely independent." In a cable to president Warren G. Harding that same year, members of the Congress explained that "Syria and Palestine should form one country because they are mostly inhabited by the same Arab race [and that] many Syrians and Palestinians in the United States . . . would be ready to return to their countries provided the latter were entirely free." They went on to decry the mandate system as a mere "pretext for the colonizing designs of France and England."[38]

While the prospect of hundreds of thousands of Syrians abandoning their homes and business ventures en masse and returning to the Middle East from the United States was an exaggeration, the acknowledgment of the diaspora as a potential constituency in a future independent nation nevertheless is important. Much like Lotfallah's nod to Syrians "in Egypt and abroad," it is evidence of the transnational public sphere that stretched intercontinentally between far-flung mahjar communities in North Africa, Europe, the Americas, and beyond. As this example illustrates and Fahrenthold astutely observes in her study of mahjar political networks in the World War I era, "with the Ottoman government's hostility to Syrian journalism during the war, emigrants living [abroad] gained increasing control over the Syrian press, gaining power to define what it meant to be 'Syrian' or 'Lebanese' in a post-Ottoman context."[39] In the postwar era, these voices continued to engage in what Fahrenthold refers to as "discursive warfare for the right to define and represent the community abroad."[40] Albeit subtly, and with a great deal of social tact, we see women from organizations such as the AFSO engage with these debates.

When the women of the AFSO wrote to Michel Lotfallah, they demanded that certain stipulations be observed in the distribution of their charitable donation. "These funds are meant to aid the destitute individuals in Palestine, regardless of their race or religion," they wrote.[41] At a time when Arab and Syrian Nationalist discourses were being fueled by resistance to Jewish resettlement in Palestine, the AFSO insisted in no uncertain terms that their money was meant to be distributed equally to "the destitute" (*damnificados*), regardless of race or creed. Alternatively, we can also interpret the AFSO's correspondence with Lotfallah in a different, more politicized, light. After stating the stipulations for disbursement of their aid, the language of the AFSO's letter became much murkier. They alluded to the fact that the Pro-Palestine Victims Aid Commission may have already been disbanded and essentially gave Lotfallah carte blanche to use the funds as he deemed appropriate. Thus, without saying as much, they nevertheless tacitly acknowledged that they had remitted money that very well might be acting as a donation for Lotfallah's political, rather than beneficence, projects. Having remitted the money to him a full eight months after the earthquake took place, they must have had a very good idea that this money was by no means the type of first-responder aid that they had remitted in the past to tsunami and famine victims. Interpreted in this light, the AFSO's letter to Lotfallah looks much more like an encoded donation to a nationalist project rather than apolitical correspondence between the figureheads of two charitable agencies.

While there was certainly a bureaucratic process that delayed international remittances, this alone does not sufficiently account for the lag time in the AFSO's letter to Lotfallah. Once the women made the decision to mobilize, they clearly had the power to do so expeditiously. When a fire broke out in the Nasr

Theater in Damascus on June 20, 1928, and destroyed a nearby hotel and one hundred houses, the AFSO promptly addressed the situation. They made the formal call for donations at an assembly on July 30, and by August 19 they were already remitting their first wave of donations to Damascus.[42] In this case, it is also fruitful to read the AFSO's actions against the grain of Middle Eastern sociopolitical context that acted as a backdrop for the Nasr Theater fire. The Nasr was one of the first cinemas in the mashriq to offer sex-segregated matinee showings in order to attract audiences of Muslim women. The June 20 fire mysteriously broke out in the projection booth within an hour of one its first women's matinees. Twelve people died, presumably among them women who had arrived early for the matinee, but authorities were quick to dismiss the blaze as accidental. "Accidental or not, the fire was a portent. Coinciding with the controversy of women's public presence ignited by [a recently published] book on unveiling, it ushered in an era of increasingly violent conflict about female moviegoers," notes Elizabeth Thompson in her study of gender and citizenship during the Mandate period.[43] Thompson contends that the cinema was "drawn into the turf wars among male groups, becoming a gendered and spatial boundary line of their ideological differences."[44] In protest, Christian and Muslim women alike from Beirut to Hama proceeded to brave "many a battle in pursuit of their favorite movie stars, against the message that they were making a dangerous transgression into the new public and that they required a new, political kind of paternalistic protection."[45] Once again, under the pretext of charity, the women of the AFSO mobilized and intentionally involved themselves in the politicized, and sometimes violent, fray of social unrest that characterized the post-Ottoman era in the Middle East. To accord outright a deeper significance of feminist solidarity to this episode is too far of a stretch in light of the limited documentation that the archive provides us. Nevertheless, together with other evidence such as the Lotfallah exchange, it is possible to puzzle out certain continuities in the Arab Argentine women's propensity to mix politics with their performance of good works.

We can also couple these instances with archival evidence from local Argentine projects that point to the politicized perceptions that at least some women had of their beneficence and community work. The following reflection from Victoria Jaulé, president of the Sociedad Femenina Sirio Libanesa de Río Cuarto, Córdoba Province, makes it clear that women's groups beyond the most powerful Buenos Aires institutions such as the AFSO and PSLBA also perceived their work as having a politicized cultural mission. Jaulé wrote,

Just like in other regions of this country, the formation of . . . aid societies are the first decisive steps in the direction of a better sociability, and an undeniable indicator of a cultural rebirth which will come to erase the remnants of selfish commerce. . . . [Until recently] Arabs living on Argentine soil lived completely distracted from ideological and social mobilization.[46]

Not only did Jaulé relate the work of her beneficence organization to the notion of "cultural rebirth," but she also saw it as an avenue for influencing a shift in the core values of her ethnic community away from what she characterized as an obsession with economic insertion. It is also clear that Jaulé and her compatriots in the Río Cuarto organization believed that women would play a crucial role in this cultural shift. Founded in 1931, the Sociedad's mission was, in Jaulé's words, "to unite the feminine enthusiasm in the collectivity." To that end, they proposed the construction of a social and recreational center exclusively for Arab Argentine women.[47] Before she penned these words, Jaulé contributed regularly to prominent mahjar periodicals. In contrast, her other contributions came in the form of romantic poetry or prose that tended to be confined to portions of periodicals designated as "Literary Gems," or "For Ladies." Thus, for at least one young Arab Argentine woman in the provinces, the realm of beneficence provided her with a platform to speak boldly about her ethnic community's values, future, and women's importance in shaping the contours of a unique, diasporic, Arab identity.

Across the spectrum of projects undertaken by women's beneficence organizations—from building hospitals, to responding to natural disasters, to fostering the arts—women in the mahjar positioned themselves as guardians and protectors of their community. The scope of their endeavors suggests that they defined their community by the yardstick of common ties to a homeland in the mashriq, not by fixed geographic boundaries. Based in Buenos Aires, associations such as the PSLBA and the AFSO looked outward toward the most remote peripheries of the mahjar's diasporic geography for moral and material support. This strategy is what propelled forward the projects that they executed in both Argentina and abroad. The official statutes of the AFSO declared the organization's commitment to establishing schools and headquarters in the provinces and territories, and in moments of crisis they clearly mobilized this web of contacts that they built.[48] In the grandiloquent language of the PSLBA, the provinces served as their "true pillars," their "columns of gold."[49] This knowledge does not change the fact that Buenos Aires was undisputedly one of the principal economic, demographic, and intellectual hubs of the mahjar, hemispherically speaking. However, this examination of the activities of Buenos Aires–based beneficence makes it clear that it was this hub's dynamic relationship to diasporic nodes across the provinces and territories that often enabled large-scale community-building and institutional projects and relief work. Honing our focus on women's beneficence work as a window into links between central and peripheral diasporic geographies also offers us an alternative model to the traditional centering of business and political relationships between men.

This new focus encourages us to see women's performance of philanthropy as a set of values and course of concrete actions that bind together distant diasporic nodes in tangible ways. Women like Wacila de Adre, Estela de Chacar, Nagibe Abud, and many other participants whose names have faded from archival holdings also used their beneficence activities to leverage claims as participants in the construction of community identity—as (Arab) Argentines and global citizens. Occasionally, we get glimpses into how, on a personal level, women's participation in philanthropy could lead to opportunities for asserting their stake in the diaspora's relationship to broader ideals of social and national progress. We saw this in the words of Victoria Jaulé of Río Cuarto, who saw the forging of a women's organization in her town as a path toward heightened social consciousness. We see the echoes of this language come through in other moments as well, buried in otherwise prosaic descriptions of meeting minutes, funerals, or accounts of fundraisers. One small archival window into these moments comes alongside the death notice of the young Rosa Nélida Asef, who died unexpectedly in 1932. Before her untimely death, Asef led the Sociedad Hijas de Líbano (Daughters of Lebanon Society) in her hometown of Tres Arroyos, Buenos Aires Province. During her leadership of the Sociedad, Asef spearheaded numerous community events, presided over the organization's elections, and managed the finances of both monetary and land donations made to the Sociedad between 1928 and 1932. In the wake of a difficult winter in 1929, she organized a clothing and food drive after observing the unusually high number of needy men and women of all ages who suffered hunger and unemployment. "We are the daughters of Eve," she announced to the attendees of one fundraising event, emphasizing their identity as a women's organization in her opening remarks. Later that year, after a violent earthquake shook Argentina's Cuyo region, Asef gathered multiple rounds of aid donations to remit to victims in the town of Villa Atuel, Mendoza. The Sociedad received a personalized letter of thanks from Carlos Borzani, the Buenos Aires–based federal official charged with managing the turmoil following the earthquake.[50] Upon Asef's unexpected passing, fellow board members organized a public homage to her, orchestrating a large graveside gathering. After hanging a bronze plaque on her sepulcher, the Sociedad's new president, Raquel Abud, addressed the gathered crowd. She made a long speech in memoriam of her friend and colleague. Abud conjured up memories of her friend as a strong leader, guardian, and visionary. She lauded her as an effective protector (*eficaz protectora*) of their organization. At length, she spoke of Asef's "noble character" that drove her to push for "brave efforts toward the growth and progress of the organization."

Following Abud's remarks were those of another member of the Sociedad, Yamile Behal. The audience met the speeches with hearty approval. Though fleeting, this moment showcases the ways in which women gained opportunities to be center-stage through their beneficence work. In this case, the memorial ceremony for Asef was widely attended by community members in Tres Arroyos, and a write-up of the event made it into the pages of at least one Buenos Aires-based periodical.[51] It also represented a chance for women like Abud and Behal to speak about the leadership of their friend and colleague. Asef was indeed someone who worked tirelessly to make her mark on many communities in their time of need: her diasporic community, her local community, and a broader Argentine community that stretched from Tres Arroyos to Villa Atuel.

While this chapter has focused primarily on the case studies of organizations in the federal capital, it simultaneously invites us to think about the ways in which the activities of groups like PSLBA and AFSO were part of a broad network of women's beneficence organizations that blanketed the Americas. It also reminds us of the need for nuanced, gendered perspectives of community building and institutional organizing in diasporic populations. Through regional and transnational philanthropy, women in the mahjar asserted ownership of their community's "enterprising spirit." Their projects also allowed them to claim space in Argentina's increasingly diverse ethnic landscape that was dotted ever more densely with the architectural and institutional manifestations of mass migration. When the PSLBA broke ground on new construction at the Hospital Sirio Libanés site in 1937, even the president of Argentina, General Agustín Pedro Justo, was present—a detail that confirms the visibility and prestige that these women's organizations achieved with their philanthropy. In this case, beyond forging a new institution within their diaspora community, this moment represented these women's assertion of a place in the Argentine nation as well as they presided over a ceremony that was attended by national and community leaders alike.

Similarly, when women of the AFSO engaged with political actors in the Middle East or selected particular works of Nahda theater to showcase, they claimed a space in the political and cultural milieu that bound together mashriq and mahjar at that particular moment. Taken in this light, perhaps we can even see these actions as part of a larger struggle for emancipation among Arab Argentine women that dates back to the earliest generations of the diaspora.[52] At the very least, these stories reveal women's work as a lens for delineating important connections between diasporic populations in the provinces and the federal capital. In some cases, the records of their philanthropic activities also provide rare insight into the lives and choices of other groups, such as rural and nonelite Arab Argentines, who are all too often relegated to the peripheries of mahjar historiography. In this sense, the history of women's philanthropy in the mahjar is yet one more component in the intricate archival composite that we must weave in order to more holistically understand the diversity of experiences that played out in the diaspora.

5 South-South Visions in the Cold War

By the middle of the twentieth century, questions of alignment, sovereignty, and new forms of South-South—or Third World—solidarities drew Argentina into the Global Middle East in new dimensions amid the reality of the Cold War. The gaze of many Argentines—those with and without roots in the Arabic-speaking eastern Mediterranean—fixed on Arab world geographies beyond those traditionally linked to Argentina by way of the nation's history of mass migration. We can begin to explore these new entanglements by starting with the events of a particularly momentous year for Argentine and Middle Eastern politics.

In July 1952, international media rushed to record the revolutionary and tragic events that unfolded in Egypt and Argentina over the course of a few days. On July 23, young Egyptian army officers ousted King Farouk and set Egypt on the path to revolution. Three days later, and across the Atlantic, populist leader Juan Domingo Perón lost his wife and main political ally, Eva, to cancer. He was at that point approaching the end of his first six-year presidential term. By the end of July, both Argentines and Egyptians found themselves amid national transition—a new phase of the Peronist national project and a new revolutionary state. For many in the Argentine mahjar, the events of 1952 led to opportunities for advocating a closer relationship between Argentina and the Arab world. For non-Arab Argentines (government officials and private citizens alike), this early Cold War moment held the possibility of building new Global South political and economic relationships.

This chapter analyzes the developing relationship between Argentina and Egypt in the years surrounding the 1952 Egyptian Revolution.[1] By interweaving diplomatic, mahjar, and anti-imperial activism histories, this chapter provides evidence of the intellectual links and institutional networks that join Egyptian history to Argentina. During this time, the spheres of Arab and Latin American state actors, mahjar communities, and broader anti-imperialist activisms of the early Cold War era overlapped and were mutually influential. Furthermore, the set of relationships, mirrored rhetoric, and organizational exchanges highlighted here represent an early moment of Global South exchange in the lead-up to the Non-Aligned Movement's (NAM) galvanization by the early 1960s. This approach differs from previous treatments of Argentine–Middle Eastern international relations in its chronological scope, geographic focus, range of archival material, and attention to the significant role of diaspora communities in mediating South–South dialogues between Argentines and Egyptians. Evidence gleaned from diplomatic archives, the diasporic press, and personal correspondence points to Argentina as a previously unacknowledged linguistic register, intellectual base, and source of aid for the Egyptian revolutionary project.

The 1952 Egyptian Revolution, followed by the rise of President Gamal Abdel Nasser, inspired many Argentines to articulate a connected history between Egypt and Argentina. Many also envisioned a connected future between these nations and peoples. By situating these unfolding events within the broader context of the early Cold War era and nascent NAM, we arrive at a new perspective on this global moment. The fact that many important Latin American leaders hoped fervently for South–South solidarities at this moment has never been in question. In this regard, one need look no further than Cuba's post-1959 attempts to export its revolutionary model and Che Guevara's optimistic courtship of Afro Asian leaders such as Nasser and Ghana's Kwame Nkrumah. Solidarities of the Global Left—both hoped-for and real—proliferated in the newly christened Third World, especially surrounding landmark moments of transregional anticolonial movements. These included the 1955 Bandung Conference (from which Latin America was conspicuously absent). While a rundown of Latin America's formal diplomatic history leaves the impression that, on balance, the region arrived rather late to the rising NAM, this overlooks the profusion of smaller-scale South–South exchanges.

It is true that Latin America did not begin to send delegations to the formal reunions of the central African Asian international committee that arose from Bandung—the Organization of Solidarity of the Peoples of Africa and Asia (OSPAA)—until OSPAA's 1966 Havana meeting.[2] In the Argentine delegation to the meeting, the presence of the Left was prominent.[3] This was undoubtedly a key moment in the mobilization of a Global Left within international organizational engines such as OSPAA(L). However, there also existed another set of complex tricontinental solidarities that predated this mobilization. In Argentina, these came in the form of cultural exchanges, activisms, and overlapping developmentalist ideologies. Diaspora communities, anti-imperialists, state actors, and Perón himself (during both his presidential terms of 1946 to 1952 and his subsequent exile) sought to mediate and foster these tricontinental solidarities. In return, Egyptians (both politicians and nonstate actors) recognized Argentina and Argentines as connected to the longer Egyptian struggle for sovereignty against imperial forces. Many envisioned a time line of continuous anti-imperial action ignited by the 1952 revolution that intensified shortly after with the 1956 Suez Canal crisis. Methodologically, this chapter's case study of the Egyptian Revolution provides a model for tying diasporic histories into Latin American diplomatic and cultural narratives.

Though often absent from scholarly literature on the Latin American mahjar, the burgeoning relationship between Argentines and Egyptians from the early 1950s on was part of the much longer historical relationship between the Americas and the Arabic-speaking eastern Mediterranean. As Chapter 3 explored in depth, the public sphere of the South American mahjar stretched not merely to the Levantine geographies to which the diaspora could trace its heritage. This was not merely a transnational back and forth but, rather, a circulation of a transregional nature. Circulating networks of journalists, artists, and other mobile actors moved among Egypt, the Levant, and Argentina from the early twentieth century. Histories of this transnational public sphere that bound the Middle East to the mahjar tend to emphasize the pre–World War II era, however, and as a consequence, there exists a relative silence when it comes to postwar dynamics of diaspora communities, host countries, and home regions. Approaching the 1950s from a diasporic, anti-imperialist perspective enables us to address this paucity in scholarship while simultaneously building on the constellation of migration and diaspora scholarship that has shaped our knowledge of the earlier twentieth century.

Piecing together a history of Argentine–Egyptian relations also builds on studies that examine the political and diplomatic ties between these world regions. This task contributes to a larger historical field of South–South cooperation and connections that unfolded against African, Asian, and Latin

American backdrops during the Cold War.[4] Analyzing the role of diasporic Arabs in the connected history of Argentina and Egypt bridges migration and diplomacy literature, bringing the diaspora into our understanding of the state and civil society after World War II.

By bridging these fields, we see how the tides of public opinion and political posturing appeared among Latin Americans of all stripes who saw an Arab reflection of their own situation. Formal diplomatic correspondence between Argentine, Syrian, Lebanese, and Egyptian bureaucrats during World War II and Perón's first term in office reveals a rich story when read in tandem with the Arab Argentine press, academic treatises, and international nongovernmental organization reports from the 1940s and 1950s. This was an era in which both Arab and Latin American nations experienced the rise of mass politics, populist leadership figures, and a keen awareness of the emerging postwar global order. During this time, the Argentine state made clear efforts to cultivate strong diplomatic relationships with many Middle Eastern nations beginning in 1945—with Egypt in particular.[5]

To delineate Argentine–Egyptian relations during this period, this chapter integrates analyses of the actions of politicians, intellectuals, and local Argentine agitators of Arab descent. I explore three dimensions of Argentine–Egyptian relationships: (1) Arab Argentine journalistic and translation projects that offered a rhetorical register to Egyptian revolutionaries, (2) diplomacy by state officials and self-appointed citizen-diplomats, and (3) anti-imperial solidarities. The sections that follow posit the connected history of Argentina and Egypt as a starting point for reconstructing Latin American–Middle East relations at the dawn of the Cold War.

Egypt 1952 in the Mahjar

Diasporic institutions and press organs from the Arab Argentine community responded to the 1952 Egyptian Revolution with extensive press coverage. The response of mahjar journalists to events in 1950s Egypt reveals diasporic viewpoints on the relationship between Argentina and Egypt. It also exposes state-level exchanges and transnational information networks that otherwise remain hidden. As discussed in Chapter 2, from the nineteenth-century immigration boom onward, Argentina boasted a vibrant array of diasporic press organs run by Italians, Spaniards, Germans, and Middle Eastern collectivities, among others. Newspapers and magazines routinely intermingled news stories on Argentine politics and current events with news from the homeland—in the case of the Middle Eastern newspapers, Syria and Lebanon. This Levantine focus mirrored the demographic composition of the Southern Cone mahjar, where there were almost no Egyptians to speak of save the few individuals occupying diplomatic posts at the Egyptian legation in Buenos Aires (established in 1947). Despite the lack of a direct heritage tie, however, events in 1952 pushed Egypt into the spotlight of Argentina's mahjar press.

The Arab Argentine community's outpouring of attention to the 1952 revolution and its aftermath did not stem from a strictly national heritage–based empathy. Rather, the shower of commendations that the young Egyptian men of the Free Officers Movement received from many mahjar press organs was the result of a twofold affinity that many individuals felt. Arab Argentines identified as both Argentines *and* Arabs as they extolled those who dismantled the monarchy, ushering Egypt into a new era. They were part of a broader movement among Argentine citizens and statesmen to recognize Latin America and Africa-Asia as world regions with a common history and destiny. Simultaneously, they represented a diasporic limb of the large-scale mobilizations in support of the Egyptian project that occurred across the African-Asian world.

Expressions of this deep identification with the Egyptian cause took numerous forms in the diasporic press. These included emphatic comparisons between Argentine and Egyptian leaderships, the juxtaposition of Egyptian and Argentine current events, and instances of symbolic adoption of Egyptian identity. This identification with events and people in Egypt spurred diasporic Arabs in Argentina to cultivate networks of communication between Argentina and Egypt. They engaged in translation projects and press campaigns that ultimately resulted in rendering Peronist doctrine accessible to an Arabic-speaking audience.

The few academic works that look comparatively at Argentine and Egyptian history in the mid-twentieth century focus on similarities or links between Presidents Perón and Nasser. Diasporic press coverage of the 1952 revolution reveals that Arab Argentines eagerly drew comparisons between Argentine and Egyptian leaders even before Nasser came to power. When news reached Argentina that Farouk had fallen and a Sudanese-Egyptian army general by the name of Mohammad Naguib was the front man for a series of sweeping reforms to be carried out in Egyptian society, Arab Argentine writers immediately drew connections. In Buenos Aires and in the provinces, journalists in the Arab Argentine press jubilantly compared Generals Naguib and Perón.

They also drew parallels between the political trajectories that they predicted for Argentina and Egypt.

One of the most enthusiastic tracts on the similarities between Perón and Naguib appeared in Tucumán's *El Eco de Oriente*, owned and edited by the highly mobile Nallib Baaclini. "Egypt Has Her Own Perón Now," proclaimed Baaclini's 1953 article.[6] The piece included an interview transcript of his conversation with Egyptian journalist Ahmed Mattar, who was residing in Argentina and serving as a functionary of the Egyptian legation. Not only does this example demonstrate the perceived similarities in leadership between Naguib and Perón, it furthermore provides evidence of documentation and communication circulating between Argentine and Egyptian political actors and diasporic mediators.

The constant theme in Baaclini's interview with Mattar was the resemblance between Naguib and Perón—in their action, philosophy, and even physical appearance. Mattar concluded that "Naguib . . . is the Perón of Egypt! You Argentines can understand Naguib perfectly, because you have had to fight doggedly, as we have, for your liberty, and you have achieved [this] thanks to your magnificent leader, who is similar to Naguib."[7] Repeatedly, Mattar insisted on the reciprocal nature of the affinity that he sensed between the two men. Both he and Baaclini carefully noted that it was not merely the case that Naguib resembled Perón. In equal measure, Perón was like Naguib— thus placing the two men on equal footing as world leaders connected in the struggle for sovereignty, *patria*, and *pueblo*. When asked what Naguib was doing for his patria, Mattar pointed to the parallel rhetoric of social justice that he observed in both leaders: "In his discourses, he has employed words and concepts that remind us of the great Argentine president."[8] In addition to highlighting parallel aspects of Naguib and Perón's bearing and rhetoric, the article also made clear that concrete exchanges of information and political strategy were taking place between the Egyptian and Argentine leaders.

Mattar reported that he had spoken with Naguib at length about the Peronist project and acted as a courier of "abundant documentation" from Buenos Aires to Cairo. Specifically, he mentioned that on his upcoming trip to Egypt, he would be "carrying in his suitcase [Perón's] *Segundo Plan Quinquenal*."[9] Perón's First and Second Five-Year Plans (*Plan Quinquenal*, 1946, 1952) were landmark documents in his administration that outlined political, economic, and social goals for the nation. This provincial Arab Argentine newspaper's interview with an Egyptian functionary is an important link in helping us grasp the mechanics of communication and exchange between Arab and Latin American states outside formal diplomatic realms. As Hishaam Aidi notes in his comparative study of Egyptian and Mexican corporatism, "After the 1952 Revolution, Egyptians—leaders and laymen—had looked toward Latin America for solutions and prescriptions for economic autonomy and freedom from the neocolonial yoke."[10] Until now, however, scholarship has yet to produce a clear picture of the exact workings of these exchanges and communications networks. The diasporic press provides information about the communication and exchanges between Arab Argentines and their Egyptian counterparts that gives concrete dimension to the more ephemeral claim that Egypt "looked toward" Latin America during this period. It also reveals diasporic actors (like Mattar or Baaclini) who were interlocutors in important exchanges of documents and information for Egyptians (like Naguib) engaged in the revolutionary project.

A few provinces away from Tucumán, the Córdoba-based newspaper *Mundo Árabe* used a different method of juxtaposing Egypt and Argentina for its readers. Its focus was not on Naguib and Perón themselves but, rather, on key aspects of their agrarian and economic programs. On consecutive pages, it presented lengthy articles about agrarian reform in the two nations—one penned by an Argentine journalist and one by Officer Gamal Abdel Nasser. Thus, readers could inform themselves about the Argentine Institute for the Promotion of Trade and the Plan Quinquenal in counterpoint with Naguib's agrarian reform and the Egyptian *fellah* (agricultural laborer).[11] The gains for Argentina's agrarian sector under Perón were "similar to [those for] Arab nations currently living in a fecund time of popular progress, redemptive revolution," concluded the editor of *Mundo Árabe*. With this, editors deftly converted a discussion of the possibilities for Argentine agrarian reform into evidence of significant similarities between Argentina and "Arab nations living in a time of revolution"—obviously, a reference to Egypt. This conspicuous coincidence of subject matter in consecutive articles on Egypt versus Argentina was not unique to *Mundo Árabe*; other examples include a pair of articles on paper factories and their labor unions in the two nations that appeared in Tucumán's *El Eco de Oriente*.[12]

In some newspapers, eager to show the Arab Argentine collectivity's closeness to the Egyptian cause, journalists adopted the symbolic label of *la colectividad siriolibanesa y egipcia* (Syrian-Lebanese and Egyptian collectivity) when speaking of their heritage community. The number of Egyptian civilians living in Argentina was not in fact significant, yet beginning in 1952, some Arab Argentine press organs, such as the *Diario Sirio Libanés* and *Assalam,* often made equal mention of the Syrian, Lebanese, and Egyptian heritages of their community. Taken together with examples of diasporic voices articulating similarities and connections between Argentina and Egypt, the adoption of a symbolic Syrian–Lebanese–Egyptian identity by some press organs suggests the desire to position diasporic Arabs as specially qualified interlocutors between Argentina and Egypt. This was an exciting moment for a heritage community attuned to opportunities to draw Argentine attention to the Arabic-speaking eastern Mediterranean. From the outset of the 1952 revolution, Arab Argentines strategically positioned themselves as mediators and facilitators of the South–South dialogues that they hoped would follow.

As Raanan Rein and Ariel Noyjovich demonstrate in their work on ethnicity and citizenship discourse under Perón, this position as interlocutors between Argentina and the homeland was one that Perón actively encouraged in diaspora communities such as the Jewish, Japanese, and Arab collectivities.[13] Thus, in part we can see the Arab Argentine desire to act as intermediaries between Argentina and a revolutionary Egypt as a response to a newly opened political space in Argentina, in which the national leadership actively courted the support of immigrant groups formerly excluded from national imaginaries of citizenship. Beyond this factor, to further understand why many Arab Argentines wanted to see Argentina and Egypt as legitimately connected and why they wished to mediate this new relationship, we must also historically contextualize the events of the 1950s in the Middle East. Beyond the favorable conditions that a Peronist Argentine political landscape created for some ethnic minorities, broader processes of imperialism and decolonization struggles had an impact on the Middle East and its diaspora.

Arab Argentine Relations

The circulation of both private citizens and state-sanctioned diplomacy between Argentina and Egypt after 1952 was not new. It built on and was facilitated by diasporic networks of Arabs in Latin America since the early twentieth century. Middle Eastern governments recognized the utility of these networks when it came to fundraising or drumming up political support in the transnational public sphere of the diaspora. As World War II ended, Latin American and Middle Eastern nations hoped to improve their positions in the new world order by strengthening regional alliances. In the Middle East, the formation of the Arab League embodied the desires of many who wanted to usher in a new era of sovereignty and self-determination after decades of European mandates and intervention. Leaders from Syria, Lebanon, and Egypt ramped up their diplomatic visits to Latin American nations, and official delegates of the Arab League, as well as of the Higher National Committee (HNC) of Mandate Palestine, made extensive international tours in the Americas. In 1947, press organs across Argentina reported on the HNC's activities as its members visited the offices of provincial press organs and Arab immigrant associations.[14] From 1946 onward, important HNC and Arab League delegates such as Mahmoud Fawzi (Arab League assistant general of military affairs) regularly traveled across the Southern Cone with an entourage of Arab Latin American intellectuals.[15]

The goal of these visits, and the subject matter of the discourses delivered by members of Arab League governments, was the marshaling of Latin American moral and monetary support for causes such as the liberation of Palestine from British control and, later, support for the Egyptian government after 1952. Thus, by the time of the Egyptian Revolution and Nasser's rise to power in the 1950s, many Arab Argentines were already tapped in to networks of pan-Arab economic, intellectual, and political solidarity. This created pathways for the facilitation of communication between important Egyptian and Argentine officials as dramatic sociopolitical shifts took place in Egypt.

In the 1940s and 1950s, Arab Latin Americans worked diligently to open pathways for diplomats and delegates who wished to spread their message and solicit monetary support for their projects. The organization with the widest transnational reach was without a doubt the Permanent Committee of the First Panarabic Congress in America. One of the stated goals of this group was to promote the "indestructible ties" that historically bound Latin Americans and Arabs and to endeavor to "make these links even closer." The organization boasted representatives in Argentina, Brazil, Uruguay, Paraguay, Bolivia, Colombia, Venezuela, Mexico, and the United States. Argentine members of the congress acted as translators and guides for Arab League envoys such as the 1947 official delegation of Arab states that toured Central and South America.[16] From the mid-1940s, the Congress's Permanent Committee maintained a media presence in Argentine newspapers through letter campaigns surrounding important events in the Middle East and North Africa.[17] The committee also petitioned the Argentine Ministry of Foreign Relations at pivotal moments regarding decisions to open diplomatic relations with Lebanon, Syria, and Saudi Arabia.[18] By 1952, political actors in the Arab League already had a tradition of incorporating outreach to diaspora communities in North and South America into their political campaign and rhetoric. After the revolution, leaders like Naguib and Nasser followed suit.

Just prior to the Egyptian Revolution, the first years of Perón's presidency came at a time of heightened activism and organizing within the Latin American mahjar. A year after he took office, the United Nations would vote on Resolution 181, the Plan for the Partition of Palestine. In the lead-up to the 1947 vote, the Arab League, alongside many individual Middle Eastern states, sent official delegations and representatives to liaise with Latin American nations in hopes of swaying them toward voting against partition. On these visits, Arab Argentines acted as tour guides and self-appointed retinues for visiting diplomatic missions.[19] Though largely unsuccessful in swaying Latin American votes firmly against partition, it is notable that of the ten nations that abstained from the partition vote, six were Latin American. In fact, the powerhouses of the Spanish-speaking Latin American bloc—Chile, Mexico, and Argentina—all abstained.[20] The Arab Argentine press avidly followed the actions of the UN Special Committee on Palestine. Arabs in the diaspora read abstention as an indication of pro-Arab leanings and repeatedly tied the Palestinian question to other liberation and anti-imperialist struggles going on elsewhere on the globe in the 1940s and 1950s—despite Argentina's establishment of diplomatic relations with Israel in 1949. In the wake of 1952, at least one Palestinian Argentine saw the revolution as a hopeful turning point in both the fate of Palestine and the future of Arab–Latin American solidarities. Issa Nahkleh, a Palestinian member of the Arab Higher Committee (the political organ of Arab Palestinians for part of the British Mandate period, 1936–1937), immigrated to Argentina following the 1947 Palestinian Nakba.[21] He founded the magazine *América y Oriente* with the express purpose of facilitating Arab–Latin American conversations about mutual anti-imperialist agendas post-1952. At the state level, Perón's government trod a careful line on the issue. Perón and the Foreign Ministry cultivated relationships with Arab League states while alternately granting audiences to representatives from the Jewish Agency (a nonprofit organization founded in 1929 to link Jewish communities around the world), as well as pro-Israel groups. The strategy appeared successful enough: Argentina's election to the UN Security Council only two months before the partition vote was largely attributed to wide Arab bloc support.

The following year, the 1948 Arab–Israeli war resulted in Egyptian defeat and represented the Arab League's strategic failure. In Egypt, this served as a blow to King Farouk's legitimacy, and Palestine became a key symbol in the rhetoric of Generals Naguib and Nasser in the wake of the revolution.[22] In part, we can view enthusiasm on the part of Arab Argentines to act as interlocutors in the wake of the 1952 revolution as a continuation of their activist tendencies since the beginning of Perón's administration. Meanwhile, ideologies of pan-Arab identity received mixed reviews among different groups within the Argentine mahjar, and the deployment of Arab nationalist or pan-Arab unity language varied between press organs of diverse political and geographic origins. Nevertheless, the ripples of different brands of Arab nationalism made their way throughout the diaspora's transnational public sphere and form an important part of the historical context for Arab Argentine interest in Egyptian affairs in the 1950s.

In the entanglement of Argentine and Egyptian history in the mid-twentieth century, key dates such as the 1948 partition or the 1952 revolution can serve as useful fulcrums. They allow us to construct a panorama of intersecting interests, pressures, and influences that drove civilians and politicians to act in certain ways. These temporal fulcrums can ultimately be more useful than side-by-side comparisons of particular actors—for example, Perón versus Naguib or Nasser. In this case, using 1952 as a fulcrum allows us to extend our analysis of Argentine–Egyptian relations beyond the confines of Perón's presidency (1946–1955), and beyond the realm of state-sanctioned diplomacy. Between Argentina and Egypt, we can see a clear network of communication and institutional exchange that arose following 1952. These bidirectional webs of exchange incorporate overlapping spheres of diplomatic, anti-imperialist, and diaspora histories. We find archival evidence of their existence in the Arab Argentine press, Foreign Ministry records ,and intellectual publications.

Tracing State and Civilian Communication

Throughout the 1950s, the Arab Argentine press publicized the role of their community in the translation of Peronist political writings into Arabic and their subsequent transmission to Egypt. While translation projects for key Peronist doctrine documents were already underway in 1952, the revolution gave these projects a sense of urgency and relevancy. The revolution opened new paths of circulation between Argentina and Egypt for Arabic translations. In Córdoba, Professor José Guraieb undertook a translation of Perón's landmark Justicialist doctrine into Arabic after being granted official permission to do so by the Ministerio de Asuntos Técnicos de la Nación (National Ministry of Technical Affairs). Guraieb drew motivation from what he described as the "social and cultural evolution" unfolding among the "Arab peoples." He felt an urgency and relevance in his work: "In the Near East, people are talking about Perón's Justicialismo. It has been the subject of conferences and official reports by Argentine ministries who have travelled to Arabic-speaking nations. . . . The logical next step is for us to present the entire work, organic and complete, to these friendly countries."[23]

By 1954, Guraieb completed the translation, and the diaspora press heralded the news alongside reports of Nasser's ascension to the presidency. Nowhere in this press coverage did there appear significant acknowledgment of the rockiness that the Naguib-to-Nasser transition involved (whereby Nasser placed Naguib under house arrest and assumed executive office in June 1956); rather, the focus remained on the potential role of Arab Argentines in mediating relationships with the evolving Egyptian government.[24]

In Buenos Aires, Lebanese Argentine writer Malatios Kouri produced an Arabic translation of *La Razón de mi Vida*, Eva Perón's autobiography. In May 1952, though Eva was gravely ill with cancer, the Peróns hosted a reception at the Casa Rosada, the presidential palace, for numerous Arab Argentine delegates, as well as diplomatic representations from Syria, Lebanon, and Egypt. Authorities from the board of directors of the Argentine Confederation of Lebanese Institutions presented General Perón with two copies of Kouri's translation of the autobiography. In separate, previous ceremonies, Syrian and Egyptian diplomats had gifted him copies of the same text after Perón received them in private audiences.[25] Arab Argentine press organs such as *Assalam* and *El Diario Sirio Libanés* reported on these events with great fanfare, dedicating front-page spreads in both Arabic and Spanish to the receptions in the Casa Rosada. The coverage revealed that members of the collectivity voluntarily financed the distribution of thousands of Arabic copies of the autobiography to co-nationals across Argentina. Diplomatic delegations from Syria and Lebanon took advantage of the translations produced in the diaspora and carried copies of the autobiography home to distribute in the Levant. Yet again, the characteristic circulation of people and print media connected Arab Argentines not only transnationally to goings-on in the Middle East but also to one another across rural and urban space.

Argentine officials also took interest in the events in Egypt leading up to, and in the aftermath of, the Free Officers coup. Evidence of this interest ranges from military surveillance reports to Perón's personal correspondence. From Perón's first presidential term, his government expended large amounts of bureaucratic energy in its economic and diplomatic relationship with Egypt. Argentina formally opened diplomatic relations with Egypt in 1947, and a flood of correspondence between Argentine dignitaries in Buenos Aires, London, and Cairo ensued. As the relationship between King Farouk, the military, Egypt's nationalist liberal Wafd Party, and British interlopers became increasingly strained, Argentine diplomats documented the rapidly shifting political panoramas.

Their reports were more extensive and detailed than those of any other Argentine diplomatic mission in an Arab country at the close of the 1940s. One 1949 report from envoy Francisco Bengolea to Minister of Foreign Relations Hipólito Jesús Paz even closed with a slew of reconnaissance-like photographs that Bengolea took to document a large military parade in Cairo that was presumably meant to demonstrate military might in the wake of Egypt's defeat a year earlier in the Arab-Israeli War. Bengolea went so far as to meticulously list the type and quantity of aircraft participating in the formation flying during the march: "2—Meteor Gloster [sic]/1—Vampire/12—Hurricane/10—Lockheed/6—Commander/6—Dakota/15—Spitfire/3—Stirling."[26] Regional politics in the Arabic-speaking eastern Mediterranean felt extremely tense—but also exciting—to Argentine diplomats who arrived there as the 1940s drew to a close. "I had the Middle East in my hands," reflected Guillermo Aníbal Speroni, who arrived in Cairo as Argentina's newly appointed ambassador to Egypt, Saudi Arabia, and Ethiopia in 1949. Speroni arrived as Israel, Egypt, Syria, Lebanon, and Jordan signed armistice agreements to formally end official hostilities of the Arab-Israeli War. In the ambassador's words, it was the most exciting posting of his entire diplomatic career; the Middle East was, at that moment, "a continent on the move." Furthermore, Speroni clearly saw Peronist political doctrine as viable and influential in the Egyptian context in the years leading up to the formation of the NAM. In his eyes, Perón's Third Position philosophy of nonalignment in a Cold War world was "the true precursor of the NAM . . . even if the [NAM leaders] didn't want to admit it."[27]

As president and into his exile, Perón made overtures to the Egyptian government and people, often drawing from the diaspora community for interlocutors or couriers. He held exclusive interviews for Egyptian journalists traveling to Buenos Aires and sent cultural ambassadors to Egypt in the years following 1952. In 1953, Egyptian journalist Farog Gobran traveled to Buenos

Aires, where Perón granted him a lengthy interview. Gobran reported afterward, "I have been received in the [Casa Rosada] by the . . . most powerful man in South America. Perón has asked me to send this message of good will to the Egyptian people [and] spoke to me about the surprising similarity between the Argentine and Egyptian peoples." The mahjar press eagerly picked up the news story of Perón's audience with Gobran and obtained transcripts of their meeting. At the end of the interview, Perón referred to Argentina and Egypt as "sister nations."[28] Between his reception of both Arab Argentine and Egyptian representatives (civilian and state sponsored), Perón sent the message that he stood in solidarity with Arab and Egyptian causes, even if his foreign policy tended toward a more neutral official stance.

In addition, Perón sent cultural ambassadors to Egypt, including the prominent journalist Luis María Albamonte. In 1953 Albamonte traveled throughout the Middle East and North Africa at Perón's behest, arriving in Cairo in time to celebrate the first anniversary of the Egyptian Revolution. He was received by Egyptian officials, including General Naguib and his wife. Naguib spoke of his admiration for Perón's patriotism and requested a copy of the Segundo Plan Quinquenal, as well as of various other documents articulating Peronist doctrine. In response, the Egyptian legation in Buenos Aires promptly organized the acquisition of this documentation and forwarded it to Cairo.[29] By tracing the paths of nonstate actors like Gobran and Albamonte, who formally or informally played the role of citizen-diplomat between these two nations in the 1950s, we can more clearly perceive the origins of official diplomatic exchanges that took place during this period. These journalists had the ability to act as cultural ambassadors between foreign governments and everyday Argentine or Egyptian citizens when they returned from their travels and relayed their perceptions of life abroad.

Albamonte, for example, undertook a speaking tour of Argentina following his 1953 journey to the East. In December of that year, in Santiago del Estero, he gave a presentation about his recent travels and spoke at length about his time in Egypt. The provincial government sponsored the event, which packed a large theater.[30] Aside from serving as a civilian envoy to Cairo in 1953, Albamonte was the rector of the Buenos Aires School of Journalism and director of *El Laborista*, the newspaper that served the working-class, union-based Labor Party. In 1955 Albamonte would accompany Perón during his exile from Argentina. His voice carried the weight of a prominent intellectual, and his favorable review of his experiences in Egypt could reach a wide audience.

Attuned to the prospect of stronger Arab–Latin American ties, diaspora communities were often the first to report on political overtures by citizen-diplomats. Only a few weeks after the Egyptian Free Officers ousted Farouk, a message from Egyptian diplomat and secretary-general of the Arab League, Azzam Pasha, appeared in Tucumán's *La Gaceta* and *El Eco de Oriente*. He outlined similarities between the Latin American and Arab blocs in the context of their representation in the United Nations, stating, "The countries of Latin America have affinities and interests in common in terms of their collective defense, geographic proximity, linguistic unity and cultural ties" with the Arab bloc countries. He compared the two areas' history of regional solidarity by drawing a parallel between the Act of Chapultepec and the Alexandria Protocols. The former referred to a 1945 pan-American treaty signed at the Conference of Chapultepec in Mexico City that acted as a precursor to the 1947 Rio Pact, a security agreement invoked in the name of hemispheric defense as the Americas entered the Cold War era. In a similar vein, the Alexandria Protocols, signed by the five founding Arab League states in 1944, promoted the coordination of foreign policy and national defense agendas by the pact's signatories. Commenting to the Argentine press, Azzam conspicuously omitted the detail that in 1945 Argentina refused to sign the Act of Chapultepec. Instead, he chose a revised version of events to emphasize similarity between Latin American and Arab regional history for his Argentine audience.[31] Azzam's statement is evidence of Egyptian officials' desire to portray affinity between Latin American and Arab identities and histories.

General Naguib also reached out to the Argentine public through Arab Argentine press organs. In a May 1953 meeting with *América y Oriente*'s Cairo-based correspondent, Naguib gave an interview that concluded with remarks about the future of Arab–Latin American relations: "Egypt welcomes all friendly nations which extend their hand and aid [Egypt] in her struggle for liberty. We want to maintain friendly and cordial relations with these nations. We will exert our most concerted efforts to realize cultural and economic treaties. This is the way in which we view [Latin America]."[32] By the end of that year, steps toward Naguib's promise of cultural treaties with Latin American nations materialized. A December 1953 news brief in Córdoba's *Mundo Árabe* reported, "The Iberoamerican Cultural Center has been inaugurated [in Cairo]. Present at the ceremony were Argentine, Brazilian, Chilean, Uruguayan, Portuguese, French and Spanish diplomatic representatives. It was announced that the Spanish language will be taught in the Center's

Foreign Language School."[33] Here we see the rhetoric of solidarity and affinity backed by concrete initiatives from the revolutionary government, such as the establishment of the Cultural Center.

Channels of communication also extended beyond the diaspora to the realm of the state, yet this dimension of the South–South dialogue tends to be ignored by the scholarly literature prior to Nasser's rise. Naguib also contacted Perón and his cabinet directly on multiple occasions between 1952 and 1954. In commemoration of the first anniversary of the revolution, he wrote to the Argentine Congress to express his "sincerest thanks, and affirmations of the greatness of the Argentine nation."[34] His thanks were in response to a lavish celebration of the Egyptian Revolution that took place at the Teatro Nacional Cervantes in Buenos Aires. The event filled the ornate theater, which was "decked out in a profusion of flags and Egyptian national symbols." In attendance were important functionaries such as Minister of Foreign Relations Jerónimo Remorino (successor to Paz), Minister of the Interior Ángel Borlenghi, Eduardo Vuletich—secretary-general of the main trade union federation, Confederación General de Trabajadores—and Egyptian ambassador Mahmoud Moharram Hammad.[35] A few months prior to the celebration, when Hammad returned to his Buenos Aires post after a Cairo visit, Naguib sent the following message to be relayed directly to Perón: "Naguib is a fervent admirer of Perón and his masterpiece—that which he is elaborating for the greatness of his patria and for the triumph of the Third Position." He concluded his message with a reference to the anti-imperial struggle that would define the revolutionary government in the years after 1952: the battle for control over the Suez Canal. He decried British incursions into Egyptian territory: "The Egyptian people are fighting to dislodge the English from the strip of land that extends along the banks of the Suez, and which is totally Egyptian in fact and by right."[36] Over the course of the 1950s, anti-imperial struggle was one of the most prevalent topics in both Argentine and Arab discourses on the common trajectories of the Egyptian and Argentine peoples.

Perón in Exile: Arab Argentines as Interlocutors

Recently, historian Diego Olstein has called for scholars to "[bring] history out of the national box" by considering Perón's 1946–1955 administration in global perspective.[37] One strategy for globalizing our understanding of Peronism is to plot lines of comparison between national leaders or international policy doctrines. To this end, scholars have already noted overlaps in rhetoric and corporatist policy between Peronism and Nasserism. Robert Bianchi described Nasserism as "a fascinating and often intentional Egyptian counterpart to Peronism."[38] Accordingly, the memoirs of Free Officer Abdal Latif al-Boghdadi confirm that during the transition from the leadership of the Revolutionary Command Council (RCC) headed by Naguib to that of Nasser, elite circles of the armed forces regularly debated aspects of Peronism as they discussed the maintenance of military rule versus the return to multiparty politics.[39] In foreign policy, Diego Olstein and Hishaam Aidi have noted the similarities between Perón's and Nasser's philosophies of nonalignment in a Cold War world (Perón's "third position" and Nasser's "positive neutralism").[40] In retrospect, Nasserism certainly shared many defining features with Latin American populism, as articulated by Elie Podeh and Onn Winckler. These included "the central role of the charismatic leader and the special bond with the masses; the authoritarian nature of the regime, with its various techniques of mobilization among broad stratums; and the regime's eclectic use of ideology."[41] Collectively, scholarship renders a compelling picture of similarities between Peronist policy and early Nasserist Egypt.

This focus on parity of style, however, often elides the mechanics of influence between the two leaderships and risks situating the two as spontaneously parallel phenomena. The activities and memories of state actors such as Ambassador Speroni, alongside Arab interlocutors such as the journalist Mattar, show a concerted intention to incorporate Argentine modes and ideas into the Egyptian revolutionary project beginning with Naguib's tenure and continuing through the rise of the NAM. Furthermore, relying on the periodization of Perón's time in office or the Egyptian Revolution only from Nasser's assumption of power in 1954 risks limiting our understanding of the entangled nature of Argentine–Egyptian history outside the confines of these temporal guideposts. At the beginning of the period, it ignores the important exchanges during Naguib's tenure, and from its end, it precludes networks of solidarity that continued to function well after Perón's 1955 exile.

With respect to the pre-Nasser era of the revolution, the eagerness of both Argentines and Egyptians to recognize their countries as "sister nations" (in Perón's words) is clear. Although Perón was driven into exile when his first two presidential terms ended with a coup in 1955, some eight months after the RCC appointed Nasser president, he continued to strive for a closer relationship with important members of the Egyptian government. Even while he was in exile, the Arab Argentine community managed to facilitate Perón's contact with Egyptian political actors. In addition, the opportunities that the Arab Argentine community had created for him to interact with Egyptian diplomats during his time in office created lasting contacts for him while he was in exile in the Dominican Republic and then Madrid. In sum, the diaspora community had already laid the foundations for a lasting relationship between Argentine and Egyptian politicians that would extend beyond the limits of Perón's presidential rule.

A flurry of correspondence that Perón dispatched to Egypt in 1959 provides insight into his continued interest in Argentine–Egyptian relations well into his exile. In one letter, penned from the Dominican Republic, Perón wrote to Nasser. He conveyed admiration for Nasser's "patriotic enterprise," adding that he had carefully followed the revolution since its inception.[42] Later, Perón wrote from Madrid, where he remained until his return to Argentina in 1973. Syrian Argentine businessman Jorge Antonio, one of Perón's closest financial advisors, accompanied him for much of his exile in Madrid, and recalled that Perón "had great sympathy and good dealings with the Arab nations while he was in exile. . . . He was a personal friend of Nasser, and they wrote back and forth often. I was his interpreter and went to Egypt various times in order to relay things from Perón to Nasser, and from Nasser back to Perón."[43] In other letters to Egypt in 1959, Perón repeatedly noted his use of Arab Argentine businessmen as couriers for mail to Egypt. Before he went to Madrid, Elias Abud, a prominent Syrian Argentine from Buenos Aires, traveled to Ciudad Trujillo to ferry his letters to Cairo.

Perón also contacted important functionaries in the Egyptian government such as Zeki Djebi and Hassan Ismail Fahmi—respectively, minister of foreign relations and director of the Latin America Foreign Ministry Division.[44] In his letters to both men, he assured them that he had kept abreast of the trajectories of their diplomatic careers since meeting them personally in Argentina. As with Nasser, we witness the facilitating role of Arab Argentines in creating avenues for exchange between their national leadership and Arab politicians. Before being ousted, Perón had had opportunities to encounter these two diplomats at functions hosted by members of the Arab Argentine community. Fahmi, who served as military attaché to the Egyptian legation in Buenos Aires in the 1950s, and Djebi, the first official Syrian minister in Argentina, were regular attendees at mahjar voluntary association dinners and celebrations.[45] Djebi had close ties with members of the Arab Argentine community who, for many years, had lobbied for Syria and Argentina to open diplomatic relations and celebrated Djebi's 1945 assignment to his Buenos Aires post. It was Djebi who conferred the Syrian government's highest medal of honor, the Order of the Umayyads, upon Eva Perón in April 1952, only a few months before her death, amid great celebration from mahjar press organs.[46] By 1959, the Syrian diplomat found himself working in Cairo after Egypt and Syria's official declaration in February 1958 that they would federate as the United Arab Republic (the federation lasted from 1958 to 1961).

In his letter to Djebi, Perón leaned heavily on the language of nonalignment, promoting the vision of a united Arab world, "happy owner of her own destiny." He remarked on the "triumph of Nasser, surrounded as he is by the great powers, without allowing himself to become trapped by the powerful interests of his aligned enemies."[47] Once again, Perón employed the language of the NAM, still in its infancy in 1959. (It was not until 1961 that the NAM was formally established at the Belgrade summit meeting.) To Fahmi, tactfully reassuring an Egyptian audience that Peronism still wielded power in Argentina, he wrote:

> The pueblo has begun to rebel.... As of 16 September 1955, there were 5,000,000 Peronist votes we could count on. Now there are more than 7,000,000. Soon everyone will recognize the great benefits for the people and the country that come from Peronism in power. Sooner or later, recuperation of the government is inevitable. In the meanwhile, it is with great satisfaction that I share the triumph of Egypt in this tremendous struggle which signifies total popular and national liberation.[48]

While he was writing from exile in 1959, Argentina was experiencing economic recession, military-imposed austerity measures, and civil unrest. Perhaps spurred by these uncertain times on the home front, Perón reached out to Egyptians, whom he perceived as strategic global allies in the future of the Peronist movement. The content of Perón's correspondence demonstrates that he not only admired the Egyptian revolutionary project and its key leaders, but, furthermore, was concerned that the Egyptian government should recognize the sway that he held in Argentina despite his exile.

By 1960, there is evidence that Perón explicitly advised followers in Argentina to view the cooperation of other Arab bloc countries (not just Egypt) as an example to emulate. To militant labor organizer and *Resistencia peronista* member Avelino Fernández, he wrote:

The world today . . . forms a single unit, as divided as it may seem. What is happening in Algeria resonates on other continents, and what Russia and the United States do . . . has repercussions across the rest of the globe. There is a deep woven interdependence, first because of economic interests, and now because of ideological interests. Restrictive nationalities that raised impassable borders between countries have ceased to exist, and the realization that everyone's destiny is at stake has driven the formation of national blocs.[49]

He cited Africa and the Middle East as primary examples of regions that formed regional alliances, such as the Arab League. Analysis of Perón's exile correspondence to both Egypt and constituents in Argentina adds new layers on two fronts to the study of Argentine–Egyptian relations in the twentieth century. First, it demonstrates the continued role of diasporic Arabs in mediating the relationship between Peronism and Nasserism even after the Revolución Libertadora coup that ended Perón's presidency in 1955; second, it represents a step toward excavating a broader regional history of informal relationship to the NAM during the early Cold War. Perón's fascination with the Egyptian project closely resembled that of other Latin American leaders at the turn from the 1950s to the 1960s. Examples of this regional trend include Che Guevara, with his three-month tour of fourteen Bandung Pact countries, including Egypt in 1959, what one scholar deemed Mexico's early 1960s "flirtation" with the NAM,[50] and Jânio Quadros, president of Brazil for seven months in 1961, of whom John Karam notes that he was "particularly fond of" Nasser and "declared what he called Brazil's . . . Independent Foreign Policy" before being overthrown by the military.[51] Much as Karam argues in the Brazilian case, in Argentina we see a Latin American leader who "learned the keywords of nonalignment" and "eventually used [that language] to frame . . . increasingly closer ties with the Middle East."[52] This brings us to our final temporal fulcrum for constructing an entangled Argentine–Egyptian history at midcentury: the 1956 Suez Canal conflict.

Suez

As tensions over the Suez Canal zone escalated throughout the mid-1950s and came to define the early Nasser years, the canal became a flashpoint for comparison and identification with anti-imperialist sentiments in Argentina before and after Perón's exile. It is instructive to provide a brief review of the Suez

Canal conflict as context prior to analyzing this moment as an important flash-point for many Argentines.

The Suez Canal symbolized unique forms of transnational solidarity and historical parallels for diverse sectors of Argentine society, as well as the transnational public sphere of the mahjar. Argentines took an interest in these events in Egypt for various reasons: cultural or ethnic heritage ties, a sense of relevance to the labor movement, or as fellow citizens of a global periphery. This nuanced perspective challenges previous views on the influence of Nasser-era politics in Latin America that downplay the possibility of variegated forms of empathy or solidarity on the part of Latin American citizens with the specifics of the Egyptian cause.[53]

By 1956, the Suez Canal had been in operation for nearly a century under de facto British control via stakeholding in the Suez Canal Company and the Constantinople Convention declaration that had placed the Canal Zone under British protection since 1888. When Nasser nationalized the Suez Canal Company in July 1956, his actions were part of a series of Cold War power plays involving figures such as US Secretary of State John Foster Dulles and British Prime Minister Anthony Eden. As the RCC sought to consolidate the revolution after 1952, they pushed forward an agenda of large-scale agrarian reform, industrialization, and sovereignty from European occupation of the Canal Zone. The leaders of the RCC, the Soviet Union, and United States knew that the necessary infrastructure and energy needs for this agenda were linked to the completion of the Aswan Dam, a major hydroelectric project. Between 1955 and 1956, Nasser stubbornly adhered to his political stance of "positive neutralism," attempting to obtain funding from both the United States and the USSR to advance construction at Aswan—a position that irked US strong-men such as Dulles. In early July 1956, Dulles abruptly withdrew the $56 million funding package previously offered for the dam project. He banked on the ability of the United States to call a Soviet bluff regarding more than a billion dollars in arms deals and construction loans, but as a gamble to humiliate Nasser, it was a resounding failure. Soon after, on July 26, came Nasser's announcement of his decision to nationalize the Suez Canal Company as a means of subsidizing Aswan. Throughout the Global South, people who had long struggled against colonial and imperial yokes celebrated Nasser as a hero and avidly followed the conflict.

Support for Egypt's position in the Suez Canal conflict spread quickly. In the Levant, hundreds of thousands of people rallied in popular support of

Nasser.[54] Following the canal's nationalization, Israeli, British, and French forces invaded Egypt in hopes of regaining control. The Egyptian military managed to keep the waterway blocked to all shipping, and Israel, France, and Britain withdrew from Sinai and the Northern District of the Canal Zone under heavy pressure from the United States, the Soviet Union, and the United Nations. In the eyes of many international onlookers, the withdrawal was a watershed moment for General Nasser. He became a symbol of global anti-imperialism. Across the Global South, many attributed his successful maintenance of the Canal Zone to his strategy of nonalignment, a move that ultimately pitted the United States against its European allies. For many Arabs in the Middle East, Nasser's triumph invigorated their hope for the liberation of Palestine through a combination of nonalignment—a strategy that appeared to have the power to counter imperialism—and armed struggle. This episode's magnitude in the global struggle against imperialism, as well as its implications in the Arab–Israeli conflict, reverberated in Latin America and throughout the mahjar's public sphere. These events in the Middle East drew attention from and inspired the involvement of people across the globe—with and without diasporic connections to the traditional geographic bounds of the region. The shifting politics, boundaries, and social mobilizations that ensued were transregional, and thus invite us to think of the Middle East globally: from the Canal Zone to the vast terrain of the Americas, Europe, Asia, and Africa.

From Panama to the Southern Cone, there were marches and demonstrations in support of Egypt after the Suez affair. In Buenos Aires, public manifestations began the night of the tripartite invasion, and marchers chanted, "Argentina with Egypt!"[55] In the following months, Arab Argentine heritage organizations, intellectuals, and university students echoed this sentiment. Indeed, by 1956, the 1952 revolution's agenda and trajectory were more central to civilian discussions of imperialism, nonalignment, and international diplomacy than ever before. "I believe that the struggle for the Suez Canal had a great deal of positive influence in the colectividad," recalled Syrian Argentine writer, intellectual, and political activist Fernando Nadra. "When the British and the Israelis attacked, this raised up the figure of Nasser before all of us, and there was a great movement in support of the Egyptian cause—the cause of the Arabs."[56] For some Arab Latin Americans, their views of the Egyptian victory at Suez were influenced by deeply personal connections to a Palestinian homeland. At least one person went so far as to cable Nasser directly. Her message read: "President Nasser. Cairo, Egypt. Invoking your brave spirit, I beg the Egyptian people not to give up an inch of your stake. This attitude will save Palestine, my homeland. Nazarena Lama, Santiago [de Chile]."[57]

At the associational level, Arab Argentine organizations mobilized to express solidarity with Egypt or a pan-Arab cause. In 1956 two long-running organizations, the Club Honor y Patria (established 1932), and the Patronato Sirio-Libanés (1928), merged to form the Honor and Fatherland Club, Union of Arab-American Peoples. The long-dormant Federation of Arab Bodies in the Argentine Republic issued a communiqué on August 15, 1956, in response to the invasion and called for a general strike by members of the collectivity in solidarity with Egypt. Charitable organizations mobilized with campaigns such as that of the Islamic Center Women's Commission in Buenos Aires, which raised funds to send to Egyptian victims of the fighting in Suez.[58] Other groups held public meetings to discuss and honor Nasser's decision to nationalize the canal, including the Homs Club of Buenos Aires; the Argentine–Arab–Latin-American Congress for Solidarity, Peace and Freedom; the Arab Argentine Home Association of Berisso; and the Lebanese House of Buenos Aires; and they organized press conferences hosted by the Syrian and Egyptian legations and the Rotary Club of Cairo.[59] From charity campaigns to heritage associations that adopted new names, a focus on Nasser's anti-imperialist nonalignment and an evocation of solidarity between Argentina and Egypt were the salient themes. In 1956, these themes defined discourses of anti-imperialism in the writings of Arab Argentine intellectuals, university conferences, and the labor movement. Solidarity with Egypt was a common language that appeared in the 1950s, bridging different sectors of Argentine society. Though the Egyptian context was new, it was a register that meshed seamlessly into the preexisting tradition of invoking the right to sovereignty as a key component of national dignity that had appeared in Argentine political discourse since the nineteenth century.[60]

Comparisons between British incursions in the Suez Canal and the Islas Malvinas (Falkland Islands, according to the British) were one way that people expressed the affinity they perceived between Argentine and Egyptian realities. These comparisons appeared before the Suez conflict, in Perón's assessments of the 1952 revolution, and they proliferated after Nasser's declaration of nationalization. As early as 1953, Perón responded to a message from General Naguib proclaiming that it was "the struggle for liberty for the people which links the sentiments and aspirations of [Argentina and Egypt]":

Great Britain occupies the Canal Zone by force in the same manner that she occupies the Malvinas. . . . The situation is the same. It is like a thief who one day
steals a dog and the next day comes back and demands that the owner provide
him with the leash as well. A country can't be half independent—either it is or
it isn't.[61]

This comparison also appeared centrally in the book by Arab Argentine intellectual and Arab League liaison officer Ibrahim Hallar published during the
Suez conflict: *The Dreams of Colonel Nasser Are White and Sky Blue, Like the
Emblem of the Argentine Nation.* Seizing on the Suez–Malvinas theme, Hallar wrote: "If we imitate the example of the Egyptian people in expelling the
English from our Malvinas, we will not be committing any crime against that
country; on the contrary, our spirit would become fortified, our Argentinista
conscience would affirm itself more and more each day."[62] For Hallar, "imitat-
ing" Egyptian actions was something that could deepen and affirm Argentine
anti-imperialist consciousness.

Voices from the Argentine Left and labor movement shared this language,
despite their political differences from the traditionally more middle-class
and centrist Arab Argentine political and journalistic circles. The Argentine Communist Party (PC) was openly pro-Arab during the tripartite invasion (largely owing to the USSR's support of the canal's nationalization), and
pro-Nasser articles appeared regularly in their principal press organs, such
as *Nueva Era*.[63] Press coverage often framed Argentina and Egypt as bound
together in a unified working-class struggle against imperial interests. Particularly vocal was Fernando Nadra, who extended his comparison of the
Argentina–Egypt binary to encompass a regional Latin American history of
landscapes physically scarred by imperialism. In the aftermath of the Suez
struggle, he wrote:

The managers of this foul enterprise (as wealthy in dollars and pounds
as they are in the blood of the people), which is based upon the "Western
rights" over the Suez Canal, are the same people who are the beneficiaries of
the Panama Canal, of the fruit trees and the cane fields of the Caribbean, of
the Bolivian situation, of Chilean copper, of Brazilian coffee, of Argentine
meat and wheat . . . and of so many other riches produced by the sweat and
misery of Latin Americans. . . The cause of the Egyptian people is our cause.
We could not seriously be patriots, we would not be doing everything in our

power to assure our own national independence, if we did not feel for the cause of independence of other peoples.[64]

For Nadra, the basic unit of human suffering on which the two canals were constructed was an inescapable factor that bound these two world regions together via a common history of exploitation.

Meanwhile, in the Labor Party's official newspaper, *El Laborista*, more than eighty articles on Egypt and the canal appeared in September and October 1956 alone. Founded by Peronist union leaders in 1945 but forcibly dissolved in 1946 by Perón, Argentina's Labor Party reappeared after his exile in 1955 under the leadership of Cipriano Reyes. Reyes, a union leader in the meat-packing warehouses, was on the frontlines of organized labor that brought Perón to power, but he was subsequently repressed by the regime once it began to drastically consolidate political parties under the all-subsuming Justicialist Party. When Reyes reappeared as a central figure in the neo-Peronist Labor Party in 1955, he represented a movement that was deeply critical of the current military dictatorship, was pro-labor, yet opposed to Perón serving as the movement's figurehead.[65] Only weeks after Nasser declared the nationalization of the Suez Canal Company, Reyes began to make appearances at pro-Egypt, Nasser-themed events. On August 19, 1956, Reyes acted as a guest speaker at the Association for Arab Culture in the Argentine Republic, and a few days before that, he was the guest of honor at an homage to Nasser hosted by the Homs Club. Similar associations emerged among politicized groups of university students that, though largely unaffiliated with the Labor Party, shared the language of a connection between Argentina and Egypt.

In November 1956, the Buenos Aires branch of the University Reform Movement (MUR) published extensive analysis of current events in Egypt and the Middle East. They emphasized the widespread popular solidarity toward Egypt, citing the profusion of lively discussions, marches, conferences, and publications from university faculty and students. At the University of Buenos Aires, demonstrations in support of Egypt took place at the medical and law schools, and universities in the federal capital broadcast special radio transmissions to express students' "instinctual solidarity with the Egyptian people."[66] To articulate their solidarity with "not just Egypt . . . but the Arab world," the MUR turned to the language of Argentine economist Raúl Prebisch, whose structuralist approach to global economics emphasized a core–periphery dichotomy: "Being as we are a `peripheral country,' we have a responsibility to support . . . without reservation the attitude assumed by the Egyptian leader, given that [his action] embodies an anti-imperialist struggle of which all Latin American nations in general, and Argentina in particular, are currently a part."[67]

Overall, the enthusiasm for Nasser's Suez agenda expressed by university groups, taken alongside that of Argentina's Labor Party and PC, indicates that Argentines who identified with the Nasserist agenda were not simply Peronists interested in elevating a perceived Arab version of their own former leader. Nor were they strictly Argentines of a broader Left; veneration for Nasser came from within the ranks of the Argentine military even after the 1955 coup. Argentine journalist Rogelio García Lupo observed that by 1959, "Nasserism exercised an irresistible attraction on young [army] officials."[68] A decade after Argentina began its formal diplomatic relationship with Egypt in 1947, the Suez moment generated an amalgam of pro-Egypt solidarity extending far beyond Argentina's mahjar. This support, often expressed as a belief in an Argentine–Egyptian connection, appeared across sectors of Argentine society with distinct social and political agendas yet shared a language of solidarity with Egypt and, to some extent, the NAM.

Traditional diplomatic history would at this moment outline a vision of Argentina turning away from the NAM and the Arab world. After all, in the wake of Perón's exile, the foreign policy of the leaders of the Revolución Libertadora was much more openly aligned with US interests. But approaching this era instead as an intermingled panorama of civilian groups and their relationship to the idea of Egyptian sovereignty provides a different vision of this historical moment. In the end, it is not necessary to view the potential divergences between Argentine political rhetoric versus policy versus expressions of popular sentiment as contradictory in themselves. Indeed, it is within these modes of relating to Egypt and its revolutionary process that we witness the overlapping, and sometimes oppositional, programs and postures that circulated in Argentina, and the wider Global South, during the Cold War.

Through this analysis of three dimensions of the developing Argentine–Egyptian relationship at midcentury, we can observe that Argentine people and politics were influential in the Egyptian revolutionary project. From diasporic interlocutors to activists and diplomats, Argentines offered a discursive model, intellectual base, and demonstration of Global South solidarity with Egypt.

These solidarities ran far deeper than previously acknowledged by the literature on Argentine–Egyptian relations, and they preceded the rise of the NAM. This is not merely a case of spontaneous discursive similarities between national leaderships. Rather, we can trace lines of transmission and influence in the realm of political theory and praxis made possible by preexisting traditions of anti-imperial activism and through diasporic networks linking South America to the Arabic-speaking eastern Mediterranean. Thus, overlaying a history of Argentine international relations with narratives of human migration and mobilities allows us to achieve a more accurate rendering of the state of Arab–Latin American relations during this period. It also reveals the diverse ways in which historical events in the Arab world resonated with, and mattered to, Argentines from diverse ethnic, social, and political sectors. This entanglement should serve as an invitation for further exploration of Argentines and their place in a broader Global Middle East—beyond the case study taken up here. There are many other connected histories to be told and stitched together with this one—for example, the connected histories of Argentina, Israel, and Palestine during this pivotal midcentury moment and beyond.

Methodologically, constructing these bridged histories draws us closer to a new historical model of international relations that goes beyond diplomacy and interfaces with other realms of social and cultural life. Narratives of travel, diaspora, and anti-imperial activisms come to bear on this new international history of Latin America and the Middle East.[69] This relational model reveals the meaningful ways in which these two regions have been entangled beyond state-sanctioned diplomacy through (among other things) avenues of migration and anti-imperialism. In short, we arrive at yet another dimension of Argentina's place in the global Middle East as the twentieth century unfolded.

Ultimately, we cannot fully measure Latin America's movement toward or away from global phenomena solely by observing the tides of statecraft. We must also consider how the state's diverse public identified itself in relation to these global trends or events, such as the Egyptian Revolution, Suez, or the NAM. As Karam notes, Latin American states learned the language of the NAM and used it as they inched closer to Arab nations over the years.[70] This chapter has made clear that nonstate actors and groups (whether of the Arab diaspora, the Left, or deposed political parties) also learned and deployed this language for their own ends. Methodologically, the connected history of two nations opens the field of their respective national histories to new vantage points, suggests Sanjay Subrayhaman.[71] We thus reveal "multifaceted interactions, beyond . . . political partitions (national or imperial) and on various scales." By "moving laterally [we] identify connections that had been hitherto hidden or unseen."[72] In this light, the study of Argentine–Egyptian history serves as an invitation to other scholars of Latin America, Africa, and the Middle East to venture a lateral step and illuminate new dimensions of the multifaceted networks that have historically bound these regions together. For scholars of migration and diaspora, this exercise proposes a model for integrating ethnic and diaspora histories into regional histories of diplomacy and dialogues about alignment that took place in the early Cold War era.

6 Enduring Ties

The rich transregional relationships, networks, and solidarities that took shape between Argentina and the Middle East over the course of the twentieth century are not phenomena strictly relegated to the past. The notion of Argentina in a Global Middle East is a living, evolving landscape of moving people, things, and ideas. These historical ties endure and will no doubt continue to shape Argentine realities and futures in ways that range far beyond the case studies of this book. This final chapter serves as an invitation to explore a series of further arenas—new jumping-off points—for envisioning Argentina's entanglement in South-South networks, circuits, and horizons.

To this end, we might consider three forms of linkages related to contemporary Argentine realities that have their roots in historical mobilities of material goods, traveling people, and circulating ideas. The first is the movement of commodities along South-South lines, using the case of the long-robust Argentine yerba mate export market to Syria. The second arena is that of discourses and actions surrounding twenty-first-century scenarios of mass displacement in light of the Syrian Civil War that began in 2011–. This massive humanitarian disaster has reconfigured the possibility-scapes of millions of Syrians who have found themselves displaced internally or as international refugees roughly during the time period that this book was being researched and written. This displacement is not only the elephant in the room while writing a book on Syrian migration in historical perspective, but it also has brought new migrant populations into contact with historic diasporic communities across Latin America. The third arena is that of contemporary artistic collaborations that result in the creation of South-South cultural spaces.

In our final frame of reference, we return to the dynamics of "Art in Motion" that we first visited in Chapter 3. Here, we examine a series of film festivals and conferences starting in 2012 in Buenos Aires that seek to highlight and develop South-South ties among broader Latin American, Middle Eastern, and North African—that is, Arab world—publics. The individuals at the helm of these cultural-intellectual projects are at the forefront of new movements to recognize the idea of the Global South as much more than academic jargon.

By knitting together these three frames for honing our perspective on Argentine and Middle Eastern entanglements past and present, we see that the movement of people, things, and ideas is not merely the process by which diasporas such as the mahjar coalesce. Rather, these are the building blocks for larger transregional relationships that, once we recognize them, have the ability to help us desegregate notions of presumably fixed divides among world "regions" delineated by a Cold War generation of area studies scholarship. In this chapter, these three frames of reference for Argentine-Middle East relations lead us on a tour through the projects, markets, and individual trajectories of the various forms of mobility that link, rather than divide, these geographies. Ultimately, this new perspective allows us to globalize our vision of Argentine history in a way that helps us better understand the multiplicity of ways in which the nation's contemporary economy, culture, and politics of human movement are intimately enmeshed in South-South circulations of people, commodities, and cultural production.

Frame 1: Yerba Mate and South-South Commodity Circulation

Perhaps Argentina's most iconic foodway, the ubiquitous practice of drinking yerba mate tea takes place throughout the country. The hallmark ritual involves imbibing hot tea brewed from loose leaves (*yerba*) in a small vessel (the *mate*, traditionally a gourd but alternatives include wooden, metal, glass, or even plastic). Those partaking in the beverage drink through a metal or wooden straw (the *bombilla*) that filters out the finely ground tea leaves. Though this activity can be performed by individuals, it is a markedly social, communal practice. In groups, the mate is passed from person to person in a circle, with frequent replenishment of hot water and optional spoonfuls of sugar depending on individual preference. Periodically, writers and travelers have remarked on the fact that this foodway is readily observable in the Levant as well—particularly in Syria, but also in Lebanon. More than any other group, Syrian Druze communities south of Beirut and east of Damascus can be found preparing yerba tea in their mate vessels.

Scholars have remarked in passing on the connection between Levantine mate consumption and histories of transnational migration. For the Argentine government, the preponderance of the mate ritual in the Middle East takes on new dimensions of importance when considered in the realm of large-scale agro-export trade relationships. After major cereal and viticulture-related exports, yerba mate is one of Argentina's biggest agricultural exports. Syria represents the largest international market outside South America. In 2018, when Argentina's Instituto Nacional de Yerba Mate (National Institute of Yerba Mate) announced that the country had reached a record high in international exports—up a whopping 44 percent from the previous year—Syria topped the list of importers. Of the approximately 7 million tons of yerba exported that year, Syria brought in some 4.9 million, with Lebanon, France, the United States, and a handful of other destinations trailing far behind in their imports.[1] The roots of this twenty-first-century commodity chain that links South America to the Middle East are grounded in the early twentieth-century arrival of mahjar populations in Argentina's northeastern Mesopotamia region. Its future, too, may very well be tied to processes of migration and displacement that are unfolding in the eastern Mediterranean.

The geography of Argentina's yerba mate industry takes us once again out of the hub cities and to the peripheries of the mahjar. Primarily grown in the humid Mesopotamia region, most yerba mate cultivation takes place in the provinces of Misiones and Corrientes. As we explored in Chapters 1 and 2, Middle Eastern migrants reached the heart of Argentina's yerba mate–producing region early in the twentieth century. Thanks to the expansion of both the main arteries of the national rail network as well as narrow-gauge, moveable Decauville-style track, Ottoman Syrians were able to make their way throughout the Mesopotamia region. Information gleaned from a combination of government reports and mahjar business directories reveals that these migrants became directly involved in the production process of yerba mate as a commodity, from the early stages of cultivation and agricultural labor on through its processing and distribution.

One of our earliest insights into the presence of Middle Eastern migrants in the ranks of yerba mate harvest workers comes from the reported presence of so-called turcos observed by labor inspectors deployed from Buenos Aires by the Departamento Nacional de Trabajo (DNT; National Labor Department). A precursor of Argentina's Ministerio de Trabajo, Empleo y Seguridad Social (Ministry of Labor, Employment and Social Security), the DNT was the 1907 creation of President Jose Figueroa Alcorta. It served as a centralized bureaucratic body for gathering, assessing, and publishing data gathered about "relations between labor and capital and the legislative and administrative reforms capable of improving the material, social, intellectual, and moral situation of workers."[2] To this end, the DNT sent inspectors to yerba plantations, sugar mill operations, workers' barracks, and company stores and into interviews with laborers, managers, and industrialists across the country. The presence of Middle Eastern workers and contractors in Mesopotamian yerba mate and yerba-related industries appears in the reports generated by these DNT inspectors as early as 1914.

In that year, the DNT sent inspector José Elías Niklison on a tour through the upper Paraná River (Alto Paraná) region of Misiones Province to observe the operations of various agro-industrial enterprises from sugar cane, to yerba mate, to lumber. This was one of several long inspection trips that Niklison undertook for the DNT with the specific assignment of assessing the state of Indigenous labor in rural Argentina in several provinces and national territories.[3] In his Misiones foray, Niklison penned extensive descriptions of his observations and interactions with those involved with every level of production at each site he visited over the course of early 1914.

In order to observe the mechanics of the labor contracting process, Niklison spent time at the provincial capital of Posadas. A bustling port on the Paraná River, Posadas was a way point for much of the regional labor migration that supplied workers to growing yerba mate and other agricultural industries that required rotating seasonal labor during planting and harvest periods. Workers chiefly from Paraguay and elsewhere in Argentina arrived at the Port of Posadas by boat before being dispersed to their final destinations. Those chiefly responsible for connecting this incoming labor supply with the rotating demands of plantation managers were middlemen known as *conchabadores*. These contractors awaited the arrival of boats at the port and then vied for contracts with workers by promising small cash advances. Then they proceeded to deal directly with the contracting managers or firms and collected a small kickback of between 3 and 5 pesos per head for arranging transport for the laborers to their final destination. The profit in this transaction came, in reality, not from this small head tax but rather in side deals made between conchabadores and their clients. Conchabadores sold them food and other provisions as part of the transaction at whatever price they could manage to negotiate. Both Niklison and the local police force viewed the work of these conchabadores as dubiously exploitative of the laborers (*peones*) who passed through Posadas en route to jobs primarily at local yerba mate farms (*yerbales*). Local law enforcement kept lists of businessmen who operated part-time as conchabadores in addition to running other businesses. As Niklison observed, Middle Eastern conchabadores figured prominently in these lists:

> There are good and bad conchabadores, but certainly more of the latter. According to information from the police, there are currently nineteen [conchabadores] of different nationalities. Those who operate most successfully are the turcos, of whom they have a record of six in current operation. Almost all of them are the proprietors of small or large general stores [*ramos generales*], and this helps to considerably augment their inflated profit margins.[4]

Both *Niklison*'s and the local law enforcement's observations of turco labor contractors hold the same tone of skepticism tending toward anti-turco sentiment that we see in other DNT reports of the era (such as those explored in Chapter 1 from the Chaco, Jujuy, Salta, Formosa, and Tucumán). Niklison didn't bother to remark, for example, that the number of *argentino* and *paraguayo* contractors he observed outnumbered the presence of the so-called turcos two to one, instead choosing to focus on the presence of the latter group and speculate as to their profiteering motives. Regardless of this bias, however, his recorded observations do provide a baseline for confirming the presence of a relationship between Arab Argentine entrepreneurs and labor migrants destined for regional yerbales in the early twentieth century.

As Niklison noted, his list of Posadas conchabadores contained the names of six "turco" businessmen: Jorge Simon, Antonio Faischi, Luis Guainchi, Antonio Julián, Felipe Chemes, and Lazaro Chemes.[5] The latter three of these all registered their general store (*ramos generales, tienda y mercería, almacén*) businesses in mahjar directories between 1917 and 1942, coinciding with Niklison's observation that conchabadores tended to be the owners of this type of small business in addition to acting as labor contractors.[6] The last two names in this list were likely related to the sizable Chemes family, which registered more than thirty businesses spread across Misiones Province and dozens more in the broader *alto paraná* region during this same period. It would appear that Felipe Chemes went on to become involved in the movement of people and goods—perhaps across Misiones or along the Paraná River—as he changed his registered business listing to *Transportes* by 1942. In regard to mobility, it appears that Lazaro Chemes was himself somewhat mobile, making at least one transatlantic trip in the decade following Niklison's report.[7] When he reentered the country in 1926, port officials recorded his profession as *comercio*. It is impossible to know if this trip was business, chain migration, or otherwise related, but these small clues do point toward a vision of a larger group of Arab Argentines who staked their business interests at least partially in the growing industry of yerba mate cultivation and labor.

Elsewhere in Niklison's reports to the DNT, we gain clues as to the presence of Arab Argentines not only as conchabadores but as manual laborers in industries related to the region's yerbales. While the inspector's reports did not name turcos specifically in his observations of yerbales' labor force, he did acknowledge their presence in yerba-adjacent industries such as the timber sector. Clearing or "opening" forest land through the process of logging was one of the industrial practices that made way for the expansion of yerba mate cultivation. Many large companies ran forest clearing operations alongside agricultural operations while simultaneously expanding infrastructure (such as Decauville rail track) into their targeted agricultural areas.[8] In the same 1914 report that featured Niklison's observations of Arab Argentine conchabadores, he also noted the presence of Middle Eastern laborers for these large forest-clearing companies such as the Compañía de Tierras y Maderas del Iguazú. In one instance, Niklison took detailed notes on worker testimonies regarding what several laborers viewed as unfair labor conditions in the rural Puerto Segundo area of Misiones Province starting in late 1913. After managers at the Compañía de Tierras y Maderas del Iguazú refused worker demands for an afternoon *mate cocido* break, a biweekly pay schedule, and improved medical attention for injured workers, laborers decided to strike in the last days of November 1913. By that point, the situation was heated, and major national press organs such as *La Prensa* and *La Nación* dispatched correspondents to cover the developing situation. Journalist Raimundo Fernández of *La Nación* recorded the following account from a group of six Spanish workers who appeared before a local justice of the peace, and Niklison included it in his report back to the DNT:

> On the 29th [of November] at 12:30, we watched as almost all of the turcos descended, each with his bundle of belongings [*lingera*] hoisted on his shoulder. We tried to inquire as to what they wanted, and they said that if they didn't get paid the earnings they were owed, they would all go [*se marchaban todos a reclamar*] and demand to be done justice. [They said that] one of them was in

possession of sufficient money such that they could all board the first steamboat that would take them [to the relevant authorities]. Later that night, we saw them once again, and they said that they had been paid some of what was owed them. We too, refused to work, and told the administration that they should pay us, too. . . . Our pleas were not attended to, and so we continued to strike on the 30th. At around 7 in the morning on the 30th, the engineer [boss] appeared with a Winchester in hand [to scatter the encamped strikers].[9]

Beyond the fact that this testimony gives us rare insight into an episode of labor action undertaken by proletarian Arab immigrants in rural Argentina, it also speaks to the range of ways in which Arab Argentines did work related to the production of this agricultural commodity. If we return now to migrant-produced archival sources from the following decades, we can broaden our vision of the multiple overlaps between mahjar and mate histories.

By the early 1940s, there is clear evidence of Arab Argentines who worked at each stage of the yerba mate agricultural production chain from cultivation, to processing and warehousing, to wholesale distribution and individual sales. The 1942 *Guía de Comercio Siriolibanés* reveals the presence of these operations spread across at least five provinces: Misiones, Formosa, Tucumán, Córdoba, and Buenos Aires. In Misiones, two growers registered their agricultural enterprises in the business directory. In the tiny municipality of Itacaruare, Manuel Asis reported that he was a yerba mate grower (*cultivador de yerba mate*). Itacaruare was a remote agricultural outpost a few miles up a tributary of the Uruguay River that drew some seasonal agricultural labor, potentially even on Asis's land. Only one other individual listed business there in 1942: a lone almacén owner by the name of Luis Jalil. Almost directly across the province from Itacaruare was the riverine port town of Santa Ana. There, another yerba mate grower, Andrés Adad, registered his presence in the 1942 *Guía*. Adad appears to have worn several hats—as a fruit and yerba mate grower and middleman distributor (*acopiador*), as well as a bakery owner. Fifteen years prior, Adad was living and working some 50 kilometers downriver in Posadas, where he owned a general store (*mercadería general*) and was surrounded by several Arab Argentine businesses of the same ilk. By the 1940s, he was clearly branching out and trying his luck in a much more agricultural setting. After harvest, cultivators like Jalil and Adad would have to thoroughly dry the clipped yerba in a double process of flash-drying, followed by a longer curing procedure (the *sapecado* and *secado* processes). Then they would grind it themselves into a more or less coarsely ground consistency, thus rendering *yerba canchada* or *yerba molida*, respectively.[10] This processing may have taken place on site; indeed, this was likely especially for smaller operations. Larger yerbales, however, would sometimes direct their dried product to a mill (*molino*) for the final processing stage.[11] In the capital of Formosa Province, at least one such mill was under Arab Argentine ownership: that of Julián Cura, who registered his Molino de Yerba Mate in the *Guía de Comercio*. Relatively far from the yerbales of Misiones, Cura's mill was most likely linked to large-scale yerbales in Paraguay. Yerba in need of processing could have been easily transported by boat southward along the navigable Paraguay River to Formosa, which lies some 130 kilometers downstream.

After the first round of milling, yerba canchada is ready to drink, but usually it is packaged and left to cure for up to an additional six months prior to the second round of milling into yerba molida, the most common form of yerba mate purchased by consumers worldwide.[12] Before bulk distribution to wholesalers and vendors, large sacks of yerba mate are warehoused en route to their final sale destination. At this stage of the production chain as well, we see Arab Argentine business owners such as Juan A. Nacud of Pergamino (Buenos Aires Province) and Elías Dip of San Miguel de Tucumán. In 1942, both reported owning these storehouses (*depósitos*). In both cases, they appear to have started out as dry goods and sundries proprietors on a smaller scale (Nacud owned a tienda y mercería in 1927 and Dip a *mercería y tejidos* shop) before ramping up their investment in yerba storage and distribution.

After sacks of yerba left storehouses like those of Nacud and Dip, they most often traveled to countless dry goods, general, and grocery stores across the country. However, some of that product went directly to distributors dealing specifically in the sale of coffees and teas. This was the business model, for example, of Salim Simes, who identified himself as a seller of coffee and yerba mate. Simes first registered as a tienda owner in 1927, where he owned a business on Itzuaingó Street in the heart of Córdoba's historic microcentro neighborhood. By 1942, he reported himself as a business that dealt specifically with coffee and yerba sales (*venta de yerba y café*). Along with his counterparts in other provinces—like Adad (Misiones), Nacud (Buenos Aires), and Dip (Tucumán)—Simes is another example of an Arab Argentine entrepreneur who appears to have transitioned to a livelihood that dealt more directly with yerba mate production, processing, or sales over the course of the late 1920s to early 1940s. Over this same period, the Argentine yerba economy was undergoing an expansion as it overtook Brazil as chief producer in the wake of that country's corresponding shift toward coffee production.[13]

By the 1930s, Argentina regularly exported large quantities of yerba to several international destinations. Christine Folch notes 1935 as a particularly significant turning point in the yerba mate industry, as this was the year that the government established a parastate institution to standardize mate production and sale regulations: the Comisión Reguladora de Producción y Comercio de la Yerba Mate (Regulating Commission on the Production and Trade of Yerba Mate.[14] The commission also tracked export tonnage to primary yerba mate consumer markets. Larger export markets were primarily those created by neighboring Latin American consumers: Bolivians, Uruguayans, and Chileans above all. Syrian exports stood out, though, from the commission's earliest reports through the early 1940s. Syrian exports (sent to both current-day Syrian and Lebanese destinations) exceeded all other export markets with the exception of Bolivia from 1936 to 1939, tapering slightly during 1940–1941 (quite possibly due to rising complexities in transatlantic trade during World War II). It is challenging to trace with more precision the moments and capacities of participation of Arab Argentine individuals and firms in the cultivation of a taste for yerba mate and the set of social practices that accompanies its consumption. To this end, further research, ideally involving oral histories, promises the possibility of nuance to some of these narratives linking mate consumption and migration patterns. Juxtaposing these oral histories with other archival information on the growth of the yerba export industry would likely advance this line of inquiry. In fact, if we look to one such set of family memories from a contemporary Syrian Argentine yerba mate grower in Misiones Province, we can already detect potential connections between his family's mobility practices in the twentieth century and the growth of yerba mate as a desired commodity in the Middle East.

As of 2018, Omar Kassab ran a major yerba mate export business that annually exported thousands of tons of product from his yerbales to Syria. In comparison to the majority of the actors whose histories stitch together the chapters of this book, Kassab is a relative newcomer to Argentina. He arrived in 1986 from Syria, a few years into the presidency of Raúl Alfonsín and the country's return to democracy following the military junta dictatorship (1976–1983). Kassab made his way to Misiones Province, where other members of his family were already living. In a classic example of chain migration, Kassab's father emigrated first, making the trek from the small city of

Yabroud, north of Damascus, to Misiones at some point earlier in the twenti-eth century. Eventually, three of his eight children would follow suit—among them Omar (b.1967), who arrived in Argentina after an older brother came first. In a thirty-minute interview with Canal 12 (a regional public television and radio channel that serves Misiones, Northern Corrientes, and neighboring areas of Brazil and Paraguay), Kassab shared his understanding of how the practice of yerba mate consumption became a habit in his hometown of Yabroud. The image that he renders in this June 2018 interview connects the histories of migrants who moved back and forth between Argentina and the Middle East over the course of the twentieth century, with Kassab's own feelings about the special connection between his Syrian homeland and the Argentine landscape that he makes his home and where he has staked his economic interests.

Kassab recounts that his father first came to Argentina with a friend Miguel and several others from the town of Yabroud. Among these migrants from Yabroud were individuals such as thirty-one-year-old Mohamad Ahmad Kabbour, whom immigration officials recorded as entering Argentina in October 1930. He registered his profession then as an agricultural laborer/farmer (*peón/agricultor*).[15] He may very well be one of the members of the Kabbour family of Yabroud mentioned by Kassab as a known associate of his father in those early years of an incipient mate trade between Misiones and their hometown. Indeed, today, the Kabbour Group company is one of the large yerba mate exporters to Syria.[16] After twenty-five or thirty years, "[several of these individuals] were doing well economically, and they traveled back to Yabroud," he relays to the Canal 12 reporter. It is at this point that Kassab paints a picture of how those visiting family members brought the practice of consuming yerba mate back to Yabroud after decades of living in Argentina:

> They brought mate with them, yerba, so that they could continue drinking it there. [They brought] all of the things that they liked, because they were used to it. They shared it with their family, and people enjoyed it. . . . [When it was time for them to return to Argentina] of course each of those travelers left their mate, their yerba [in Yabroud]. And people started sending requests, letters, saying "please send us some yerba mate", [and they would send these requests] when someone was traveling [from Yabroud] back to Argentina.

In this manner, claims Kassab, yerba mate began to travel back to Syria via informal family and village networks. In the years that followed, "Many people carried yerba in suitcases, on their travels, in parcels, or [sent it] in the mail," he explains. By the early 1970s, Kassab's father and Miguel, now his business partner, must have decided that the taste for yerba mate in the Yabroud District and surrounding Qalamun Mountains region was sufficiently ingrained as to create a potentially profitable trade market. According to Kassab's memory, it was 1972 or 1973 when they sent their first shipping container of mate from Argentina to Syria, destined for eager consumers in Yabroud and its surrounds. The Syrian market was of course already a well-established front for mate exports by 1972. In fact, it had been for a few decades according to the figures published by the national Comisión Reguladora for the national yerba industry. Nevertheless, personal recollections like those of Kassab have the potential to help us contextualize the connections between migrant mobilities and the growth of what Folch has identified as modern financial circuits that have almost entirely evaded the Global North.[17]

When Kassab reflects on his personal trajectory that took him from Yabroud to the town of Comandante Andresito in far northern Misiones Province, he focuses on the aspects of Mesopotamian Argentina that make him feel connected to his home area of Yabroud and the Qalamun Mountains. More than the travel of people and goods that connect these regions through trade and family ties, Kassab expresses ideas of connectedness between these two places that are at once more ephemeral yet perhaps experienced more viscerally. In comparing his home in Comandante Andresito to Yabroud, Kassab states, "Yabroud has the same feel. People follow similar daily rhythms—they sleep the siesta, they drink mate. I like it here . . . the presence of nature, greenery, the yerba, the people."[18] Perhaps the fact that Kassab maintains some of his own rhythms and traditions from Yabroud helps him to feel this way. At the end of his interview with Canal 12, he shares some verses from the Koran that he has displayed in his home and then gives an in-depth cooking demonstration in which he makes an array of typical Levantine dishes—hummus, tabouleh, baba ghanoush, and kibbeh nayeh, a raw minced beef dish. Though it goes unremarked in the interview transcript, other scenes in the footage from Kassab's home include the preparation of a *nargileh* (a traditional water pipe for tobacco) and several shots of Kassab and associates watching Arabic-language news channels. These details subtly reiterate for us the fact that yerba mate as a South-South commodity chain not only connects Argentine and Middle Eastern economies but also encourages the development of cultural spaces—in this case, a Syrian home space created in the northern jungle of Argentine Mesopotamia. It is in spaces like these that Argentina truly becomes part of a Global Middle East.

Frame 2: Contemporary Displacements, Associational Nodes

As we move from this brief examination of yerba mate as a South-South commodity to our next exploration of twenty-first-century Syrian refugee mobilities, it bears mentioning that there is some overlap between these two forms of contemporary entanglement. The future horizons of yerba mate exports to the Middle East to a certain degree map to the massive population shifts wrought by large-scale human displacement within the region. Specifically, this section deals with massive-scale migration within and out of Syria since the March 2011 onset of the civil war. This war has its origins in a series of protests against the Bashar al-Assad government that were met with increasingly violent suppression by government forces and international allies. What began as part of the broader regional Arab Spring pro-democracy uprisings that started in 2010 devolved over the following years into a humanitarian disaster that has shaped large-scale regional mobilities and displacement both inter- and intra-regionally. Five years in, the United Nations High Commissioner for Refugees (UNHCR) identified more than 13 million Syrians in need of humanitarian assistance: some 6 million internally displaced persons and 5 million international refugees.[19] These processes of massive displacement inevitably have an impact on Argentina's twenty-first-century entanglements with Middle Eastern economies, cultural spaces, and migrant circuits. In small ways, it also shifts the panorama of Latin American cultural practices present in the Middle East and North Africa as these practices accompany big groups of moving people. For example, Argentine governmental agencies like the National Food Safety and Quality Service (Servicio Nacional de Sanidad y Calidad Agroalimentaria, SENASA), as well as yerba mate producers like Omar Kassab, are thinking seriously about how the presence of millions of Syrian refugees in Turkey or Egypt might mean that yerba culture might become more widespread in the Arabic-speaking eastern Mediterranean. Conversely, they have worried about the tightening of yerba markets in Syria that has been concomitant with moments of intensified arms conflict.[20] "Right now, we [exporters] follow [these populations on the move], in order to provide them with yerba mate," Kassab stated to a Posadas-based journalist several years into the civil war.[21] In short, contemporary patterns of migration and displacement continue to shape the development of this South-South commodity circuit nearly a century after early, informal circulation of yerba mate in suitcases, letters, and mail parcels. This is not to say that Argentine citizens and agencies simply see this humanitarian disaster in terms of a market opportunity, for this is certainly not the case. Rather, bringing up these connections between, ultimately, the circulation of people and things is yet another reminder of the overlaps that exist between the multiple transregional spheres of mobility that have bound these world areas together since the early years of the mahjar.

Twenty-first-century migration due to the Syrian Civil War has also brought new groups of migrants into contact with earlier generations of the Transamerican mahjar. In the process, new arrivals end up interfacing with mahjar institutions that have long histories of migrant aid and advocacy. This is true in the specific case of Argentina and also characterizes contemporary scenarios of Syrian refugee arrivals in Latin America more broadly. In each case, a combination of federally funded support systems and nongovernmental networks and actors has shaped the experiences of Syrian refugees since 2011. The continued presence and visibility of Middle Eastern heritage communities in receiving countries like Argentina, Brazil, and Chile have put these diasporic communities in the spotlight as potential interlocutors between new migrants, host societies, and governmental bodies. Associational nodes established by early generations of the Latin American mahjar (such as voluntary organizations, beneficence groups, religious institutions, and hometown clubs) have engaged in twenty-first-century advocacy efforts, and in some cases have entered debates on visa and asylum policy. In Argentina, one instance of this type of involvement came from heritage organizations concerned with the parameters of the government legislation aimed at regulating the process of Syrian refugee entry and integration into Argentina after 2011. The Programa Especial de Visado Humanitario para Extranjeros afectados por el conflicto de la República Árabe de Siria (Special Humanitarian Visa Program for Foreigners Affected by the Conflict in the Syrian Arab Republic, Ministerio del Interior, Obras Publicas y Vivienda) was established in 2014 by the Dirección Nacional de Migraciones (DNM) under the umbrella of the Ministry of the Interior, Public Works, and Housing. Known colloquially as Programa Siria, the DNM created this protocol with the following stated objectives: "To facilitate the entry into the Argentine Republic of foreigners impacted by the armed conflict in Syria. [These include] persons of Syrian nationality and their families, or of Palestinian nationality who are habitual residents of Syria and have received assistance from the United Nations Relief

Works Agency for Palestinians in the Near East (UNRWA)."[22] The early itera-tions of Programa Siria—under the second-term administration of Cristina Fernández de Kirchner—included the controversial stipulation that appli-cants had to prove a family tie or meaningful preexisting relationship (*ser fa-miliar o tener un lazo de afinidad*) with an Argentine wishing to sponsor their visa application. Updates to the protocol removed this stipulation, ostensi-bly smoothing the visa process for a wider range of potential applicants. This streamlining process was by no means flawless, but an increase in Syrian refu-gee arrivals did follow in 2017 nonetheless. By March 2014, Argentina's DNM and Comisión Argentina para Refugiados y Migrantes (Argentine Commis-sion for Refugees and Migrants) reported the arrival of 417 Syrian refugees.[23]

In some cases, applicants to the early version of Programa Siria found his-torical mahjar associations to be facilitators in their connection to potential sponsors. In other cases, these voluntary associations served as convergence points for newly arrived migrants. In Buenos Aires, a young woman who went by the pseudonym of Leila reported that her great uncle acted as her sponsor so that she could immigrate to Argentina some two years after the civil war's violence began to rapidly escalate. In this case, her great-uncle's local Arab Ar-gentine heritage organization, Asociación Kalaat Yandal, helped facilitate the process. Founded in the 1930s by the first group of Syrian immigrants hailing from the village of Qal'at Jandal, the association was founded with the aim of creating a space where Syrian immigrants could gather, speak their language, eat typical Syrian food, and keep in contact with others who immigrated to Argentina from their hometown. More than seventy years later, it appears that this heritage association was looking to once again assert that mission. In the lead-up to her departure from Syria, Leila communicated frequently with her great uncle and his family. "I chatted with my great-cousins all the time and they were telling me about their lives in Buenos Aires. . . . I wasn't afraid to come here by myself, as I felt I knew them already, and they were telling me great things about Argentina," she stated after her arrival.[24] Much as we saw earlier in the twentieth century, the response of mahjar voluntary associations in the wake of humanitarian disasters is not confined to major population centers like Buenos Aires. Across the provinces, associations have sought involvement in refugee resettlement and ongoing advocacy, includ-ing the Centro Sirio Libanés de Gualeguaychú (Entre Ríos), Sociedad Sirio Libanesa San Luis, Asociación Sirio Libanesa de Misiones, Colectividad Árabe de Oberá (Misiones), and Sociedad Sirio Libanesa de Santiago del Estero. In

Gualeguaychú, the Centro Sirio Libanés took out an advertisement in local newspapers to solicit the collaboration of other groups interested in resettling refugees. The advertisement, titled "[The Situation in] Syria [elicits pain] in all of us [*Siria nos duele a todos*]," stated:

> Faced with this grave problem, the Center has resolved to take up contact with municipal and ecclesiastical authorities in order to put itself at their disposition, and offer any required collaboration regarding the humanitarian assistance program. [We make this known to] all of the Centro's associates, and to the community in general, that if—because of regions of heritage, friendship, etcetera—you should agree to receive a refugee or refugee family [through the visa program], know that you can count on us at the Centro to support you in any way that we can.[25]

In neighboring Misiones Province, the Posadas-based Asociación Sirio Libanesa de Misiones met with migration officials from the local DNM office to discuss Programa Siria and the Sociedad's role as an interlocutor. After this meeting with authorities, Asociación president Luis Alberto Chemes appeared on a local *Radio Libertad* show to talk about the role of his organization as a facilitator for dialogue about the refugee situation in Syria and the future possibilities of Misiones responding to humanitarian needs at the provincial level. He opened the interview by noting that his organization was founded in 1924, with "one of the objectives in its legal framework being that of the provision of aid toward all immigrants coming from the Arab world." After describing in broad brushstrokes the conflict in Syria, he connected the future prospects of refugees' resettlement in Argentina with the actions of the Arab Argentine heritage community and its organizational bodies:

> In Argentina we have the whole legal framework [Programa Siria] ready to receive refugees. Now we, as an institution that is home to the Arab community (especially Lebanon and Syria), are in dialogue to organize with [DNM authorities] so that when this possible arrival of refugees occurs, we have raised the funds and have everything prepared to be able to provide a home for those who choose to come to this country. But this process doesn't happen overnight. This is a long legal and technical process [that we must undergo to] be able to place refugees throughout the length and breadth of the country, should they come. The provinces of Salta, La Rioja, Catamarca, Santiago del Estero, and Tucumán have the greatest concentration of Syrian descendants in this country, and also

of course Rosario and Buenos Aires. So what are our next steps? Well, we are assessing the legal and material means available to us, making use of the Asociación, and the national [DNM] office.

It is also clear that Chemes viewed his role as association president as one that prepared him to speak directly to the Misiones general public about the polemic of Syrian refugee settlement in local context. By the end of his interview, he took on a reassuring tone, seemingly invested in ensuring his listeners that refugee resettlement would be planned, ordered, and top-down in its organization. At the same time, he called on the moral obligation of the diaspora and articulated the conditions of the civil war as a humanitarian crisis:

> These days we are following the media, going to meetings, and getting ready for when we get [approval to host Syrian migrants]. We are staying alert, and as an organization we receive information—for example [updates on] the situation of migrants in Europe. This is a humanitarian question that no one can escape. We, as an organization, and as descendants [of Arabs], are evaluating our resources so that when [refugees arrive], it will be an ordered process. We have to do it this way, because with the emotions of the public, we can't take any chances—we have to do things well. We are thus prepared to keep dialogues open, and continue organizing—for the benefit of those [migrants] who will come here.[26]

Outside the provincial capital, in the small town of Oberá, more misionero descendants of mahjar migration came to the fore to publicize efforts to interface with Syrians wishing to settle in their province. In this case, representatives from the Colectividad Árabe de Oberá association traveled to Posadas to meet with DNM officials as they prepared to receive a small group of Syrian refugees in 2015. The primary mission of the Colectividad Árabe is cultural diffusion—its main yearly event being the management of the Casa Árabe restaurant and activity space at Oberá's famous Fiesta del Inmigrante. Though a much younger organization than the Posadas-based Asociación Sirio Libanesa de Misiones, the Colectividad Árabe (established 1992) appeared to have some similar goals when it came to the provision of aid and advocacy for twenty-first-century refugees. Colectividad president Alejandro Quesini, much like Luis Chemes in Posadas, went on air for a local radio program to talk about the Colectividad's work with one Syrian woman who hoped to relocate her family to Oberá. Quesini's on-air comments alluded to his organization's interactions with DNM delegates and reiterated their close involvement with the bureaucratic protocols required under Programa Siria: "It's a very bureaucratic protocol, but there is a good outlook toward this immigration, so we're happy to be able to participate in [refugee resettlement], the nature of which is sad, but our idea is to collaborate and do our part." The precipitating event for Quesini's meeting with local DNM delegates was the application of Mabel Maja, who had immigrated from Syria to Argentina in 1971 and now wanted to sponsor the visas of family members under Programa Siria. The Colectividad Árabe association, though not the prospective sponsor of Maja's family, positioned itself as spokesperson to the local press during the process. Quesini assured the local radio host that Maja had completed all of her paperwork and that she and her family members were in constant communication, using digital social networking platforms like Whatsapp to relay photographs of their visa paperwork back and forth. "We are so proud to be the first Arab community in the province to take part in this theme . . . we have everything in order [*todas las patas en la mesa*]: we have the interested party, [Maja,] and for our part as a nonprofit organization [we act as] a nexus [between Maja and] migration authorities . . . , and the Ministry of Human Rights."[27] Though it is sometimes difficult to suss out the precise mechanics of the role that groups like the Colectividad Árabe and Asociación Sirio Libanesa play in the bureaucratic nitty-gritty of individual resettlement cases, it is clear that they often envision themselves as interlocutors and publicly position themselves as such.

In San Luis Province, we see a similar dynamic of a historic heritage association acting as a resource center and interlocutor during the arrival of new Syrian refugees after 2011. When a local artist in San Luis sponsored the visa of "Lana," a young artist from Damascus, the local Sociedad Sirio Libanesa de San Luis hosted festivities to welcome her and her husband, Majd—the province's first two Syrian refugees.[28] "This was a nice gathering, a [chance for a] reunion with their country [Syria]," reported Sociedad member Julio Raba to the local press. "They got together with young people from the community and they also had the chance to get to know the experience of Syrians who arrived in San Luis during the past century," he added. Thus, for at least some members of the Sociedad, the orchestration of these activities was clearly linked to an opportunity to connect mahjar histories to contemporary migrant realities.

A few months prior to Lana and Majd's arrival, a representative from the Sociedad Sirio Libanesa made a statement on the local Canal 13 news regarding the impending arrival of Lana and Majd, as well as plans for subsequent arrivals. They made it clear that they were engaged in concrete preparations for the arrival of refugees who would need services and support:

> We are going to offer them help with everything that they need—as is only right [*como se corresponde*]. There have been offers of lodging, including offers from within our Sociedad. . . . We are going to rent some lodging for [Lana and Majd] for a year, until they are able to integrate. We also have language instructors who are going to collaborate, and we are talking to a local school about [working with children who arrive in the future].[29]

After Lana and Majd's arrival, the Sociedad continued efforts with subsequent families and even provided employment for at least one new arrival.[30] Attention to these basic needs of language instruction, employment, and housing is the same type of support that Arab Argentine heritage organizations across the country provided to new arrivals. In the case of this San Luis organization, it began doing so in 1928 as the Sociedad Sirio Libanesa de Socorros Mutuos. This is not to suggest that there has been an unbroken pattern of aid and advocacy from the early twentieth-century mahjar to the twenty-first century across the board for heritage associations. It is clear, however, that these earlier formations are still meaningful for civic engagement. They also continue to serve as platforms for Argentines with Middle Eastern roots who wish to assert themselves as interlocutors in the broad scope of Argentine–Middle Eastern relations—in this case, represented by the formulation of national, provincial, and local responses to a humanitarian crisis. In San Luis, affiliation with this historic mahjar association also opened pathways for collaboration with the local government on the Corredor Humanitaria project, which provided a legal framework for bringing refugees to San Luis and coordinating support services once they had arrived. Part of the Corredor Humanitaria project involves San Luis citizens who register as member supporters (*adherentes activos*) and signal their willingness to volunteer housing, translation services, language training, child care, and a host of other services as needed.[31]

This concerted leveraging of civic participation from local communities is not unique to the Arab Argentine heritage community of San Luis. We see this pattern elsewhere as well, such as the involvement of members of the Asociación de Libaneses y Sirios de Misiones, who, in conversation with the Syrian embassy, coordinated the generation of a registry of names of local individuals willing to host or provide work for prospective refugees.[32] Similarly,

the Sociedad Sirio Libanesa de Santiago del Estero (founded in 1931) coordinated a registry of citizens willing to open their homes or provide resources
to prospective refugees. Sociedad president Eden Habel Sapag described the
campaign as "in solidarity with the Argentine government" and conceived in
the wake of several Syrian refugees who came to Santiago del Estero in part
because they had family ties to the area.[33] While these examples typify the initiatives of heritage associations in preparation for Syrian Civil War refugees,
there were also plenty of concrete services orchestrated by heritage associations once people arrived. In many cases, historic associational nodes of the
mahjar continued to serve as hubs for refugee socialization, advocacy, and
resource organizing. It is worth noting at this juncture that although an associational node might help to facilitate migration, this does not automatically
mean that nodes play important ongoing roles in the new sociocultural milieus that refugees build once they arrive. For example, "Leila," who migrated
to Buenos Aires in part due to the help of her great uncle's hometown club,
Asociación Kalaat Yandal, later reported that she didn't choose to attend any
events at the organization after her arrival. In contrast, the function of associational nodes in other resettlement cases remained central to the lived social
experience of refugees after they relocated to Argentina.

In Buenos Aires, the Centro Islámico de la República Argentina (CIRA)
made a concerted effort to offer useful ongoing services to Syrian refugees
displaced to Buenos Aires. Spanish-language classes, occupational training,
and legal assistance are among the services that CIRA has offered to Syrian
families displaced to the federal capital. Much as these associational nodes
have functioned since the early twentieth century, CIRA also creates spaces
of sociability by providing services. When a group of refugees from Yabroud
arrived in Buenos Aires a few years after the 2011 escalation of violence, they
found in CIRA a space to come together and share news of their hometown,
mutual acquaintances, family, and so on. "We decided to come to Argentina,
because it was the only door open to us," related Hussam Deen Hamdan to
La Nación in 2015. "From the first day [of being here] and onward, I think
about Syria. We have relatives, my husband's whole family is there, and we are
always worried, but what can we do?" added Hamdan's wife, Susana Cristina
Hassoun. For this couple, Argentina's open door was made all the more accessible due to the fact that Hassoun was born in Argentina and lived there
until the age of three before moving with her family to Yabroud. Half a century later, Hassoun found herself living in the same house on Avenida San

Juan where she spent her early childhood—but this time with her own family. Argentina was not their destination of choice—first they were displaced to Lebanon, where they unsuccessfully sought visas for relocation to other Middle Eastern countries. "I even miss the rocks in the streets [of Yabroud]," lamented Hamdan. "I have visited lots of countries, but I've always had the intention of returning home. It was always so easy: you bought a ticket and you went back. But now it's very difficult to return to Syria; it's very dangerous. Two of my brothers were kidnapped; I was next." Other Yabroud families displaced to Buenos Aires include Emaad Al-Kassab and his daughter, Walaa, who decided to flee after Walaa nearly boarded a public bus that was later hijacked. Expressing a similar concern for her daughter's safety, twenty-nine-year-old Khawla Saibaa described her fear for the well-being of her toddler daughter, Lamar: "People just aren't used to this. . . . There is no flour, no chicken, no rice, no water. There is shelling. I can manage to withstand these things, as an adult, but my daughter can't."[34]

These are but a few examples of the pattern of emotional trauma and threat of physical violence that accompanies the act of departure for many, if not all, post-2011 Syrian refugees in Argentina. These difficult circumstances only add to the challenges of building new lives (or lives-in-waiting for those who hope to return home eventually) on Argentine soil. For Hassoun, Hamdan, and the El-Kassab and Saibaa families, the CIRA represented a place where they could spend time with other families from Yabroud. Twice-weekly Spanish classes thus became part language-learning sessions and part information-sharing opportunities. We can imagine that similar scenarios have played out in other places where associational nodes create these sociocultural spaces.

The provision of language courses and occupational training for Syrian refugees was by no means unique to Argentine mahjar organizations in the wake of 2011, but rather part of a hemispheric trend. In Chile, Club Sirio Unido (established 1928) and the Sociedad de Beneficencia Siria (established 1913) collaborated to provide loans, Spanish classes, free legal assistance, and organized social activities for some forty Syrian refugees as of 2018.[35] In Brazil, some more recently founded organizations such as the Liga da Juventude Islâmica Beneficente do Brasil and the Do Pari mosque of São Paulo (established 1995) offered language classes and provided services to aid new arrivals in the navigation of Brazilian bureaucratic systems.[36] In Paraguay, the Asociación Líbano Siria de Socorros Mutuos of Encarnación (established 1926) collected funds to rent a house and provide basic services for a Syrian family of seven.[37] Where mahjar heritage communities elsewhere in the hemisphere have not necessarily organized at an institutional level, many still engage in other forms of advocacy. For example, in Mexico City, some five hundred Mexicans of Arab heritage participated in a September 2015 protest outside the Secretariat of Foreign Affairs, in which they called on their government to expedite policy initiatives that would provide asylum for Syrian refugees.[38]

In light of these examples, we gain some perspective on mahjar heritage community and associational node advocacy in Argentina as part of a wider regional pattern of sustained South-South connections between historic communities and new refugee mobilities. It is, of course, easier to track these instances of visible solidarity than it is to document private discord and quiet abstention among potential diasporic interlocutor groups—indeed, ongoing ethnographic research needs to be done about the reception (or lack thereof) of displaced Syrian refugees who find themselves in Latin America amid historic mahjar populations with ties to similar geographies. We will doubtless find this to be a varied social-political terrain.

In Argentina, we can see how these connections also have the potential to become recognized by state agencies that hold the power to drive new refugee and migration policy. In the years following the initial promulgation of Programa Siria, for example, the DNM openly acknowledged that the legal framework was an evolving bureaucratic arrangement. The agency recognized that various interlocutors had involvement in the evolutionary process of the program and specifically noted that "in the implementation of Programa Siria, different organizations within the Syrian-Lebanese community have collaborated, [including] the Centro Cultural Islámico de Argentina, the Confederación de Entidades Argentino-Árabes (FEARAB), and the Administrative Council of the Orthodox Church of San Jorge."[39] In other words, partially responsible for the evolution of Programa Siria are diasporic voices that have helped to shape national dialogues about the future of refugee resettlement in Argentina. Outside the central offices of the DNM in Buenos Aires, provincial migration officials (*Delegados de Migraciones*) often end up being the ones to liaise with local heritage communities and their institutions. In Misiones, DNM delegate Daniel Domínguez of Posadas appeared on the local news alongside Asociación Sirio Libanesa de Misiones president Luis Alberto Chemes to brief the public on the current state of Programa Siria in relation to the provincial Misiones context. In this press conference, he announced that the DNM and the Asociación Sirio Libanesa were committed to the following form of collaboration:

> [We are] exchanging positions, updates, news, [and addressing] the total reach and advances of Programa Siria . . . and law no.126.165 on refugees by Co.Na. Re. [Comisión Nacional de Refugiados]. . . . The message here is perfectly clear: the Misiones DNM delegate and the Asociación Sirio Libanesa (as represented by its president) stand together before this international predicament whose ripples we are beginning to feel in this country. . . . We are preparing ourselves to receive future refugees in the best manner possible. . . . We [the DNM] are on the legal side of things, to ensure that the process is coherent, timely, and effective, and the Asociación Sirio Libanesa play a role in the realm of psycho-emotional support. We mustn't forget that . . . many of these migrations are forced—individuals end up escaping a situation of vulnerability, and they need not only the kind of aid that this country has historically provided . . . but rather they also need emotional support. For this reason it was very opportune that we were able to have this discussion with [Luis Alberto] Chemes today.[40]

Perhaps one motivation for officials like Domínguez to work openly with heritage communities is that these citizen groups can leverage resources and support that may not necessarily be within the reach of a state agency. In observing the state of refugee resettlement in Argentina, UNHCR officials have pointed out the challenges that refugees face once they successfully navigate Argentine visa requirements. Officials from the Buenos Aires UNHCR legal office have noted that in contrast to relatively accessible health care and education, employment and housing remain uncertain prospects for many refugees in Argentina.[41] Provision of housing and employment possibilities is precisely the sort of services that many mahjar heritage communities have sought to address since 2011—with more or less concrete actions depending on the local situation.

An examination of policies such as Programa Siria can also give us a window into some of the ways in which Argentina has entered twenty-first-century global dialogues and initiatives related to migration, displacement, and international responses to humanitarian crises. This has the potential to help us understand possible futures of South-South connections, of new ways in which Argentina might link to the Middle East via the circulation of people, things, and ideas. In conjunction with the steps that the Argentine government took to establish and then evolve Programa Siria since 2011, they also formed ties to intergovernmental organizations such as the International Organization for Migration (IOM), the UNHCR, and the Global Refugee Sponsorship Initiative. Since May 2017, Argentina has been a participant in the joint IOM-UNHCR Emerging Resettlement Countries Joint Support Mechanism (ERCM). This program's main goals are (1) providing a mechanism for governments to access financial and expertise resources to support refugee resettlement, (2) assisting emerging resettlement countries in assessing the sustainability of their program and identifying vulnerable areas in their policy, and (3) channeling technical expertise and good practices from experienced resettlement countries, international organizations, and nongovernmental organizations to emerging resettlement countries.[42]

A 2018 ERCM-funded summit on refugee resettlement that took place in Buenos Aires identified community involvement as a priority area in their list of challenges for expanding Programa Siria's capacity for placement and resettlement. At this same summit, DNM's director of social issues, Federico Agusti, emphasized the importance of partnership with community groups (such as mahjar heritage organizations) when he stated to attendees, "Programa Siria is a blueprint for resettlement that is based in public-private cooperation via an alliance between civil society and the incorporation of various actors in order to assemble a network of support for migrant and refugee families." Echoing this sentiment, UNHCR's deputy, Kylie Alcoba Wright, emphasized that one of the greatest strengths of Programa Siria is its "articulation generated between national and provincial authorities, and with other actors from civil society."[43] In the case of another organization, the Canada-based Global Refugee Sponsorship Initiative (established 2016), the Argentine government received technical advice and resources for the planned formalization of Community Refugee Sponsorship across several provinces, with examples like the San Luis Corredor Humanitaria project as models.[44] Meetings about prospective provincial programs in Mendoza and Salta took place in August 2018 and brought together local, federal, and UNHCR, ERCM, and IOM officials with local groups and institutions invested in sponsoring refugee resettlement.[45] These types of provincial initiatives have already presented opportunities for local mahjar heritage community involvement and suggest the potential for ongoing, or even expanding, avenues of participation and collaboration between communities of diasporic interlocutors, the Argentine government, and intergovernmental organizations. We would do well to further investigate the ongoing ways in which, as Jessica Stites Mor and Paul

Silverstein have noted, "worlds not left behind" shape the "reverberations of conflict in the Middle East within communities in Latin America and vice versa."[46]

Frame 3: Contemporary South-South Cultural Spaces

South-South spaces of artistic and cultural production serve as our final frame for examining the enduring ties between Argentina and the Middle East. Contemporary projects by artists are strong attestation to the continued existence of a transnational public sphere that connects Middle Eastern and Latin American cultural production. Furthermore, the transregional cultural spaces that come out of artistic collaborations remind us that South-South movement of people, things, and ideas continues to result in productive, generative links among these world regions—beyond the realms of economic exchange or response to humanitarian crises. This is, in and of itself, a compelling reason to study contemporary South-South cultural connections in historical perspective. In short, the idea of a connection between Argentina (or Latin America) and a broader Arab world remains meaningful to many Argentines. Thus, the transnational public sphere that first flourished in the context of peak mahjar migration and the subsequent formulation of international networks at the beginning of the late nineteenth century continues to evolve. The cast of characters that engages in the debates, artistic innovation, or philanthropic advocacy constitutive of this transnational public sphere has continuously shifted over time. They range from early twentieth-century traveling comedians and opera singers, to 1960s student movements interested in Third World connections to Asian and African counterparts, to twenty-first-century cinematographers in transregional conversation with colleagues. Consistently across these diverse examples, the circulation that this transnational public sphere continues to engender represents the fundamental dynamic of constant movement and exchange between these world regions rather than an intrinsic boundedness. To illustrate one manifestation of the contemporary transnational public sphere at work, we now turn to filmmakers and the South-South cultural space that cinema has the ability to create.

Beginning in 2007, the Cine Fértil film collective began organizing an ongoing series of events in hopes of opening spaces for South-South encounters: artistic, cultural, and intellectual. Their work resulted in a series of film festivals coupled with conferences and roundtables that started in December 2011 with the inaugural Festival Latinoamericano de Cine Árabe. Since then, the activities have progressively gained steam, drawing large international audiences to subsequent LatinArab festivals and garnering governmental and private support from across the globe. By 2013, LatinArab reached an audience of some thirteen thousand spectators, and what began as a gathering based in Buenos Aires has been transformed into a traveling festival. After launching in the capital, the group went on to tour several provinces with LatinArab Gira, a special traveling version of the festival . Sites visited included Córdoba (yearly from 2010 to 2015), Rosario (2015, 2016, 2018), La Rioja (2014), as well as San Miguel de Tucumán, Catamarca, and San Juan (all in 2015). Elsewhere on the continent, they visited São Paulo and Rio de Janeiro (both in 2014), as well as Barranquilla, Colombia (2016). In the Middle East and North Africa they have presented LatinArab Gira and participated as invited presenters at several international film festivals. Sites include Amman, Jordan; Marrakech, Morocco (2013); and Tunisia's capital (2018). "We do these tours because the project isn't 'BuenosAiresArab'—it is 'LatinArab'. It has a regional, rather a bi-regional, dimension," stated LatinArab cofounder Christian Mouroux in 2018.[47]

International recognition of their work reached a new peak in July 2018, when the group accepted an award from UNESCO in honor of its contribution to the promotion of diverse Arab cultures.[48] A selection of contemporary Middle Eastern and North African cinema alongside panels, workshops, keynote talks, and seminars comprise each edition of LatinArab. In conjunction with LatinArab, cofounders Edgardo Bechara El Khoury and Mouroux established the Observatorio LatinÁrab working group, defined as "a relational South-South academic space for the production, review, and diffusion of research, projects, and reports—qualitative as well as quantitative—on the cultural flows and exchanges between the Arab World and Latin America."[49]

Observatorio LatinÁrab links the need for these spaces of South-South artistic and cultural exchange to other arenas of twenty-first-century South-South ties. These include the four Summits of South American Arab Countries (ASPA) that took place in Brazil, Qatar, Peru, and Saudi Arabia between 2005 and 2015. These biregional forums convened heads of state from Arab League and South American nations to address economic, cultural, environmental, science and technology, and social issues.[50] Partially in response to this type of formal biregional meeting, Observatorio LatinÁrabe's mission encourages the amplification of other forms of organized interaction between Latin America and the Middle East/North Africa regions: "We believe in a vast universe of possible cooperations and cultural exchanges with the Arab World that are based in the growing linkages between the diverse countries of these two communities of nations."[51] The relationship between this stated mission and the belief that contemporary Latin American–Arab relations is embedded in a history of migratory networks is also clear. In this regard, they note the "historic presence of Arab communities in the processes of formation and constitution of many of the countries in Latin America." Their mission statement goes on to directly connect the idea of migratory histories and contemporary international relations: "As such, [historic] Arab cultural contributions to America have been one of the principal mechanisms for establishing current ties that promise to become even tighter between these regions." Specifically, they reference the "large migration of Lebanese and Syrians at the end of the 19th century" as an important antecedent that, in their view, set the stage for contemporary transregional relations. Thus, a cognizant referencing of the mahjar and previous iterations of South-South encounters undergirds the Observatorio's formal objectives.[52]

As part of its mission, Observatorio LatinÁrab works in conjunction with the organization's film festival to organize "conference series, seminars, and [graduate-level university] courses" on Latin American–Arab biregional relations, Arab culture and art, and film studies. A 2017 mini-conference hosted as part of the Seventh LatinArab Festival illustrates how these activities can reinforce the notion of connectivity between historical and contemporary Latin American–Arab encounters. A half-day gathering, From Algiers to Buenos Aires, featured a discussion of the collaborations between Global South filmmakers that preceded the foundation of LatinArab by nearly a half-century. Between December 1973 and May 1974, a series of meetings took place in Algiers, Buenos Aires, and Montreal with the goal of consolidating the Third World Cinema Committee. In attendance were filmmakers from across Latin America, Asia, and Africa who were interested in discussing the role of cinema in the construction of anti-imperial, Third World solidarities. The first meeting, held in Algiers in December 1973, followed on the heels of the September 1973 Fourth Summit of the NAM hosted in the same city. Some forty-five filmmakers attended the meeting, most hailing from South American and African nations that included Argentina, Bolivia, Brazil, Cuba, Chile, Colombia, and Uruguay on the Latin American side, alongside African representatives from Egypt, Guinea, Guinea-Bissau, Congo, Mali, Morocco, Mauritania, and Senegal.[53] Notable Middle Eastern representatives also hailed from Palestine and Syria, including the director of Syria's National Film Organization, Hamid Merei, who served as one of the organizing members of the Third World Cinema Committee.[54] Argentina's representative at the Algiers meeting was Jorge Giannoni, a film director whose work has been inspired by his travels through Palestine in the late 1960s. In Algiers, Giannoni helped to facilitate dialogue about forms of co-production between Third World filmmakers that would obviate the dependence on US and European funders, and thus foster the creation of a South-South transnational film market.[55]

Following the 1973 Algiers meeting, a smaller group convened at the Universidad de Buenos Aires (UBA) in May 1974. They met at the Instituto del Tercer Mundo Manuel Ugarte, a short-lived intellectual project that formed in August 1973 but was essentially disbanded by the end of 1974 after the death of Perón. During its brief existence, the institute managed the Third World Cinematheque within the UBA's archives. Overall, the institute dedicated itself to the study of and academic exchange with countries in Africa, Asia, and Latin America by sponsoring research, coordinating study-abroad opportunities, and inviting visiting international scholars.[56] Mor points out that the institute functioned as the "official vessel of the Third World Cinema movement in Argentina [a movement that] situated the struggle of filmmakers against the forces of imperialism within a frame of solidarity with the universal underclass's revolutionary impulses. It held regular film series, presenting films from the Third World to the largely university audience."[57]

In the years following the brief florescence of these South-South sociointellectual efforts under the auspices of institutions like the UBA, public state-sanctioned space for these types of Third Worldist synergies became deeply restrictive during Argentina's military dictatorship from 1976 to 1983. The resilience and continued exchanges between Argentine and Middle Eastern actors through this period is a topic that merits a study of its own. Regardless of the setbacks that Argentines like those involved in the institute and the Third World Film Committee faced in subsequent decades of military repression aimed in part at those who envisioned common emancipation horizons with other regions of the Global South, it is clear that the legacy of those imaginaries persists today in contemporary projects of South-South solidarity such as LatinArab. In this vein, the 2017 Argel a Buenos Aires conference hosted by LatinArab at its film festival focused discussion on the central themes of the 1974 Buenos Aires meeting: the contribution of cinema to processes of national liberation, the decolonization of screens of the Third World, and the

struggle against "cultural alienation." Panelists, including Saad Chedid, former director of the Instituto del Tercer Mundo, addressed the ways in which
these themes remain pertinent to contemporary Latin American realities "in
a world that is ever more alienated by capitalist praxis and imperialist discourse."[58] If we think more broadly about the lines of connection between
cultural-intellectual projects like LatinArab and Third World cinema movements a half-century earlier, we once again return to the role of travel and
mobility that lies at the center of both of these projects.

In both the case of Cine Fértil's various LatinArab endeavors and efforts
in the 1970s to build models of South-South coproduction through a Third
Worldist approach, the projects took shape as their organizers actively moved
about among Global South geographies. The practice of travel allowed Third
World Cinema Committee members like Jorge Giannoni to formulate vantage
points on the connection between the lived experiences of imperialism and
oppression. As committee members traveled from Algeria to Buenos Aires to
Montreal in 1973 and 1974, this meeting-in-motion provided them a mobile
venue in which to consider the ways in which shared experiences of imperialism and marginalization had the power to collapse vast geocultural distances
from Africa, to Asia, to Latin America. The development of Cine Fértil's projects happened through the act of building a network of funders, collaborators,
and audiences across multiple continents visited over the course of several
years. El Khoury reflects on the early years of underground film showings that
eventually led up to the creation of LatinArab:

> First, we started with university showings, but we knew that we wanted to do
> something bigger. We began to get to know the ropes of how to secure institu-
> tional support in Argentina. Traveling to a film festival in Abu Dhabi in 2010
> [helped crystallize our plan regarding] our project, and we were able to secure
> support afterward from INCAA [the Argentine National Institute for Film and
> Audiovisual Arts].[59]

The practice of traveling also makes logistical sense for the continued growth
of Cine Fértil and LatinArab projects. "We go on tour with our festivals in
order to generate a South American network, and generate synergies between
institutions and artists," explained El Khoury. "And practically speaking,
there is a public interested in seeing Arab cinema beyond just those in Buenos
Aires. And there are potential collaborators that we can only meet by going
out into the 'field' to physically meet them," added Mouroux.[60]

These interrelated processes of travel and cultural-intellectual production are not altogether dissimilar from patterns that we identified earlier in the activities of diasporic artists who moved between mashriq, maghreb, and mahjar in the early decades of the twentieth century. We can recall the extensive tours of the Oriente Film crew, who circulated among South American mahjar landscapes in the 1920s, 1930s, and 1940s. Similarly, these patterns might remind us of the careful cultivation of connections with communities of artists and performers in hubs like Cairo and Beirut that helped to shape the careers of individuals like opera singer Selim Zeitun and comedian Gibran Trabulsi. The work of the 1974 Third World Film Committee, and the productions of Cine Fértil, are of course different in some key ways from the activities of Oriente Film or the theatrical events orchestrated by Trabulsi. Principally, work done by Cine Fértil or Third World filmmakers differs from these earlier examples in that it was not envisioned and executed by strictly diasporic actors—even though notable figures like El Khoury and Chedid are both of Middle Eastern heritage. "We are not 'of the colectividad', but . . . as we went along, we learned that what we were doing wasn't new. There was [Syrian journalist] Américo Yunes, who traveled to the [interior] to bring projections of Arab films in the 1950s at venues like Cine Atalaya; there was the Oriente Film crew even earlier," explained El Khoury. "Even if we weren't always conscious of all of these historical flows, we feel that if they hadn't existed as a context in which we ourselves were in formation, then I think that our project wouldn't have turned out the same" interjected Mouroux. "We're not creating anything new [by creating bridges between Latin America and the Middle East]," concluded El Khoury. "When you put it in this perspective, everything [our work] becomes a little easier."[61]

It is necessary that we group these contemporary and historical examples together into a cohesive discussion of the broader panorama of bridging imaginaries that have entangled Latin America and the Middle East for more than a century. Conceptualizing Argentina and its relation to the idea of a Global Middle East is not simply a question of elucidating histories of migration; rather, it requires a critical examination of the ways that those historical migratory links mapped to other currents of South-South circulation of people, things, and ideas over time. It also requires a rigorous assessment of how this migratory lens can help to frame contemporary South-South relations across a broad spectrum of scenarios—from commodity circuits, to migration policy, to cultural production. Conceptualizing these South-South projects as the products of sustained mobilities helps lead us to new ways of framing their resulting cultural productions, markets, or migration pathways as grounded in this movement rather than in a particularity of space-time-place.

The three frames presented in this chapter are in no way an exhaustive study of contemporary commodities, human displacement, and cultural spaces that entangle Argentina in an imaginary of a Global Middle East. These windows into the historical roots of contemporary people, things, and ideas in motion are just the beginning of much more work to be done. Nonetheless, from these brief examples—yerba mate trade, refugee resettlement, and transnational artistic networks—we can see in sharp relief the ways in which Argentina's past and present entanglements with the Arabic-speaking eastern Mediterranean come to bear in an array of twenty-first-century arenas. This is the promise of applying a transregional, migratory lens to our vision of Argentina as embedded in the histories and social processes of a wider Global South community. Moving forward, it is vital that we intentionally interrogate the links between migratory contexts and those areas of South-South relations that we are only recently beginning to better apprehend as key theaters of Global South relations. As Mor notes, economists acknowledge that we have a nebulous grasp of how Latin America and the Middle East interact—and this despite an estimated $40.6 billion in annual trade, positioning the Middle East as a major player in regional economies.[62] Scholars of biregional trade relations have gone so far as to posit the potential for new monetary orders that could arise from South-South trade networks. "This is not your grandmother's Third Worldism," warn economists Omar Dahi and Alejandro Velasco. We are at a critical moment in which "South-South ties, including South-South trade agreements, [emanate] from multinational corporations interested in South-South economic liberalization to solidify global commodity supply chains." South-South tariffs, point out Dahi and Velasco, represent one of the last remaining obstacles for universal free trade in a world of crumbling North-North and North-South tariff barriers. These barriers present obstacles not only to production processes but also to multinational corporations that wish to use Global South countries as launching pads for export.[63] As South-South economic futures appear to be hinging on the generation of new agreements and organizations such as the Federation of Arab–South American Chambers of Commerce and the Consejo Para las Relaciones Entre el Mundo Árabe y América

Latina y el Caribe, we would do well to analyze these new formations in the context of longer historical processes of migration and exchange.

Moving forward, historians of the mahjar would do well to consider the ways in which twenty-first-century conflicts have had the power to reshape diasporic identities and the rearticulation of imagined diasporic communities in distinct local contexts. This may very well serve to help us rethink key moments of similar rearticulation at past historical junctures of war, mass displacement, or humanitarian crisis since the late nineteenth-century migration boom. Recent interdisciplinary collaborations of political scientists, economists, and anthropologists have laid bare the ways in which diasporic pasts come to bear on contemporary constructions of identity in particular ways in the wake of events such as the Syrian Civil War. Cecilia Baeza and Paulo Pinto point out that "the transformation of the internal dynamics of the Syrian-Lebanese communities in Argentina and Brazil through their mobilization around the Syrian conflict illustrates how diasporic communities are defined by their ability to endure through a process of reinvention over generations." More research is needed to elucidate the ways in which these reinventions both link diaspora communities across space and depend on the "mobilization of material or symbolic links to homelands that are invested with moral dimensions."[64]

Concerted interdisciplinary collaborations will be necessary as we move toward this better, tandem understanding of diasporic histories and futures. As we increase collective production of knowledge that transcends institutions and disciplines—and, necessarily, geographic space—we move closer to an intellectual process with more commonalities to the very nature of migration processes that, by definition, routinely transcend boundaries and borders. Even within the much smaller tent of Latin American historiography, scholars of the mahjar will do well to engage in new ways with adjacent subfields beyond the typical interface with intellectual or urban history and seek out dialogue with other bodies of work such as the history of memory or spatial histories. How, for example, might conceptualizations of memory production in postdictatorship Latin American contexts help us to recast our theorization of diasporic identity transformations in the wake of highly visible violence, trauma, and acts of state terror? Looking back at past mobilizations of diasporic communities, such as Chapter 5's examination of the Suez Canal contest, we might begin to think of these diasporic mobilizations and reformations in the interpretative framework of memory studies scholarship, such as Steve Stern's concept of memory knots on the collective body—that is, "the specific human groups and leaders, specific events and anniversary commemoration dates, and specific physical remains or places that [demand] attention to memory."[65] These new lines of analysis hold the promise of better integrating past-within-present realities and experiences not only for diasporic actors and groups, but for the larger communities, institutions, and nations in which they reside and participate. They may also lead us toward a fuller grasp of the emergent ties between homeland and host societies and governments—ties that develop in part fueled by diasporic interlocutors but grow to encompass larger sectors of societies, as we saw in this study. Just as the act of migration and border crossing has historically challenged, and simultaneously constituted, geographic boundaries and conceptualizations of space, so too might these disciplinary and methodological border crossings breed new horizons for understanding the worlds that migrants make.

Epilogue
Somos Sur

We don't need to create bridges between Latin America and the Middle East. The bridges already exist—we just need to mobilize them.

Edgardo Bechara El Khoury

In a recent essay, migration historian Barbara Lüthi called for scholars to "direct critical attention to the increasing prominence of migrations as key figures for apprehending culture and society in the present, not least by understanding the contours and shifts, continuities and disjunctures of migration policies and experiences in the past."[1] This speaks directly to the stakes of reexamining the South-South entanglements of the geographies explored in this book. Enlarging our scope of Middle Eastern–Latin American ties grows ever more critical of a task in an age of increasingly mainstream anti-immigrant reactionism, Islamophobia, and intensification of border regimes and other politics of human mobility government. We face politically motivated discourses that myopically—and almost always erroneously—link Latin America and the "Arab World" through their relationship to the threat of terrorist violence. The equation of Latin American–Arab migratory networks with the building up of transnational subversive activity has been an alarmist framework for generating fear for several decades, and has gained steam over the past decade.

Claims by US President Donald Trump in 2018 that Middle Eastern immigrants had likely "infiltrated" a "caravan" of Central American migrants headed for the US-Mexico border elicited public outcry due to their lack of evidence as well as racist underpinnings.[2] While perhaps vocalized more sensationally by the late 2010s as part of the context of the rightward shift that

Note: *Somos* sur translates as "We are the South."

characterized many international leaderships around that time, these types of claims follow a longer genealogy. Some two decades earlier, at the turn of the twenty-first century, there was a flurry of reportage on suspected terrorist links with the *Triple Frontera* region of Argentina, Paraguay, and Brazil. Subsequent academic studies refuted the legitimacy of these claims, but the specter of terrorists at the Triple Frontera nevertheless still occasionally appears in news reports. Widely consumed popular culture (such as network television crime series) does its part to resuscitate fears and misconceptions of Latin American–Middle East ties.[3] Border anxieties that guide migration policy in the Global North feed on the sensationalist equation of mass migration in the Middle East as a recent phenomenon, when in reality the region has been forged by centuries of cyclical population shifts in the form of regional circulations, and international out-migration.[4]

In this light, it is critical that we acknowledge and explore the direct relationship between current discourses or media renderings of global migration processes and South-South relations as related to historical subjects like those who appear in this book. If we can begin to see South-South relations now as part of longer historical processes, we can start to normalize their existence in ways that eventually have a chance at making their way into discourses outside academe. This is, of course, the fundamental role that historians play much more generally (not just in offering possibilities for new imaginaries of South-South relations—in particular, those related to migration systems). The hope of driving public conversation in more informed directions is by no means the only fruit born of studying ties between Latin America and the Middle East. And we certainly cannot let the desire to take on uninformed renderings of South-South relations and migrants be the sole (or even principal) force driving the formation of our research plans and subsequent writing and analysis. As others have pointed out, history (and historiography) cannot simply function in the service of politics. But at the same time, history is not just the "Other of politics." Historical thinking is a necessary step toward intervening in uninformed fixations on migrants as Others.[5] As we witness a continuing expansion of what one historian has called "epistemic communities dealing with migration issues" (academics, nongovernmental institutions, border enforcement apparatuses, and others), we have to be especially attuned to the role of academic knowledge production about migrants, migration, and other forms of connection that often represent the legacies of migratory pasts.[6] This is even more urgent if we consider the often destructive outcomes of policies that dubiously claim to simultaneously take into account both security and humanitarian concerns. Even if this is not the end goal of migration scholarship (historiography or otherwise), this knowledge can indeed end up shaping regimes of mobility (what one philosopher has recently deemed "kinopolitics") in concrete ways.[7]

In this light, we can see the stakes of new migration histories as perhaps higher than we necessarily tend to acknowledge in our classrooms, conferences, or collaborations. At this moment in which mainstream media, politicians, and other interest groups assert the increased urgency of managing migration and displacement, especially in regard to the Global South (and, even more so, the Arabic-speaking eastern Mediterranean region within that), it is important that migration histories serve as a reminder that this urgency is not often accompanied by nuanced perspective. The challenge is this: to not merely offer up a nuanced perspective but to fight for it as a form of resistance against simpler narratives characterized by erasure. By whatever means necessary—through, for example, scholarship, new forms of artistic coproduction, or pedagogy—the challenge now is to find ways to repeatedly assert that for more than a century, migration, cooperation, and exchange have been the norm between the American hemisphere and the Arab World. Through these efforts, we can have some hope of coming to understand the Americas as *part of,* rather than witness to, the movements of people, things, and ideas that have constituted both the historical processes and contemporary realities of the Middle East.

Notes

Introduction

1. Scholarship in this vein, which gained currency in the 1990s and came to be known as the "transnational turn," fundamentally shifted the way that scholars began to understand and articulate the dynamics of global migration and migrant communities. See Nina Glick Schiller, Linda Basch, and Cristina Blanc-Szanton, "Transnationalism: A New Analytic Framework for Understanding Migration," *Annals of the New York Academy of Sciences* 645 (1992).

2. Other scholars have also considered the utility of framing transnational ties as a subset of a broader spectrum of relationships. See, for example, Lynn Stephen. *Transborder Lives: Indigenous Oaxacans in Mexico, California, and Oregon* (Durham, NC: Duke University Press, 2007). Others hone their focus on instances of "translocalism" or the creation of specific "transcultural" spaces by migrant actors and their descendants. For examples and definitions, see Dirk Hoerder, "Translocalism" in *The Encyclopedia of Global Human Migration* (February 2013), https://onlinelibrary.wiley.com/doi/abs/10.1002/9781444351071.wbeghm540.

3. This perspective has increasingly characterized migration studies scholarship across several disciplines. Illustrative examples include Eiichiro Azuma, *Between Two Empires: Race, History, and Transnationalism in Japanese America* (New York: Oxford University Press, 2005); Nina Glick Schiller and Georges Eugene Fouron, *Georges Woke Up Laughing: Long-Distance Nationalism and the Search for Home* (Durham, NC: Duke University Press, 2001); Molly Todd, *Beyond Displacement: Campesinos, Refugees, and Collective Action in the Salvadoran Civil War* (Madison: University of Wisconsin Press, 2010). Newer works hinge on attention to the interplay between spatial and migration history, gendered experiences of migration, and the formulation of

shared anti-imperialist imaginaries in the Global South. For examples of recent works that address these themes, see Michael Goebel, *Anti-Imperial Metropolis: Interwar Paris and the Seeds of Third World Nationalism* (Cambridge: Cambridge University Press, 2015); Robeson Taj Frazier, *The East Is Black: Cold War China in the Black Radical Imagination* (Durham, NC: Duke University Press, 2014); Anne Garland Mahler, *From the Tricontinental to the Global South: Race, Radicalism, and Transnational Solidarity* (Durham, NC: Duke University Press, 2018); Sandra McGee Deutsch, *Crossing Borders, Claiming a Nation: A History of Argentine Jewish Women, 1880–1955* (Durham, NC: Duke University Press, 2010); Fredy González, *Paisanos Chinos: Transpacific Politics among Chinese Immigrants in Mexico* (Berkeley: University of California Press, 2017), For an overview of the evolution in migration studies historiography in recent decades, see Barbara Lüthi, "Migration and Migration History" *Docupedia-Zeitgeschichte* (June 2018), http://docupedia.de/zg/Luethi_migration_v2_en_2018.

4. On the idea of the transnational public sphere and meaning making in the mahjar, see Reem Bailony, "Transnationalism and the Syrian Migrant Public: The Case of the 1925 Syrian Revolt, *Mashriq and Mahjar: Journal of Middle East and North African Migration Studies* 1:1 (Spring 2013): 8–29; Lauren Banko, *The Invention of Palestinian Citizenship, 1918–1947* (Edinburgh: Edinburgh University Press, 2016); Stacy D. Fahrenthold, *Between the Ottomans and the Entente: The First World War in the Syrian and Lebanese Diaspora, 1908–1925* (New York: Oxford University Press, 2019).

5. The advent of postcolonial theory acted as a polestar for challenges to the construction of categories and meanings previously assigned to the globe's geographic subregions. Over the last two decades of the twentieth century, other areas of increased academic interest also helped to chip away at these delimitations; these fields included world/global history and historians of oceanic realms. For a brief discussion of the evolving relationship between postcolonial and migration historiography, see Andrew Arsan, John Karam, and Akram Khater, "On Forgotten Shores: Migration in Middle East Studies and the Middle East in Migration Studies," *Mashriq and Mahjar: Journal of Middle East and North African Migration Studies* 1:1 (2015).

6. Scholars have brought much-needed critical perspective to the term *Middle East*, which arose amid particular geopolitical conditions. The actual spatial parameters of this region, however, have been less thoroughly interrogated. See Michael Bonine, Abbas Amanat, and Michael Ezekiel Gasper, eds., *Is There a Middle East? The Evolution of a Geopolitical Concept* (Stanford, CA: Stanford University Press, 2012); Thomas Scheffler, "'Fertile Crescent,' 'Orient,' 'Middle East': The Changing Mental Maps of Southwest Asia," *European Review of History* 10 (1993): 253–272. Recently, some scholars have begun to more fully integrate histories of large-scale migration and displacement into our understanding of geopolitical formations in the modern Middle East. See, for example, Benjamin Thomas White, "Refugees and the Definition of Syria, 1920–1939," *Past and Present* 235:1 (2017): 141–178.

7. For further discussion on redrawing the boundaries of area studies via mahjar histories, see John Tofik Karam, "I, Too, Am the Americas: Arabs in the Redrawing of Area and Ethnic Studies," *Journal of American Ethnic History* 37:3 (2018): 94.

8. For earlier examples, see James Clifford, "Diasporas," *Cultural Anthropology* 9 (1994: 302–338), and Donna R. Gabaccia, *Italy's Many Diasporas* (New York: Routledge, 2000). For later application of diasporic theoretical approach to Middle East studies, see Paul Silverstein, "Anthropologies of Middle Eastern Diasporas," in Soraya Altorki, ed., *A Companion to the Anthropology of the Middle East* (Hoboken, NJ: Wiley, 2015).

9. Cecília Baeza and Paulo Pinto, "The Syrian Uprising and Mobilization of the Syrian Diaspora in South America," *Middle East Report: The Latin East* 284/285 (Winter 2017), https://merip.org/2018/04/the-syrian-uprising-and-mobilization-%E2%80%A8of-the-syrian-diaspora-in-south-america/.

10. For a brief review of the state of the field of Middle East and North African migration studies in recent years, see Elizabeth Claire Saylor and Lily Pearl Balloffet, "Editorial Foreword: Mashriq and Mahjar Today—Migration Studies at a Crossroads," *Mashriq and Mahjar: Journal of Middle East Migration Studies* 4:1 (2017): 1–3.

11. Histories of Middle Eastern migrants and their communities in the Americas include Akram Fouad Khater, *Inventing Home: Emigration, Gender, and the Middle Class in Lebanon, 1870–1920* (Berkeley: University of California Press, 2001); Ilham Khuri-Makdisi, *The Eastern Mediterranean and the Making of Global Radicalism, 1860–1914* (Berkeley: University of California Press, 2013); Evelyn Alsultany and Ella Shohat, eds., *Between the Middle East and the Americas: The Cultural Politics of Diaspora* (Ann Arbor: University of Michigan Press, 2013); Sarah M. A. Gualtieri, *Between Arab and White: Race and Ethnicity in the Early Syrian American Diaspora* (Berkeley: University of California Press, 2009); Sally Howell, "Cultural Interventions: Arab American Aesthetics between the Transnational and the Ethnic," *Diaspora* 9:1 (2000): 59–82. Recent works specifically on the mahjar in Latin America include Steven Hyland Jr., *More Argentine Than You: Arabic-Speaking Immigrants in Argentina* (Albuquerque: University of New Mexico Press, 2017); Camila Pastor, *The Mexican Mahjar: Transnational Maronites, Jews, and Arabs under the French Mandate* (Austin: University of Texas Press, 2017); John Tofik Karam. *Another Arabesque: Syrian-Lebanese Ethnicity in Neoliberal Brazil* (Philadelphia: Temple University Press, 2007).

12. In the case of Latin America, like the Middle East, scholars have critiqued the conceptions of geopolitical space imposed by Europeans as part of the nineteenth-century's spreading imperialism. See, for example, Michel Gobat, "The Invention of Latin America: A Transnational History of Anti-Imperialism, Democracy, and Race," *American Historical Review* 118:5 (2013): 1345–1375.

13. Donna R. Gabaccia, *Foreign Relations: American Immigration in Global Perspective* (Princeton, NJ: Princeton University Press, 2012).

14. For an expanded definition of the term *Global South*, as well as further readings on the subject, see Anne Garland Mahler, "Global South," in *Oxford Bibliographies in Literary and Critical Theory*, ed. Eugene O'Brien (New York: Oxford University Press, 2017).

15. For extended discussions of systems-based approaches to migration history and a discussion of these approaches in relation to broader trends in migration historiography, see Christiane Harzig and Dirk Hoerder with Donna Gabaccia, *What Is Migration History?* (Cambridge, UK: Polity Press, 2009); Dirk Hoerder, "From Immigration to Migration Systems: New Concepts in Migration History," *OAH Magazine of History* 14:1 (1991): 5–11, and Lüthi, "Migration and Migration History."

16. Michel Foucault, "Truth and Power," in *The Essential Foucault*, ed. Paul Rabinow and Nikolas Rose (New York: New Press, 2003), 300–318.

17. Michel Rolph Trouillot, *Silencing the Past: Power and the Production of History* (Boston: Beacon Press, 1995), 27.

18. Barbara Lüthi employs this term—"mental-geographic maps." See Lüthi, "Migration and Migration History," 9.

19. Other historians have also worked to denaturalize the presumption of mass migration systems as West-East during the nineteenth- and twentieth-century boom, and South-North in the later twentieth century. For example, the work of Adam McKeown brought attention to two other major migration systems in North and Southeast Asia between the mid-nineteenth century and the outbreak of World War II, effectively challenging the Atlantic-centric norm of the bulk of earlier global migration historiography. Adam M. McKeown, *Melancholy Order: Asian Migration and the Globalization of Borders* (New York: Columbia University Press, 2008).

Chapter 1

1. Juan Gabriel Labake, "Carta Entregada a Cristina Kirchner Solicitando Refugio a Desplazados Sirios," November 13, 2015, open letter, http://argentinatoday.org/2015/11/13/carta-entregada-a-cristina-kirchner-solicitando-refugio-a-desplazados-sirios.

2. Mark D. Szuchman, "Imagining the State and Building the Nation: The Case of Nineteenth-Century Argentina," *History Compass* 4:2 (2006): 318.

3. Juan Bautista Alberdi, "Bases y puntos de partida para la organización política de la República Argentina," in *Organización de la Confederación Argentina* (Buenos Aires: Besanzon, Imprenta de José Joaquín, 1858), 42.

4. Jeffrey Lesser, *Negotiating National Identity: Immigrants, Minorities, and the Struggle for Ethnicity in Brazil* (Durham, NC: Duke University Press, 1999), 14.

5. Christina Civantos posits a uniquely Argentine brand of Orientalism beginning in the nineteenth century. Christina Civantos, *Between Argentines and Arabs: Argen-*

tine Orientalism, Arab Immigrants, and the Writing of Identity (Albany, NY: SUNY Press, 2006), 37.

6. A long woolen cloak commonly worn in the region.

7. Civantos, *Between Argentines and Arabs*, 46; Domingo Faustino Sarmiento, *Viajes por Europa, Africa y America 1845–1847*: Vol. 5: *Obras de Domingo Faustino Sarmiento* (Buenos Aires: Impr. Gutenberg: 1886), 158, 15.

8. Sarmiento, *Viajes por Europa, Africa y America*, 233.

9. Article 25 of Argentina's 1853 Constitution stated in no uncertain terms that "the Federal Government will encourage *European* immigration" in particular, despite the constitution's more generally supportive preamble, which invited "*all the men of the world* with goodwill who wished to inhabit the Argentine land [emphasis added]." *Constitución de la Confederación Argentina 1853*. Preamble and Part I, Article 25.

10. David Scott FitzGerald and David Cook-Martín, *Culling the Masses: The Democratic Origins of Racist Immigration Policy in the Americas* (Cambridge, MA: Harvard University Press, 2014), 299.

11. On discrimination, see Carl Solberg, *Immigration and Nationalism: Argentina and Chile, 1890–1914* (Austin: University of Texas Press, 1970), 20, 89; Ignacio Klich, "*Criollos* and Arabic Speakers: An Uneasy *Pas de Deux*, 1888–1914," in *The Lebanese in the World*, ed. Albert Hourani and Nadim Shehadi (London: Centre for Lebanese Studies, 1992), 268–269.

12. On the US example, see Sarah M. Gualtieri, *Between Arab and White: Race and Ethnicity in the Early Syrian American Diaspora* (Berkeley: University of California Press, 2009).

13. For further discussion of the shifting classifications of European migration, see Benjamin Bryce, "Undesirable Britons: South Asian Migration and the Making of a White Argentina," *Hispanic American Historical Review* 99:2 (2019); Benjamin Bryce, "Asian Migration, Racial Hierarchies, and Exclusion in Argentina, 1890–1920," in *Race and Transnationalism in the Americas*, ed. Benjamin Bryce and David M. K. Sheinin (forthcoming).

14. Alberdi, "Bases y puntos," 67.

15. Juan Alsina, *Memoria de la Dirección de Inmigración correspondiente al año 1899* (Buenos Aires: Imprenta de Guillermo Kraft, 1900).

16. Solberg, *Immigration and Nationalism*, 20, 88, 89. For a discussion of backlash against the idea of the pack peddler in the first decade of the twentieth century, see Steven Hyland, "Arisen from Deep Slumber: Transnational Politics and Competing Nationalisms among Syrian Immigrants in Argentina, 1900–1922," *Journal of Latin American Studies* 43:1 (2001): 547–574.

17. Miguel Vidal, "Las proveedurías—Precios de venta de las mercaderías a los indios," *Boletín del Departamento Nacional del Trabajo*, no. 28 (1914), 72.

18. Vidal, "Las proveedurías," 74.

19. Mariano Aráoz de Lamadrid, "Fundamentos del contrato que antecede," *Boletín del Departamento Nacional del Trabajo*, no. 28 (1914): 42.

20. "Contrato reglamentario del trabajo de los indígenas en los ingenious de Jujuy," *Boletín del Departamento Nacional del Trabaj*, no. 28 (1914): 32.

21. Alejandro M. Unsain, "Modificación del contrato. Conclusiones," *Boletín del Departamento Nacional del Trabajo*, no. 28 (1914): 88.

22. José Elías Niklison, "Dos Grandes Empresas de la Region, Compañía Las Palmas. Capital y Trabajo," *Boletín del Departamento Nacional del Trabajo*, no. 32 (1915): 154.

23. José Elías Niklison, "Dos Grandes Empresas de la Region, Compañía Las Palmas. Horario de trabajo," *Boletín del Departamento Nacional del Trabajo*, no. 32 (1915): 158.

24. José Elías Niklison, "Dos Grandes Empresas de la Region, Compañía Las Palmas. Los Jornales," *Boletín del Departamento Nacional del Trabajo*, , no. 32, 1915): 185.

25. José Elías Niklison, "La Comisón en el Chaco y Formosa, Habitación, alimentación, vestido," *Boletín del Departamento Nacional del Trabajo*, no. 32 (1915): 112–115.

26. José Elías Niklison, "El Arreglo Grande," *Boletín del Departamento Nacional del Trabajo*, no. 35 (1917): 96–97.

27. *Memoria del Departamento General de Inmigración, correspondiente al año 1910* (Buenos Aires: Centro de Estudios Migratorios Latinoamericanos, 1910).

28. Stephen Hyland, "Arisen from Deep Slumber: Transnational Politics and Competing Nationalisms among Syrian Immigrants in Argentina, 1900–1922," *Journal of Latin American Studies* 43:1 (2001): 555.

29. José Moya, *Cousins and Strangers: Spanish Immigrants in Buenos Aires, 1850–1930* (Berkeley: University of California Press, 1998), 57.

30. A. G. Ford, "Capital Exports and Growth for Argentina, 1880—1914," *Economic Journal* 68:271 (1958): 589–593.

31. James Scobie, *Secondary Cities of Argentina* (Stanford, CA: Stanford University Press, 1988), 28.

32. Alberdi, "Bases y puntos de partida," 48.

33. Alberdi, "Bases y puntos de partida, 47.

34. David E. Nye. "Foundational Space, Technological Narrative," in *Space in America: Theory History Culture*, ed. Klaus Benesch and Kersin Schmidt (Amsterdam: Rodopi B.V., 2004), 129.

35. Gaston Gordillo, *Rubble: The Afterlife of Destruction* (Durham, NC: Duke University Press, 2014), 171–172.

36. Gordillo, *Rubble*.

37. Scobie, *Secondary Cities*, 29, 32.

38. Gordillo, *Rubble*, 174.

39. J. Valerie Fifer, *United States Perceptions of Latin America, 1850–1930: A New West South of Capricorn?* (Manchester: Manchester University Press, 1991), 45.

40. For detailed maps of the Transandine Route, Pacific Steam Navigation Co., North Eastern Railway, and more, see Frederic M. Halsey, *Railway Expansion in Latin America* (New York: Jas. H. Oliphant & Co., 1916).

41. As of 1912, Neuquén had not yet become an Argentine province and was still designated as a national territory. Neuquén officially became a province on June 15, 1955, with its first provincial constitution promulgated on November 28, 1957. For reference to the Sapag family's decision to buy land prior to the arrival of the rail line, see Hamurabi Noufouri, Rita Veneroni, and Yusef Abboud, *Sirios, Libaneses y Argentinos: fragmentos para una historia de la diversidad cultural argentina* (Buenos Aires: Fundación Los Cedros: 2004), 447.

42. Sapag family business holdings appear in *La Siria Nueva: Obra histórica, estadística y comercial de la colectividad sirio-otomana el las Repúblicas Argentina y Uruguay* (Buenos Aires: Empresa Assalam, 1917), and *Guia del comercio sirio-libanés* (Córdoba, Argentina: Publicidad Oriente, 1943). On the history of YPF and the Argentine petroleum industry, see Carl E. Solberg, "Entrepreneurship in Public Enterprise: General Enrique Mosconi and the Argentine Petroleum Industry," *Business History Review* 56:3 (1982): 380–399.

43. On the Sapag family's political dynasty, see Orietta Favaro, "Neuquinos y rionegrinos ¿Cautivos o cautivados por los sistemas políticos locales?" *Periferias: Revista de Ciencias Sociales* 15 (2007).

44. "Asumió lúcidos contornos la filmación de la Sociedad Sirio Libanésa de Salta," *Nueva Época (Salta)*, October 15, 1931.

45. Lesser, *Negotiating National Identity*, 50.

46. See Assis Feres, "O mascate," the memoirs of Wadih Safady, and "The Legend of Marataize" in Lesser, *Negotiating National Identity*, 50. For an example of contemporary scholarly emphasis on the role of the mascate in the Brazilian mahjar, see Roberto Khatlab, *Mahjar: Saga Libanésa no Brasil, Sociología Iconográfica* (Zalka, Lebanon: Mokhtarat, 2002).

47. For example, the newspaper *Ad-Difah* contained regular sections that explicated the philosophy of "Oriental Metaphysics," Sufi numerology, or the writings of Avicenna, a Persian polymath of the tenth century. *Ad Difah* (Buenos Aires), 1942–1943.

48. Juan Alsina, *Memoria de la Dirección de Inmigración correspondiente al año 1899* (Buenos Aires: Imprenta de Guillermo Kraft, 1900).

49. Michael Humphrey, "Ethnic History, Nationalism and Transnationalism in Argentine Arab and Jewish Cultures," in *Arab and Jewish Immigrants in Latin America: Images and Realities,* ed. Jeffrey Lesser and Ignacio Klich (New York: Routledge, 1998), 172. It is also worth noting that the Spanish term *mercachifle* can carry a negative connotation, with common translations being "huckster" or even "money grabber."

50. Miguel A. Yapur, *Figura simbólica y digna de respeto: "el mercachifle": Su influencia en el progreso de la Nación Argentina* (Tucumán: Sociedad Sirio-Libanesa de Tucumán, 1933).

51. The BAGS was established in 1865 and completed in 1912.

Chapter 2

1. "Un Hijo del Líbano recio pionero del Progreso del Dep. de Trancas," *El Eco de Oriente* (Tucumán), September 26, 1936, 5.

2. Steven Hyland Jr., *More Argentine Than You: Arabic-Speaking Immigrants in Argentina* (Albuquerque: University of New Mexico Press, 2017), 137.

3. James R. Scobie, *Argentina: A City and a Nation* (New York: Oxford University Press, 1964), 22–23.

4. Misiones did not gain provincial status until 1953, and its provincial constitution was not approved until 1958.

5. Rodolfo Walsh, *El Violento oficio de escribir* (Madrid: 451 Editores, 2011), 108.

6. Monsour Breide, "Gira del corresponsal de 'La Gaceta Árabe,'" *La Gaceta Árabe* (Buenos Aires), March 24, 1929, 8.

7. Cases referenced in the *Boletín Oficial de la República Argentina* editions from March 22, 1943; April 5, 1944; April 10, 1945; and December 3, 1947.

8. For example, Raanan Rein, Stefan Rinke, and Nadia Zysman, "Introduction," in *The New Ethnic Studies in Latin America*, edited by Raanan Rein, Stefan Rinke, and Nadia Zysman (Boston: Brill, 2017), 1–6.

9. James Warren, "The Iranun and Balangingi Slaving Voyage: Middle Passages in the Sulu Zone" in *Many Middle Passages: Forced Migration in the Making of the Modern World*, ed. Emma Christopher, Cassandra Pybus, and Marcus Rediker (Berkeley: University of California Press, 2007), 57.

10. *La Siria Nueva*, 26.

11. Stacy Fahrenthold, "Transnational Modes and Media: The Syrian Press in the Mahjar and Emigrant Activism during World War I," *Mashriq and Mahjar: Journal of Middle East Migration Studies* 1:1 (2013): 38, 48.

12. Hyland, *More Argentine Than You*, 86–87.

13. Monsour Breide, "Gira del corresponsal de 'La Gaceta Árabe,'" *La Gaceta Árabe* (Buenos Aires), March 24, 1929, 8.

14. "Viaje de nuestro Director," *La Gaceta Árabe* (Buenos Aires), July 8, 1928, 2.

15. Colin M. Lewis, *British Railways in Argentina, 1857–1914: A Case Study of Foreign Investment* (London: Athlone Press for the Institute of Latin American Studies, University of London, 1983).

16. In the corresponding Syrian-Lebanese business directories for 1928 and 1942, there were, respectively, fifty-six and ninety-two businesses listed. Full listings can be accessed in Alejandro Schamún, *La Siria Nueva: Obra histórica, estadística y comercial*

de la colectividad sirio-otomana en las Repúblicas Argentina y Uruguay (Buenos Aires: Empresa "Assalam," 1917); *Guía Assalam del comercio sirio-libanes en la República Argentina* (Buenos Aires, Argentina: Empresa "Assalam," 1928); Salim Constantino, *Guía de Comercio Sirio Libanés* (Córdoba, Argentina: Publicidad Oriente, 1943).

17. Data gathered from *Viajeros* listings in 1928 *La Gaceta Árabe* on the following dates in 1928: January 1, February 5, May 6, June 24, August 26, and October 7.

18. "Viaje de nuestro Director," 2.

19. "Viaje de nuestro Director," 2.

20. In the 1928 *Guía Assalam*, Ascención registered three entries, Vedia one, and Arribeños four.

21. Elias M. Amar, "Observaciones de un viaje, Comparando. Un triste recuerdo," *La Gaceta Árabe* (Buenos Aires), March 16, 1928, 1.

22. For example, see Estela Valverde, "Integration and Identity in Argentina: The Lebanese of Tucumán," in *The Lebanese in the World*, ed. Albert Hourani and Nadim Shehadi (London: Centre for Lebanese Studies, 1992), 268–269, 313–339.

23. Marta A. Saleh de Canuto and Susana Budeguer, *El Aporte de los Sirios y Libaneses a Tucumán* (San Miguel de Tucumán, Argentina: Editorial América, 1979), 36, 102.

24. "Córdoba, Tierra Prometida . . . ," *El Eco de Oriente* (San Miguel de Tucumán), March 9, 1935, 3.

25. These included a serialized novel coauthored with Simón Hamati in 1923 and a monthly literary review cofounded with Gabriel Candalft in 1922 titled *El Jardín/al-Hadiqa*. See Christina Civantos, *Between Argentines and Arabs: Argentine Orientalism, Arab Immigrants, and the Writing of Identity* (Albany, NY: SUNY Press, 2006), 210, and Hyland, *More Argentine Than You*, 94.

26. "La Jira de Nuestro Director," *El Eco de Oriente* (San Miguel de Tucumán), September 14, 1935, 5.

27. The 1917, 1928, and 1942 mahjar business directories listed seven, fifteen, and twenty-eight individuals and firms.

28. "Club Sirio-Libanés Rosario de la Frontera," *Eco de Oriente* (Tucumán), January 1936, 74.

29. "La Jira de Nuestro Director," 5.

30. "Galería Social," *El Eco de Oriente: Número Extraordinario* (San Miguel de Tucumán), January 1936, 105–111.

31. For an example from the Rustom travel narratives, see Assad Rustom, "Mi Viaje por el Norte," *La Union Libanesa* (Buenos Aires), February 1, 1945, 1.

32. Of the 1,103 viajeros, 366 also registered in the corresponding 1928 *Guía Assalam* business directory.

33. "Don Wadi Schamún Regresó de su Gira," *La Gaceta Árabe* (Buenos Aires), March 16, 1930, 4; "Señor Wadi Schamún," *El Eco de Oriente (Tucumán)*, September 19, 1936, 5; "Terminó su Gira," *El Eco de Oriente* (Tucumán), October 17, 1936, 1;

"Una animada charla con nuestro amigo don Salim Constantino," *Ad-Difah* (Buenos Aires), January 16, 1943, 5.

34. For examples of directions to cities and businesses via rail lines, see Alejandro Schamún, *Guía Assalam del Comercio Sirio-Libanés*, 128, 161, 200, 223, 283.

Chapter 3

1. Jeffrey Lesser, *Negotiating National Identity: Immigrants, Minorities, and the Struggle for Ethnicity in Brazil* (Durham, NC: Duke University Press, 1999), 54.

2. Christina Civantos, *Between Argentines and Arabs: Argentine Orientalism, Arab Immigrants, and the Writing of Identity* (Albany, NY: SUNY Press, 2006), 19.

3. Here I refer to the *mashriq* in the broader geographic sense that encompasses human and cultural mobilities through both the Levant and Egypt. For recent examples of mahjar literary history studies, see Silvia C. Ferreira, "Excavating Mashriqi Roots in the Mahjar: Agriculture and Assimilation in Raduan Nassar's Lavoura arcaica," *Mashriq and Mahjar: Journal of Middle East and North African Migration Studies* 2:2 (2014): 13–27; Jacob Rama Berman, "Arab Masquerade: *Mahjar* Identity Politics and Transnationalism," in *American Arabesque: Arabs and Islam in the Nineteenth Century Imaginary* (New York: New York University Press, 2012); Elizabeth C. Saylor, "Mapping Women Writers in the Mahjar " [digital history storymap project], accessed 2018 at https://www.arcgis.com/apps/MapJournal/index.html?appid=1e09d680f93144dc8 cb10e42abffbf79.

4. Evelyn Alsultany and Ella Shohat, eds., *Between the Middle East and the Americas: The Cultural Politics of Diaspora* (Ann Arbor: University of Michigan Press, 2013), 76.

5. Matthew B. Karush, *Culture of Class: Radio and Cinema in the Making of a Divided Argentina, 1920–1946* (Durham, NC: Duke University Press, 2012), 6.

6. Karush, *Culture of Class*, 4.

7. "Cinematografía," *La Gaceta Árabe* (Buenos Aires), January 1, 1928, 10.

8. "'Canción de Oriente' o Siria, Palestina y el Líbano de hoy," *La Reforma* (Santiago de Chile), May 20, 1932, 14.

9. "'Canción de Oriente' o Siria."

10. "'Canción de Oriente' o Siria."

11. "El Film Sirio-Libanés," *Eco de Oriente* (Tucumán), August 11, 1931.

12. "La Atracción del Oriente: El grandioso Film de La Siria y El Líbano de 1927," *La Gaceta Árabe* (Buenos Aires), June 24, 1928, 6.

13. "Aniversarios de Instituciones," Lebanese Embassy, Buenos Aires, Argentina, accessed February 23, 2014, at https://www.ellibano.com.ar/docs/.

14. "Chic-Chic-Bey se va," *La Gaceta Árabe* (Buenos Aires), January 19, 1930, 1.

15. "La obra de la 'Oriente Film' juzgada por los periódicos sirio-libanés del Brasil," *La Gaceta Árabe* (Buenos Aires), August 4, 1929, 2.

16. "Nabih Schamún, director de Oriente Film y Gabriel Trabulci (Chic-Chic Bey) se encuentran entre nosotros," *La Gaceta Árabe* (Buenos Aires), September 8, 1929, 2.

17. "La Vida de los sirios-Libanéses en las américas," *La Gaceta de Tucumán*, August 2, 1931; "Nos visita una personalidad Libanésa," *Nueva Epoca* (Salta), October 1, 1931; "Un film sobre los sirios y Libanéses residentes en Rosario," *La Capital (Rosario)*, May 7, 1931.

18. "La Vida de los sirios-Libanéses."

19. "El Film Sirio-Libanés: Un documento interesantísimo y una obra de méritos," *Eco de Oriente* (Tucumán), August 11, 1931.

20. "El Film Sirio-Libanés."

21. "Nabih Schamún, director de Oriente Film y Gabriel Trabulci (Chic-Chic-Bey)."

22. Nabih Schamún, "Impresiones de mi viaje por el Brasil," *La Gaceta Árabe* (Buenos Aires), December 16, 1928, 1 (ellipses in original).

23. Leyla Dakhli, "The *Mahjar* as Literary and Political Territory in the First Decades of the Twentieth Century: The Example of Amīn Rīhānī (1876–1940)," in *The Making of the Arab Intellectual: Empire, Public Sphere and the Colonial Coordinates of Selfhood*, ed. Dyala Hamzah (New York: Routledge, 2013), 174–175.

24. Nabih Schamún, "Impresiones de mi viaje por el Brasil: Rio de Janeiro," *La Gaceta Árabe* (Buenos Aires), January 6, 1929, 1.

25. Residents of Buenos Aires.

26. "El fallecimiento de Nabih Schamún enluta a la juventud Sirio-Libanésa," *La Gaceta Árabe* (Buenos Aires), April 27, 1930, 6.

27. "El Film Sirio-Libanés."

28. "D. Roberto Kouri traerá la gran cinta 'La Canción del Beduino,'" *El Eco de Oriente* (Tucumán), September 26, 1936, 3.

29. "Viaje de José Dial," *Ahla Usahla-Bienvenida* (Buenos Aires), no. 21 (March 1942): 10.

30. Winn writes briefly of the extent of the business holdings of the Yarur family. See Peter Winn, *Weavers of Revolution: The Yarur Workers and Chile's Road to Socialism* (New York: Oxford University Press, 1986).

31. "Película de la Manufactura Yarur Hnos," *La Reforma* (Santiago, Chile), November 19, 1938, 3.

32. See, for example, Claudia Stern, "Otherness in Convergence: Arabs, Jews, and the Formation of the Chilean Middle Classes, 1930–1960," in *The New Ethnic Studies in Latin America*, ed. Raanan Rein, Stefan Rinke, and Nadia Zysman (Leiden: Brill, 2017).

33. "Sobre el Progreso General de la Colectividad en Chile nos habla el Director Cinematográfico sr. José Dial," *Mundo Árabe* (Santiago, Chile), April 6, 1940, 1.

34. "Sobre el Progreso General de la Colectividad en Chile."

35. "Manifestación a don José Dial en Buenos Aires," *La Reforma* (Santiago, Chile), August 2, 1941, 5.

36. "Film documental de la Colonia Árabe," *La Reforma* (Santiago, Chile), January 15, 1947, 6.

37. Hamza, *The Making of the Arab Intellectual*, 172.

38. "Nabih Schamún, director de Oriente Film y Gabriel Trabulci," 2.

39. Tour routes as reported in *La Gaceta Árabe* between 1929 and 1931.

40. "Don Gabriel Trabulsi: su Obra y Méritos," *La Gaceta Árabe* (Buenos Aires), June 1932, 42.

41. "Said Yibran al-Trabulsi, 'Chic Chic Beik,'" *Assalam* (Buenos Aires), July 2, 1937, 5.

42. "¿Que le pasa al amigo Trabulsi?" *La Gaceta Árabe* (Buenos Aires), July 9, 1933, 4.

43. "¿Que le pasa al amigo Trabulsi?"

44. "Regresó de su jira artística por las provincias de Cuyo el aplaudido actor Don Gabriel Trabulsi," *La Gaceta Árabe* (Buenos Aires), January 4, 1931, 5.

45. Palmira Brummett, *Image and Imperialism in the Ottoman Revolutionary Press, 1908–1911* (Albany, NY: SUNY Press, 2000), iii.

46. Brummett, *Image and Imperialism*, 221–223.

47. Deniz Kandiyoti, "Slave Girls, Temptresses, and Comrades: Images of Women in the Turkish Novel," *Feminist Issues* 8 (Spring 1988), 42.

48. Artur Goldschmidt, *Biographical Dictionary of Modern Egypt* (Boulder, CO: Lynne Rienner, 2000), 167.

49. Najib el-Rihani, "Interview with Najib el-Rihani," *El-Mesawar Magazine* (Cairo), October 19, 1928.

50. Badia Masabni, "Interview with Badia Masabni by Layla Rostum," *Negoum Ala El-Ard Radio*, 1966.

51. Buenos Aires newspapers reported on Trabulsi and Zeitune's collaboration and tour, including *El Boletín* (Buenos Aires), September 30, 1934, and January 31, 1938; *La Unión Libanesa* (Buenos Aires), October 10, 1936; and *Assalam* (Buenos Aires), July 2, 1937.

52. Terri Ginsberg and Chris Lippard, eds., "Abdel Wahab, Mohamed (1907–1991)," in *Historical Dictionary of Middle Eastern Cinema* (Toronto: Scarecrow Press, 2010), 6.

53. For example, Palestinian-Chilean Saba Yarur, a member of the powerful Yarur textile empire, hired the Syrian singer Selim Amran to sing at his son's wedding festivities. Amran was a student of Abdel Wahab in Cairo, and after being hired by Yarur, he continued northward and gave a series of performances in the United States. See "Famoso cantante Selim Amran invitado a Chile," *Mundo Árabe* (Santiago, Chile), September 1, 1950, 6.

54. "Una Función Especial Habrá esta Noche en el Empire Theatre," *Santa Fe*, December 1, 1932.

55. "La Atracción del Oriente: El grandioso Film de La Siria y El Líbano de 1927," 6.

Chapter 4

1. Steven Hyland explores monument-building debates in Argentina's Northwestern Arab Argentine community in depth in his *More Argentine Than You: Arabic-Speaking Immigrants in Argentina* (Albuquerque: University of New Mexico Press, 2017), 133, 138–141.

2. An earlier version of this research appeared as "From the *Pampas* to the *Mashriq*: Arab-Argentine Philanthropy Networks," *Mashriq and Mahjar: Journal of Middle East and North African Migration Studies* 4, no. 1 (2017): 4-28.

3. A notable exception is Steven Hyland, "Arabic-Speaking Immigrants before the Courts in Tucumán, Argentina, 1910–1940," *Journal of Women's History* 28, 4 (2016): 41–64.

4. For examples of literature that highlight the role of hometown associations and Latin American immigrant and ethnic communities, see, for example, Elizabeth Kiddy, *Blacks of the Rosary: Memory and History in Minas Gerais, Brazil* (University Park: Pennsylvania State University Press, 2005); José C. Moya, "Immigrants and Associations: A Global and Historical Perspective," *Journal of Ethnic and Migration Studies* 31:5 (2005): 833–86; Mariusz Kałczewiak, "Becoming Polacos: Landsmanshaftn and the Making of a Polish-Jewish Sub-Ethnicity in Argentina," in *The New Ethnic Studies in Latin America*, ed. Raanan Rein, Stefan Rinke, and Nadia Zysman (Boston: Brill, 2017), 32–51; Benjamin Bryce, *To Belong in Buenos Aires: Germans, Argentines, and the Rise of a Pluralist Society* (Stanford, CA: Stanford University Press, 2018); Stacy Fahrenthold, "Sound Minds in Sound Bodies: Transnational Philanthropy and Patriotic Masculinity in *al-Nadi al-Homsi* and Syrian Brazil, 1920–1932," *International Journal of Middle East Studies* 46:2 (2014): 259–283; and Steven Hyland Jr. "'Arisen from Deep Slumber': Transnational Politics and Competing Nationalisms among Syrian Immigrants in Argentina, 1900–1922," *Journal of Latin American Studies* 43:1 (2001).

5. Examples from both contemporary and historical accounts of mahjar communities in Latin America abound. For example, see references to espíritu emprendedor made in Jesús Ferro Bayona, *Líderes en un mundo global: Una mirada desde la academia* (Barranquilla, Colombia: Ediciones Uninorte: 2006), 392, and Farid Metuaze, "Espíritu Árabe," *Mundo Árabe* (Santiago de Chile), November 10, 1950, 8.

6. For examples of literature on immigrant philanthropy and humanitarian aid networks in Latin America and the Middle East in the twentieth century, see Sandra McGee Deutsch, *Crossing Borders, Claiming a Nation: A History of Argentine Jewish Women, 1880–1955* (Durham, NC: Duke University Press, 2010) ; Keith Watenpaugh, *Bread from Stones: The Middle East and the Making of Modern Humanitarianism* (Berkeley: University of California Press, 2015); Benjamin Bryce. "Paternal Communities: Social Welfare and Immigration in Argentina, 1880–1930," *Journal of Social History* 49:1 (2015): 213–236, and "Los caballeros de beneficencia y las damas organizadoras: El Hospital Alemán y la idea de co-

munidad en Buenos Aires, 1880–1930," *Estudios Migratorios Latinoamericanos* 70 (2011): 79–107.

7. This term first appeared in C. W. Gordon and N. Babchuk, "A Typology of Voluntary Associations," *American Sociological Review* 24(1959): 22–29. For a discussion of the difference between and definitions of ethnic associations, instrumental associations, and immigrant institutions, see Moya, "Immigrants and Associations," 834.

8. "Una Obra en Marcha," *La Voz del Hospital* (Buenos Aires), September 1948, 1.

9. "Memoria y Balance," *La Voz del Hospital* (Buenos Aires), February 1937, 1.

10. For an example of this rhetoric of *por todos para todos,* see their call to arms in the following open letter to the Arab Argentine press: "De la Asociación de Beneficencia pro Hospital Sirio Libanés, a los hombres de corazón," *La Gaceta Árabe* (Buenos Aires), March 16, 1930, 3.

11. "Memoria y Balance General de la Asociación de Beneficencia Pro Hospital Sirio Libanés," *La Voz del Hospital* (Buenos Aires), December 31, 1935, 1.

12. Wacila J. de Adre and Estela Ch. de Chacar, "Asociación de Beneficencia Pro-Hospital Sirio-Libanés: Origen, Fundación y su Obra hasta el Presente," *La Voz del Hospital* (Buenos Aires), February 1937, 1–4.

13. For a discussion of fundraising and philanthropy work as a status symbol in Argentine society in the twentieth century, see Donna Guy, *Women Build the Welfare State: Performing Charity, and Creating Rights in Argentina, 1880–1955* (Durham, NC: Duke University Press, 2009).

14. See Deutsch's chapter on philanthropy and Zionism in *Crossing Borders, Claiming a Nation,* chap. 8, esp. 210–212.

15. "La Acción abnegada de nuestros delegados," *Voz del Hospital* (Buenos Aires), December 1946, 2.

16. Adre and Chacar, "Memoria y Balance General . . ," 2; "Suplemento Especial," *Voz del Hospital* (Buenos Aires), February 1937, 2 ; "La Acción Abnegada de Nuestros Delegados," *Voz del Hospital* (Buenos Aires), December 1946, 2.

17. de Adre and de Chacar, "Asociación de Beneficencia Pro-Hospital Sirio-Libanés"; "Memoria y Balance General de la Asociación de Beneficencia Pro-Hospital Sirio Libanés Correspondiente al año 1935," *La Voz del Hospital* (Buenos Aires), January 1936, 2–3.

18. Wacila C. de Adre and Estela de Chacar. "El Hospital Sirio Libanés de Buenos Aires," *El Eco de Oriente* (Tucumán), April 11, 1936, 4–5.

19. "Aportes recibidos por nuestro delegado oficial en las Provincias de Tucumán, Salta y Jujuy," *Voz del Hospital* (Buenos Aires), December 1947, 4.

20. "Aportes recibidos," 5; "Gira de Nuestro Delegado" *Voz del Hospital* (Buenos Aires), June 1948, 6.

21. *Población de Mendoza en los Censos Nacionales según Departamento: Años 1869—2010,* Dirección de Estadísticas e Investigaciones Económicas, Ministerio de

Agroindustria y Tecnología, Gobierno de Mendoza; Jorge R. Entraigas, "La Población rionegrina durante la época territorial. Un Aporte al conocimiento de las principales características demográficas: 1884–1955," in *Horizontes en Perspectiva: Contribuciones para la historia de Rio Negro: 1884–1955*, vol. 1 (Viedma, Argentina: Fundación Ameghino, 2007).

22. *Guía de Comercio Sirio Libanés* (Córdoba: Publicidad Oriente, 1943).

23. "Memoria y Balance General," 1935, 2.

24. This recounting of events is as stated by the commemorative plaque that remains on the hospital site today.

25. "A Nuestros Delegados y Socios del Interior," *La Voz del Hospital* (Buenos Aires), December 1944, 4; "A Nuestros Delegados y Socios del Interior," *La Voz del Hospital* (Buenos Aires), June 1948, 5.

26. For example, Deutsch writes of schools for the Argentine children of Jewish immigrants from several different countries that taught Yiddish, Arabic, and Hebrew from the early decades of the twentieth century. Bryce writes about the role of bilingual German-Spanish schools in Buenos Aires during a similar period. See Deutsch, *Crossing Borders, Claiming a Nation*, and Bryce, *To Belong in Buenos Aires*.

27. "Hablamos a los árabes," *La Gaceta Árabe* (Buenos Aires), August 25, 1929, 1.

28. "Regresó de su exitoso viaje a Chile el conocido empresario cinematográfico Don José Dial," *La Gaceta Árabe* (Buenos Aires), June 1932, 45.

29. "Hamdan: El festival del 21 de la Asociación Femenina Ortodoxa," *La Gaceta Árabe* (Buenos Aires), December 15, 1928, 2.

30. "El festival de la Asociación Femenina Siria Ortodoxa de Beneficencia 'Hamdan' en el Capitol Theatre," *La Gaceta Árabe* (Buenos Aires), January 5, 1930, 3.

31. Guy, *Women Build the Welfare State*, 8.

32. Guy, *Women Build the Welfare State*, 47.

33. For examples, see Guy, *Women Build the Welfare State*; Mine Ener, *Managing Egypt's Poor and the Politics of Benevolence, 1800–1952* (Princeton, NJ: Princeton University Press, 2003); Lynne Haney, *Inventing the Needy: Gender and the Politics of Welfare in Hungary* (Berkeley: University of California Press, 2002).

34. "Asociación Femenina Sirio Ortodoxa de Beneficencia," *La Gaceta Árabe* (Buenos Aires), June 1932, 74.

35. "Bello gesto de la Asociación Femenina Siria Ortodoxa de Beneficencia," *La Gaceta Árabe* (Buenos Aires), March 18, 1928, 4.

36. Donna Guy and Mine Ener both refer to the "acceptability" of women's philanthropy work in their studies of the Argentine and Egyptian welfare states. See Guy, *Women Build the Welfare State*, 9; Ener, *Managing Egypt's Poor*, 111.

37. Michel Lotfallah to Georges Clémenceau, January 23, 1919, in *Oberlin College King-Crane Commission Digital Archive*, http://www.oberlin.edu/library/digital/king-crane/.

38. "Syrians Present Grievances to League," *New York Times*, August 31, 1921.

39. Fahrenthold. "Transnational Modes and Media," 32.

40. Fahrenthold. "Transnational Modes and Media, 33.

41. "Bello gesto de la Asociación," 4.

42. "Asociación Femenina Siria-Ortodoxa de Beneficencia," *La Gaceta Árabe* (Buenos Aires), August 19, 1928, 4.

43. Elizabeth F. Thompson, *Colonial Citizens: Republican Rights, Paternal Privilege, and Gender in French Syria and Lebanon* (New York: Columbia University Press, 2000), 205.

44. Thompson, *Colonial Citizens*, 206.

45. Thompson, *Colonial Citizens*, 210.

46. "Río Cuarto, F.C.C.A., Sociedad Femenina Sirio Libanésa," *La Gaceta Árabe* (Buenos Aires), June 1932, 93.

47. "Río Cuarto."

48. "Asociación Feminina Sirio Ortodoxa," *La Gaceta Árabe*, 74.

49. "Memoria y Balance General" 1935, 2.

50. The letter from Interventor Carlos Borzani, and related briefs on the earthquake, see the following issues from *La Gaceta Árabe*: June 6, 1929, 5; June 23, 1929, 1; July 28, 1929, 8; and December 22, 1929, 9.

51. "Sentido Homenaje póstumo a la Srta. Rosa N. Asef," *La Gaceta Árabe* (Buenos Aires), June 1932, 59.

52. Deutsch, *Crossing Borders, Claiming a Nation*, 235.

Chapter 5

1. An earlier version of this chapter's research appeared as Lily Pearl Balloffet, "Argentine and Egyptian History Entangled: From Perón to Nasser," *Journal of Latin American Studies* 50, no. 3 (2018): 549–577.

2. At that 1966 meeting, OSPAA became OSPAAL (to incorporate "Latin America").

3. Delegates included Peronist radical John William Cooke, representatives of the Argentine Communist Party, and Marxist-Leninist vanguards. Donald C. Hodges, *Argentina's "Dirty War": An Intellectual Biography* (Austin: University of Texas Press, 1991), 95.

4. See Jessica Stites Mor, "The Question of Palestine in the Argentine Political Imaginary: Anti-Imperialist Thought from Cold War to Neoliberal Order," *Journal of Iberian and Latin American Research* 20:2 (2014): 183–197; Ignacio Klich, "Toward an Arab–Latin American Bloc? The Genesis of Argentine–Middle East Relations: Jordan, 1945–54," *Middle Eastern Studies* 31:3 (1995): 550–572. For scholarship with a transnational political focus on Middle East–Latin American relations, see Hishaam Aidi, *Redeploying the State: Corporatism, Neoliberalism, and Coalition Politics* (New York: Palgrave Macmillan, 2009); Federico Vélez, *Latin American Revolutionaries and the*

Arab World: From the Suez Canal to the Arab Spring (Aldershot, UK: Ashgate, 2016); and Luis Mesa Delmonte, ed., *Las relaciones exteriores de Siria* (Mexico City: El Colegio de México, Centro de Estudios de Asia y África, 2013).

5. In "Toward an Arab–Latin American Bloc?" Klich used diplomatic cables to demonstrate the mutual desire of Argentina and Jordan to gain international respect after World War II. Correspondence from the Argentine Ministry of Foreign Relations (AMREC) from 1939 to 1950 also documents a steady increase in secret cables, official reports, press clippings, and petitions between Argentina and Syria, Lebanon, Iraq, Saudi Arabia, and Jordan. The archived documentation on Egypt far exceeds that on any other nation. AMREC, Buenos Aires, División Política (DP), Arab States, Syria/Lebanon/Egypt, 1939–1950.

6. Najib Baaclini, "Naguib, visto por un viejo amigo: 'Egipto tiene ya su Perón,'" *El Eco de Oriente* (Tucumán), February 24, 1953, 2.

7. Baaclini, "Naguib, visto por un viejo amigo."

8. Baaclini, "Naguib, visto por un viejo amigo."

9. Baaclini, "Naguib, visto por un viejo amigo" (ellipsis in original).

10. Aidi, *Redeploying the State*, 1.

11. Enio Atilio Mastrogiovanni, "La gran obra argentina de afirmación de los derechos de los trabajadores del campo," *Mundo Árabe* (Córdoba), December 19, 1953, 9. Gamal Abdel Nasser, "La reforma agraria del general Naguib favorece la reivindicación del fellah," *Mundo Árabe* (Córdoba), December 19, 1953, 10.

12. "Sobre solidaridad sindical habló el General Perón a obreros papeleros," *El Eco de Oriente* (Tucumán), August 24, 1953, 1; "Instalarán una fábrica de papel en Egipto," *El Eco de Oriente* (Tucumán), August 24, 1953, 4.

13. Ariel Noyjovich and Raanan Rein, "Para un árabe de bien no puede haber nada mejor que otro árabe: Nación, etnicidad y ciudadanía en la Argentina peronista," *Contra Relatos desde el Sur* 14 (2016): 58; "Raanan Rein and Ariel Noyjovich," *Los Muchachos peronistas árabes: Los argentinos árabes y el apoyo al justicialismo* (Buenos Aires, Argentina: Sudamericana, 2018).

14. "Difúndese el derecho árabe a Palestina," *Los Andes* (Mendoza), November 21, 1947, 7.

15. Records of these missions appear in the Arab Argentine press and heritage association institutional records. However, the most detailed consolidated list appears in the records of the Delegación de Asociaciones Israelitas Argentinas (DAIA), the Jewish community's umbrella organisation (established 1935). After 1947, the DAIA published sporadic reports on the activities of the Arab Argentine community, cataloguing any suspicion or instance of anti-Jewish or anti-Israel activities unfolding in the Arab diaspora. DAIA, *Anti-Jewish Activities of the Arabs in Argentina* (Buenos Aires: DAIA, 1958), 10. DAIA source materials can be consulted in the Biblioteca Nacional, Buenos Aires.

16. Edy Kaufman, Yoram Shapira, and Joel Barromi, *Israel–Latin American Relations* (New Brunswick, NJ: Transaction Books, 1979), 17.

17. "La iniciación de relaciones diplomáticas con Arabia Saudita," *La Nación* (Buenos Aires), February 18, 1946; AMREC, Buenos Aires, DP, Países Árabes 22/1946, "Establecimiento de relaciones con Irak, Saudi Arabia, y Egipto."

18. AMREC, Buenos Aires, PD, Syria/Lebanon 19/1945 and 1946, "Establecimiento de relaciones diplomáticas con la República Argentina"; "Congreso panarábigo de América Latina."

19. Ignacio Klich, "Arab-Jewish Coexistence in the First Half of 1900s Argentina: Overcoming Self-Imposed Amnesia," in *Arab and Jewish Immigrants in Latin America: Images and Realities*, ed. Ignacio Klich and Jeffrey Lesser (London: Routledge, 1998), 22.

20. Raanan Rein, "Political Considerations and Personal Rivalries: Peronist Argentina and the Partition of Palestine," *Diplomacy and Statecraft* 8:2 (1997): 128. The other Latin American abstainers were Colombia, El Salvador, and Honduras.

21. *Nakba* refers to the mass expulsion/exodus of Palestinian Arabs from their homes after partition in 1947. This culminated in the establishment of Israel in May 1948 and the displacement of approximately 80 percent of the Arab population of that territory.

22. For additional historical context on the 1948 Arab-Israeli War and its geopolitical implications, see James Gelvin, *The Israel Palestine Conflict: One Hundred Years of War* (Cambridge: Cambridge University Press, 2007), 165–196.

23. "El Profesor Guraieb traducirá al idioma árabe 'La Doctrina del Justicialismo,'" *Assalam* (Buenos Aires), April 4, 1952, 1.

24. "Traduce Doctrina Justicialista en lengua Árabe," *Mundo Árabe* (Córdoba), February 27, 1954, 5.

25. "Primeros ejemplares en Árabe de 'La Razón de mi Vida,'" *Assalam* (Buenos Aires), May 23, 1952, 1; "Tendrá enorme repercusión en el mundo árabe esta gran obra," *El Diario Sirio Libanés* (Buenos Aires), May 13, 1952, 1; "La Confederación de Instituciones Libanesas, entidad que representa a la colectividad de ese país, hizo entrega ayer al Excmo Presidente de la Nación Juan D. Perón dos ejemplares del libro 'La Razón de mi Vida' de la Sra Eva Perón, traducido al árabe," *El Diario Sirio Libanés* (Buenos Aires), May 21, 1952, 1.

26. AMREC, Buenos Aires, DP, Egypt 1949, Francisco Bengolea to Hipólito Jesús Paz, November 25, 1949.

27. Mario Rapoport, *Historia oral de la política exterior argentina* (Buenos Aires: Editorial Octubre, 2015), 287–290.

28. "Declaraciones del General Perón a un periodista Egipcio: Los casos de Suez y de las Malvinas," *América y Oriente* (Buenos Aires), August 30, 1953, 10.

29. "Amistad y solidaridad argentino-egipcia," *América y Oriente* (Buenos Aires), August 10, 1953, 36.

30. "Actividades de la colectividad árabe: Santiago del Estero," *Mundo Árabe* (Córdoba), December 19, 1953, 2.

31. "La América Latina y el mundo árabe-asiático," *El Eco de Oriente* (Tucumán), July 11, 1952, 1.

32. "Declaraciones del General Naguib para América y Oriente," *América y Oriente* (Buenos Aires), May 10, 1953, 15.

33. "El Cairo, 15," *Mundo Árabe* (Córdoba), December 19, 1953, 2.

34. "El General Naguib contestó un mensaje," *El Eco de Oriente* (Tucumán), August 10, 1953, 2.

35. "Rindióse homenaje a Egipto en el primer aniversario de su liberación," *El Eco de Oriente* (Tucumán), August 10, 1953, 2.

36. "Regresó el ministro egipcio," *El Eco de Oriente* (Tucumán), June 9, 1953, 1.

37. Diego Olstein, *Thinking History Globally* (New York: Palgrave Macmillan, 2015), 9.

38. Robert Bianchi, *Unruly Corporatism: Associational Life in Twentieth-Century Egypt* (New York: Oxford University Press, 1989), 28.

39. Kirk J. Beattie, *Egypt during the Nasser Years: Ideology, Politics, and Civil Society* (Boulder, CO: Westview Press, 1994), 122.

40. Olstein, *Thinking History Globally*, 13; Aidi, *Redeploying the State*, 61.

41. Elie Podeh and Onn Winckler, "Introduction: Nasserism as a Form of Populism," in *Rethinking Nasserism: Revolution and Historical Memory in Modern Egypt*, ed. Elie Podeh and Onn Winckler (Gainesville: University Press of Florida, 2004), 28.

42. Juan Domingo Perón to Gamal Abdel Nasser, January 28, 1959, Juan Domingo Perón Papers, 1931–2002, Hoover Institute Archive, Stanford University, Stanford, CA (hereafter JDPHI).

43. Abdeluahid Akmir, *Los árabes en Argentina* (Rosario: Editorial de la Universidad Nacional de Rosario, 2011), 256.

44. Juan Domingo Perón to Dr. Zeki Djebi, January 1959, JDPHI; Juan Domingo Perón to Hassan Ismail Fahmi, January 1959, JDPHI.

45. "Se aleja de nuestro país el ministro de Siria," *El Eco de Oriente* (Tucumán), January 12, 1953, 1.

46. "Siria condecoró a la Señora Eva Perón," *Assalam* (Buenos Aires), April 18, 1952, 1.

47. Perón to Zeki Djebi.

48. Perón to Hassan Ismail Fahmi.

49. Juan Domingo Perón to Avelino Fernández, June 18, 1960, JDPHI.

50. Vanni Pettinà, "Global Horizons: Mexico, the Third World, and the Non-Aligned Movement at the Time of the 1961 Belgrade Conference," *International History Review* 38:4 (2016): 741–764.

51. John Tofik Karam, "Beside Bandung: Brazil's Relations toward the Arab World," *LASA Forum* 47:1 (2016): 26.

52. Karam, "Beside Bandung," 30.

53. Kaufman et al., *Israel–Latin American Relations*, 49.

54. James Jankowski, *Nasser's Egypt, Arab Nationalism, and the United Arab Republic* (Boulder, CO: Lynne Rienner, 2002), 83.

55. Vélez, *Latin American Revolutionaries*, 16.

56. Akmir, *Los árabes en Argentina*, 235. Nadra was a long-serving leader of the Argentine Communist Party.

57. "Petición a Nasser," *Mundo Árabe* (Santiago de Chile), August 17, 1956, 11.

58. Hamurabi Noufouri, Rita Veneroni, and Yusef Abboud, *Sirios, Libaneses y Argentinos: fragmentos para una historia de la diversidad cultural argentina* (Buenos Aires: Fundación Los Cedros: 2004), 287.

59. DAIA, *Anti-Jewish Activities*, 17–21.

60. For discussion of sovereignty in Argentine political discourse, see Michael Goebel, *Argentina's Partisan Past: Nationalism and the Politics of History* (Liverpool: Liverpool University Press, 2011), 193–197.

61. "Declaraciones del General Perón."

62. Ibrahim Hallar, *Los sueños del Coronel Nasser son celestes y blancos como el emblema de la nación argentina* (Buenos Aires: Ibrahim Hallar, 1956), 9, in Biblioteca Nacional, Buenos Aires.

63. Mercedes Saborido, "De 'defensores de una causa santa' a 'lacayos del imperialismo,'" El Partido Comunista de la Argentina y el conflicto de Suez (1956)," *Cuadernos de Historia Contemporánea* 35 (2013): 193–218.

64. Fernando Nadra, *Egipto, Suez, y el mundo árabe* (Buenos Aires: Editorial Fundamentos, 1957), 1.

65. Robert A. Potash, "Argentine Political Parties: 1957–1958," *Journal of Inter-American Studies* 1:4 (1959): 521.

66. Cuadernos de Movimiento Universitario Reformista, *La nacionalización del canal de Suez: Introducción al estudio del proceso económico-social del Medio Oriente* (Buenos Aires: Prensas Universitarias Argentinas, 1956), 7.

67. Cuadernos de Movimiento Universitario Reformista, *La nacionalización del canal de Suez*, 10.

68. Rogelio García Lupo, *La revolución Nasserista* (Buenos Aires: Proceso, 1962), 11.

69. Olstein, *Thinking History Globally*, 15.

70. Karam, "Beside Bandung," 26.

71. Caroline Douki and Philippe Minard, " Histoire globale, histoires connectés: Un changement d'échelle historiographique?" *Revue d'Histoire Moderne et Contemporaine* 5:54 (2007), 7–21.

72. Douki and Minard, "Histoire globale, histoires connectés."

Chapter 6

1. Lionel Paredes, "La yerba mate conquista Siria y China," *La Nación* (Buenos Aires), February 7, 2019. https://www.lanacion.com.ar/economia/comercio-exterior/yerba-mate-crecen-las-exportaciones-y-las-ganas-de-innovar-para-ganar-nuevos-mercados-nid2217937

2. Lorena Cordoba, Federico Bossert, and Nicolas Richard, eds., *Capitalismo en las selvas: Enclaves industriales en el Chaco y Amazonia indigenas (1850–1950)* (San Pedro de Atacama, Chile: Ediciones del Desierto, 2015), 74.

3. Other missions included his travels in the Chaco region as described I Gabriela Dalla-Corte Caballero, "La Mision Franciscana de Laishi: el proyecto del ingeniero José Elías Niklison (1910–1920)," *Historia Unisinos* 17:3 (2013): 203–215.

4. José Elías Niklison, "Investigación relacionada con las condiciones de vida y de trabajo del Alto Paraná," *Boletín del Departamento Nacional del Trabajo,* no. 26, Buenos Aires, 1914, 238.

5. Niklison, "Investigación relacionada," 239.

6. Antonio Julián registered his Tienda y Almacén in 1917 and in 1928 his Ramos Generales shop. Felipe Chemes also registered his own Ramos Generales store, and Lazaro Chemes a "Tienda y Almacén."

7. In his case, he appears to have returned with a family member: Estavani Chemes, a twenty-six-year-old housewife. The two arrived at the Port of Buenos Aires on November 6, 1926, after departing from the Italian port of Genoa. Migration record located at Centro de Estudios Migratorios Latinoamericanos, Buenos Aires. Digital Database of immigrant arrivals to port of Buenos Aires, https://cemla.com/buscador/.

8. For a description of the range of activities conducted by this type of company, see Niklison's description of the requests made by the Companía de Tierras y Maderas del Iguazú in his 1914 report. See Niklison, "Investigación relacionada," 203.

9. Niklison, "Investigación relacionada," 222–223.

10. Christine Folch, "Stimulating Consumption: Yerba Mate Myths, Markets, and Meanings from Conquest to Present," *Comparative Studies in Society and History* 52:1 (2010): 9.

11. María Victoria Magan, "Dos crisis yerbateras. Similitudes y diferencias en las circunstancias que llevaron a la creación de la CRYM (1935) y la INYM (2002)," IX Encuentro de Cátedras de Ciencias Sociales y Humanísticas para las Ciencias Económicas, Mar del Plata, Argentina, June 6–7, 2002.

12. Folch, "Stimulating Consumption," 9.

13. Folch, "Stimulating Consumption," 16.

14. Folch, "Stimulating Consumption," 26.

15. Migration record located at Centro de Estudios Migratorios Latinoamericanos, Buenos Aires. Digital Database of immigrant arrivals to port of Buenos Aires: https://cemla.com/buscador/.

16. Instituto Nacional de la Yerba Mate, "Listado de Empresas Exportadoras de Yerba Mate Argentina," May 19, 2016, http://yerbamateargentina.org.ar/.

17. Folch, "Stimulating Consumption," 8, 32.

18. Omar Kassab, "De Siria a Andresito." interview by Canal 12, "Testimonios de los Cuatro Vientos" Series, Andresito, Misiones, Argentina, June 11, 2018, https://www.youtube.com/watch?v=ivjtk87ut3k.

19. United Nations High Commissioner for Refugees, "UNHCR Factsheet on Resettlement: Syrian Refugees," March 18, 2016, https://www.unhcr.org.

20. Servicio Nacional de Sanidad y Calidad Agroalimentaria, "Las exportaciones de yerba mate crecieron un 12% en 2017: El Senasa fiscalizó envíos por 30.531 toneladas. Siria y Chile, los principales destinos" (Buenos Aires, Argentina), March 5, 2018, http://www.senasa.gob.ar/senasa-comunica/noticias/las-exportaciones-de-yerba-mate-crecieron-un-12-en-2017, For information from the 2018 SENASA report, see the summary at "El bombardeo a Siria complica las exportaciones de yerba mate," *La Política Online*, April 16, 2018, https://www.lapoliticaonline.com/nota/112410-el-bombardeo-a-siria-complica-las-exportaciones-de-yerba-mate/.

21. "La guerra en Siria potencia la exportación de yerba al mercado del Oriente Medio," *Economis*, July 21, 2018, http://www.economis.com.ar/la-guerra-en-siria-potencia-la-exportacion-de-yerba-al-mercado-del-oriente-medio/.

22. Dirección Nacional de Migraciones, Ministerio del Interior, Obras Públicas y Vivienda, "Programa Especial de Visado Humanitario: Acerca del Programa" (Buenos Aires, Argentina), http://www.migraciones.gov.ar/programasiria/.

23. Dirección Nacional de Migraciones, Ministerio del Interior, Obras Públicas y Vivienda, "Qué hacemos" (Buenos Aires, Argentina), https://www.argentina.gob.ar/programa-siria/que-hacemos.

24. Celina Andreassi, "Argentina: An Exile Destination for Syrians Escaping the Conflict," *Argentina Independent,* February 14, 2013, http://www.argentinaindependent.com/socialissues/humanrights/argentina-an-exile-destination-for-syrians-escaping-the-conflict.

25. "Diez familias de refugiados sirios serán recibidos en Gualeguaychú," *El Clarín*, September 22, 2015, https://www.clarin.com/politica/siria-refugiados-gualeguaychu-monsenor_lozano-centro_sirio_0_ryb-2fFP7x.html.

26. Luis Alberto Chemes, "La Asociación Sirio Libanesa se prepara para recibir a los refugiados en Misiones," interview with Radio Libertad, *MisionesOnlineNet*, September 8, 2015, https://misionesonline.net/2015/09/08/la-asociacion-sirio-libanesa-se-prepara-para-recibir-a-los-refugiados-en-misiones/.

27. "La colectividad Árabe hará de intermedio para el ingreso de una familia Siria," link to interview, FM 101.1, *El Aire de la Integración,* October 4, 2015 (Oberá, Misiones), http://elairedeintegracion.com.ar/la-colectividad-arabe-intermediaria-en-el-ingreso-de-una-familia-siria.

28. "Los primeros refugiados sirios reciben ofertas laborales y se anuncio la llegada de mas familias sirias," *Telam: Agencia Nacional de Noticias*, February 9, 2017, http://www.telam.com.ar/notas/201702/179313-refugiados-sirios-san-luis-ofertas-laborales.html; "Emotivo encuentro de Lana y Majb con la comunidad sirio libanesa," *Agencia de Noticias San Luis* (San Luis, Argentina), February 9, 2017, http://agenciasanluis.com/notas/2017/02/09/emotivo-encuentro-de-lana-y-majb-con-la-comunidad-sirio-libanesa/.

29. Unnamed spokesman, Sociedad Sirio Libanesa San Luis, "La Sociedad Sirio Libanesa colabora con los refugiados sirios," interview, Canal 13 (San Luis, Argentina), January 6, 2017, http://sanluistv.com/la-sociedad-sirio-libanesa-colabora-con-los-refugiados-sirios/.

30. Oscar Flores, "Lila, la bebé de una familia siria que escapó de la guerra y apostó a la vida en San Luis," *El Clarín* (Buenos Aires), April 13, 2018, https://www.clarin.com/sociedad/lila-bebe-familia-siria-escapo-guerra-aposto-vida_0_HktB_8pjz.html.

31. Gobierno de San Luis, "Comité de refugiados," *Corredor Humanitaria*, accessed December 1, 2018, http://www.corredorhumanitario.sanluis.gov.ar/.

32. "Misiones elabora un registro de familias para recibir refugiados sirios," *El Territorio* (Posadas, Argentina), September 8, 2015, https://www.elterritorio.com.ar/misiones-elabora-un-registro-de-familias-para-recibir-refugiados-sirios-3547734738269718-et.

33. Eduardo Peláez, "Abren un registro para recibir a sirios en Santiago del Estero," *Telam: Agencia Nacional de Noticias* September 7, 2015, http://www.telam.com.ar/notas/201509/119036-inmigracion-refugiados-sirios-santiago-del-estero.html.

34. "Como es ser un refugiado en la Argentina?" *La Nación* (Buenos Aires), September 4, 2015, https://www.lanacion.com.ar/1825363-como-es-ser-un-refugiado-en-la-argentina.

35. Club Sirio Unido, "Inicio" (Santiago, Chile), accessed December 1, 2018, https://www.sirio.cl); Sociedad Beneficencia Siria, "Origen," (Santiago, Chile), accessed December 1, 2018, http://beneficenciasiria.cl/2016/10/14/origen/.

36. Lily Pearl Balloffet, "Syrian Refugees in Latin America: Diaspora Communities as Interlocutors," *Latin American Studies Association Forum* 47:1 (2016): 9–14.

37. "La comunidad sirio-libanesa de Paraguay asiste a los refugiados sirios en Asunción," *El Diario* (Madrid, Spain), September 10, 2015, https://www.eldiario.es/politica/comunidad-sirio-libanesa-Paraguay-refugiados-Asuncion_0_429408105.html; "Misiones elabora un registro de familias para recibir refugiados sirios," *El Territorio* (Posadas, Argentina), September 8, 2015, https://www.elterritorio.com.ar/misiones-elabora-un-registro-de-familias-para-recibir-refugiados-sirios-3547734738269718-et.

38. Balloffet, "Syrian Refugees in Latin America," 12.

39. Dirección Nacional de Migraciones, Ministerio del Interior, Obras Públicas y Vivienda, "Integración" (Buenos Aires, Argentina), 2018, http://www.migraciones. gov.ar/programasiria/indexSiria.php?integracion.

40. Daniel Domínguez, "Reunión entre migraciones y la Asociación Sirio-Libanesa de Misiones," press conference videorecording, Agencia Hoy, September 15, 2015, http://www.agenciahoy.com/notix/noticia/informacion_general/74652_reunio-acuten-entre-migraciones-y-la-asociacioacuten-sirio-libanesa-de-misiones.htm.

41. In 2016, UNHCR official Juan Pablo Terminiello stated to a journalist for *La Nación* that "access to health and education [services] are at very high levels. That which remains unsolved is access to employment and housing." See Micaela Urdinez, "Refugiados sirios: los pocos que llegan a la Argentina tienen que empezar de cero," *La Nación* (Buenos Aires), March 31, 2016, https://www.lanacion.com. ar/1884567-refugiados-sirios-los-pocos-que-llegan-a-la-argentina-tienen-que-empezar-de-cero.

42. International Organization on Migration and UN Refugee Agency, "Emerging Resettlement Countries Support Mechanism (ERCM) Information Sheet," September 2016, http://reporting.unhcr.org/sites/default/files/Information%20Sheet%20 on%20ERCM%20September%202016.pdf.

43. "Se realizó el segundo Encuentro Nacional de Autoridades del Programa Siria en Argentina," United Nations Refugee Agency, November 2, 2018, https://www.ac-nur.org/noticias/press/2018/11/5bdcd3894/se-realizo-el-segundo-encuentro-nacio-nal-de-autoridades-del-programa-siria.html.

44. "Argentina Embraces Community Refugee Sponsorship," *Global Refugee Sponsorship Initiative Newsletter,* vol. 7 (April 2018), http://refugeesponsorship.org/_ uploads/5ad64f2331076.pdf.

45. "OIM y ACNUR se reunieron con la Mesa Siria Salta y Mesa Siria Mendoza," International Organization for Migration press release, August 25, 2018, http://ar-gentina.iom.int/co/news/oim-y-acnur-se-reunieron-con-la-mesa-siria-salta-y-mesa-siria-mendoza.

46. Jessica Stites Mor, "Refuge, Alliance, and South-South Exchange: Latin America and the Middle East," *Latin American Studies Association Forum* 47:1 (2016): 8; Silverstein, "Anthropologies of Middle Eastern Diasporas," 282–315.

47. Christian Mouroux, interview with [author], personal interview, Buenos Aires, Argentina, December 5, 2018.

48. "UNESCO-Sharjah Prize for Arab Culture awarded to Christine Tohme of Lebanon and Cine Fértil of Argentina," United Nations Educational, Scientific and Cultural Organization, May 17, 2018, https://en.unesco.org/news/unesco-sharjah-prize-arab-culture-awarded-christine-tohme-lebanon-and-cine-fertil-argentina.

49. Cine Fértil, "LatinArab: Somos Cine Fértil," Buenos Aires, accessed November 28, 2018, http://cinefertil.org/index.php/quienes-somos.

50. As of 2018, the member states of ASPA are Argentina, Bolivia, Brazil, Chile, Colombia, Ecuador, Guyana, Paraguay, Peru, Suriname, Uruguay and Venezuela, Algeria, Bahrain, Comoros, Djibouti, Egypt, Iraq, Jordan, Kuwait, Lebanon, Libya, Morocco, Mauritania, Oman, Palestine, Qatar, Saudi Arabia, Somalia, Sudan, Syria, Tunisia, United Arab Emirates, and Yemen.

51. Cine Fértil, "LatinArab: Observatorio permanente de intercambio cultural sur-sur," Buenos Aires, accessed November 28, 2018, http://cinefertil.org/index.php/observatorio.

52. These objectives are enumerated in the Observatorio's mission statement as *Objetivos Generales.*

53. Mariano Mestman, "From Algiers to Buenos Aires: The Third World Cinema Committee (1973–1974)," *New Cinemas: Journal of Contemporary Film* 1:1 (2002): 40–53.

54. Rebecca Hillauer, *Encyclopedia of Arab Women Filmmakers* (Cairo: American University of Cairo Press, 2005), 252.

55. Jessica Stites Mor, *Transition Cinema: Political Filmmaking and the Argentine Left since 1968* (Pittsburgh: University of Pittsburgh Press, 2012), 35.

56. Julieta Chinchilla, "El Instituto del Tercer Mundo de la Universidad de Buenos Aires (1973–1974)," *Iconos: Revista de Ciencias Sociales* no. 51 (January–February 2015): 47–63.

57. Stites Mor, *Transition Cinema*, 36.

58. "De Argel a Buenos Aires," Biblioteca del Congreso de la Nación, LatinArab: Seventh Film Festival, Buenos Aires, September 7, 2017.

59. Edgardo Bechara El Khoury, personal interview. Buenos Aires, Argentina, December 5, 2018.

60. Christian Mouroux, personal interview, Buenos Aires, Argentina, December 5, 2018.

61. Edgardo Bechara El Khoury, personal interview, Buenos Aires, Argentina, December 5, 2018.

62. Stites Mor, "Refuge, Alliance, and South-South Exchange," 7.

63. Omar S. Dahi and Alejandro Velasco, "Latin America-Middle East Ties in the New Global South," *Middle East Report: The Latin East* 47:204 (2017), http://www.merip.org/mer/mer284.

64. Cecilia Baeza and Paulo Pinto, "The Syrian Uprising and the Mobilization of the Syrian Diaspora in South America," *The Middle East Report: The Latin East* 47:204 (2017), http://www.merip.org/mer/mer284.

65. Steve J. Stern, *Battling for Hearts and Minds: Memory Struggles in Pinochet's Chile, 1973–1988* (Durham, NC: Duke University Press, 2006), 1.

Epilogue

1. Barbara Lüthi, "Migration and Migration History," *Docupedia-Zeitgeschichte* (June 2018), 13, http://docupedia.de/zg/Luethi_migration_v2_en_2018.

2. "Trump declares without evidence that 'Criminals and unknown Middle Easterners are mixed in' with migration caravan making its way from Honduras." *CNBC*, October 22, 2018., https://www.cnbc.com/2018/10/22/trump-says-unknown-middle-easterners-are-mixed-in-migrant-caravan.html.

3. For an example of scholars who refuted claims of terrorist cells at the Triple Frontera, see Thomaz G. Costa and Gaston H. Schulmeister, "The Puzzle of the Iguazú Tri-Border Area: Many Questions and Few Answers Regarding Organised Crime and Terrorism Links," *Global Crime* 8:1 (2007): 26–39. For an example of the appearance in pop culture of the Triple Frontera as a terrorist zone, see the following network television episode: Steven Kate, "An Eye for an Eye," National Criminal Investigative Services, March 22, 2005.

4. See, for example, Resat Kasaba, *A Moveable Empire: Ottomans, Nomads, Migrants and Refugees* (Seattle: University of Washington Press, 2009).

5. Barbara Lüthi, "Agitated Times: Why Historians Need to Question the Rhetoric of the 'Refugee Crisis,'" *Histoire@Politique* 31 (2017): 4.

6. Lüthi, "Migration and Migration History," 12.

7. Thomas Nail, *The Figure of the Migrant* (Stanford, CA: Stanford University Press, 2015).

Index